The Arts of the Twenties

The Arts of the Twenties

Gilles Néret

Painting
Sculpture
Architecture
Design
Theater Design
Graphic Art
Photography
Film

Rizzoli
NEW YORK

For my father and mother for whom the 20s were the best years of their lives.

Translation from the French by Thomas Higgins

French-language edition, *L'Art des Années 20*
Copyright © 1986 by Office du Livre S.A., Fribourg,
Switzerland

English translation:
Copyright © 1986 by Office du Livre S.A., Fribourg
Switzerland

English translation published in 1986 in the United States
of America by:
Rizzoli International Publications, Inc.
597 Fifth Avenue/New York 10017

Library of Congress Cataloging-in-Publication Data

Néret, Gilles.
　The arts of the twenties.

　Translation of: L'art des années 20.
　Includes index.
　1. Arts, Modern—20th century—Europe.　2. Arts,
French.　3. Arts, Modern—20th century—France.
I. Title.
NX542.N4713　1986　　700'.9'042　　86-42740
ISBN 0-8478-0766-5

Printed and bound in Switzerland

Table of Contents

The Roaring Twenties

The art world has a tendency to produce creative individuals who are at once heir to all that has gone before them and at the same time in revolt against their immediate predecessors.

Consequently, the Twenties really began well before 1920, a date we have chosen largely for convenience. Early traces of 1920s movements can be found from 1911 onwards, in a Malevich or a Picasso, for example, or in a Kandinsky or a Delaunay. It would take several years, however, for the inevitable turning of son against father to take form. The vegetable arabesques of Art Nouveau gave way to the circles and squares of Art Deco. But the transition was progressive; between the two, there was a curious union of swirls and cubes, curls and spheres. The Twenties were fundamentally a period of transition, witness to a new art taking over from the old. By comparing and contrasting, for the first time, all the fields of art—painting, sculpture, architecture, design, stage design, graphics, photography and cinema—and by placing them against their artistic, socio-political and scientific background, we arrive at a whole greater than the sum of the individual parts—not simply an assemblage of subjects previously separated in volumes on the shelves of an immense library, but a bringing to light of the extent of interaction between the fields, how much they complement each other, and to what degree the spirit of the age emerges from their interaction.

There is a tendency in conventional art histories—and this is true too of the great Paris-Berlin, Paris-Moscow and Paris-New York exhibitions at the Centre Georges Pompidou in Paris—to highlight only the avant-garde. This is to forget the middle-class aesthetics that govern everyday life. When Le Corbusier designed his famous tubular armchair we so appreciate today, the heart's desire of the ordinary French public was to be found—and would be for a long time to come—in the Henri II furniture by Dufayel. From this confrontation between makers and users—too often kept arbitrarily apart—emerged, little by little, a style crystallizing the era, containing both the good and the less satisfying elements.

In the 1920s, the same ordinary French person was well content with the new, low-rent housing, whose constricted size led to a new conception of space: the single room, ancestor of the living room, was transformed into a bedroom, thanks to the cozy corner; stacking chairs enabled the same space to be converted temporarily into a dining room.

Two worlds coexisted and influenced each other in the frenetic pace of living that—understandably—followed the war. The adherents of official art were still present, with their Salons and their State Commissions. Yet in all areas, even though some references to turn-of-the-century art were still in evidence, it is clear that a new art was coming into being. The beginnings of design can be discerned: a search for the functional and simple, ideas upheld not only by the Bauhaus, which called for a

1   Tamara de Lempicka: *Self-portrait.*
C. 1928. Oil on canvas, 35 × 26 cm.
Private collection, London.

2   Fernand Léger: *The Bicycle.* 1929.
Oil on canvas, 92 × 65 cm. Nadia
Léger Collection.

Squares and Rectangles

unified environment, but also by Russian Constructivism, whose objective was to bring art within the reach of Everyman.

The phenomenon was international. Berlin, Paris and Moscow were in permanent dialogue and the three poles of creativity to which the Western world turned were to be found, broadly speaking, in Germany, the USSR and in France. The American influence made its appearance and would reach its climax in the following decades.

The interaction at play between countries, between the avant-gardists and middle-class taste, was present also among the artists themselves, who could pass easily from one genre to the other. Malevich can be seen applying his Constructivist theories just as much to his paintings as to his Architectons—models that inspired the New York skyscrapers—or to the design of a simple teapot. Sonia Delaunay not only painted pictures, but also the coachwork of automobiles and dressmaking materials. In the same year, 1920, a film-maker, Charlie Chaplin, and a strip cartoon author, George McManus, dealt each in his own way with aspects of the American dream that haunted the descendants of immigrants: one with *The Kid*, the other with the imaginary adventures of the Illico family in *Bringing up Father*, published in a daily newspaper. The same artist could win fame one year in a particular field, while being less innovative in another. Thus Picasso, in 1920, became a leading light as a result of his stage sets and ballet costumes for *Pulcinella*, while in painting he was still concentrating on neo-classical themes.

So, in the Twenties, the age of the airplane and of broadcasting, Soviet Russia was in dialogue, via Paris, with Weimar Germany. Creativity flourished in every way, in all forms. The notion of high and low art disappeared. Equal importance was attached to the painting of a canvas and to the designing of a poster, the building of a house or the designing of a chair or a lamp. A sense of the past, an awareness of the present and a particular vision of the future came together to form one long chain. Design was added, on an equal footing, to the traditional fields of painting, sculpture and architecture; the Inkhuk and Unovis schools—as well as the Bauhaus—were seeking to produce useful objects for the widest possible range of people. Stage design was also influenced—with the Moscow Theater, the Paris and Berlin experiments. From East to West graphic art flooded into the streets, justifying Maiakovskii's remark "... the streets are our brushes, the squares our palettes...."

Artists became interested in photography, using it in widely differing ways, whether it was Stieglitz at the head of the American school; or Man Ray in France with his rayograms—a chance invention; or the photomontages of Hausmann, Grosz and Höch in Germany; or Rodchenko's and El Lissitzky's research in the USSR.

The cinema opened its doors to Expressionism and

Squares and Rectangles

5 Piet Mondrian: *Composition*. 1920. Oil on canvas, 75 × 65 cm. Musée national d'Art moderne, Centre Georges Pompidou, Paris.

6 Kasimir Malevich: Teapot for the Leningrad Pottery. 1922. China, H. 16.5 cm. Lomonosov National China Museum, Leningrad.

7 Walter Gropius: Bookcase for periodicals. 1923. Oak and mirror, 85 × 160 × 68 cm. Executed in the carpentry workshop of the Bauhaus. Bauhaus-Archiv, Berlin.

abstraction, attracting painters like Léger, Duchamp and Dalí. New media difficult to classify appeared: collages, frottages, sables, to name a few. The Surrealists invented a new vocabulary—that of the unconscious. Divisions between the genres faded. Surely Vladimir Tatlin's famous tower is simultaneously sculpture, architecture, a model of design, a piece of social and political decoration, built with festivals in mind, as well as being an example of graphic art? After all, not only did the tower project photos, films and slogans onto the clouds, it also, among many other functions, broadcast music and announced events to the public.

The same artist could shine in turn in fields until then separate—sculpture, town-planning, furniture or jewelry design, photography or cinema. It was an era marked by enthusiasm for all fields, and Leonardo da Vinci, had he been able to return to it, would have felt wonderfully at home.

Beyond the frontiers of schools, groups and countries, from now on artists would answer directly to each other. Whatever their label, whether they were Constructivists, Purists, neo-Plasticians, whether they belonged to the Bauhaus or the De Stijl movement, whether they swore by Dada or by André Breton, or were simply independent—would it ever be possible to be truly independent again?—whether they were geniuses, creative, adventurers of art or modest craftsmen, imitators, hangers-on or fashionable interior designers, they all played with the same rounds, the same squares and the same pyramids. They had absorbed the same Cubist or Art Nouveau lessons; they were for, they were against: they were involved. They could not avoid catching the spirit invading the new century—the spirit of headlong speed, movement and machinery.

This new race of artists set out to enrich everyday life. "We must understand that art and life are no longer separate fields," wrote the Dutchmen Van Doesburg and Van Eesteren in their work *Towards a Collective Construction* (*De Stijl*, 12, 1924, Fasc. 6/7), "That is why the idea of 'art' no longer has any meaning for us...."

Van Doesburg also wrote: "As soon as artists working in the various fields of plastic art realize the need to express themselves in a universal language, they themselves will lose their individuality. By submitting to a universal principle, they will evolve an organic style. A new style, recognizable in all objects, will emerge from a new relationship between the artist and society."

Dangerous words, if only because they were turned about and badly interpreted.

But individualism dies hard. It can participate in the universal without being engulfed in the slightest degree. Schwitters might well dream of "total art" and then, in 1920, in his house in Waldhausenstrasse, Hanover, begin his first *Merzban*, an inhabitable cross between sculpture and architecture, three stories high, which would take sixteen years to build. He also launched a review called *Merz*, in 1923, with the idea of linking Dada

8 Camille Fauré: Enamel vase.
C. 1925. H. 31.8 cm. Private collection,
New York.

9 Pierre Legrain: Binding for *Daphné*
by Alfred de Vigny. 1925.

10 Jean Dunand: Four-paneled
screen. C. 1926–1928. Decorated in
silver lacquer on black ground.

The Circle
Burst Open

and Constructivism and of publishing De Stijl's, Mondrian's and El Lissitzky's neo-Plastician and Constructivist theses. This International style created by the Esprit nouveau movement, the Bauhaus and the Soviet artists is not hard to recognize, even if it occasionally degenerates into a geometric spineless style, or into Art Deco, the result of a cross between the Modern style and the highly fashionable cubic geometry. Not that it should be despised, this style so evocative of the Roaring Twenties—years that had begun some thirteen months earlier, on November 11, 1918, at 5:30 a.m., with the armistice—synonymous with jazz, burdensome pleasures, and the artificial excitement that reigned from then on like a drug for forgetting the horrors of the war. It cannot be dissociated from the life of the era and, however dubious its products may be, they should not be ignored. This International style could even be seen on chimney pieces, in the form of "superb objets d'art," female statuettes frozen in an arabesque, similar to the type that can be won at fairs, but made out of expensive, noble materials, for the use of a rich middle class. It penetrated wealthy apartments as furniture of eclectic design, violent wall hangings and commonplace jewelry. Effect was placed before quality. These objects still sell for astronomical prices in sales rooms today. On the one hand there were the "innovators"—"finders" through the rarified visions or the abstract research of Malevich's Suprematism, through Tatlin's Constructivism in the USSR, Mondrian and the De Stijl movement in Holland, through Purism in France and Italy and through the Expressionism of Beckman, Grosz, Dix, and Schad in Germany, echoed by Roualt or Soutine in France. On the other there were the "followers," who transformed discoveries and turned them into fashion. There is a fundamental conflict and yet the constants of the era are present in both the purest creations and the most superficial.

"Architects, sculptors, artists, we must all return to our trade. There is no such thing as 'professional art.' Artist and craftsman are indistinguishable in nature. The artist is simply an inspired craftsman. In rare moments, moments of sudden clarity, unwittingly, as a gift from heaven, the work of his hands becomes art. But every artist must have a certain technical ability. That is the real source of the creative imagination. Let us form a new sort of confederation, without the distinction between classes which creates a wall of disdain between artist and craftsman. Together, let us design and carry through the new architecture, the architecture of the future, in which painting, sculpture and architecture will be a single unity, rising to the sky from the hands of millions of workers, the crystal symbol of a new faith."

This profession of faith, where humility vies with the noblest ambition, this flight of lyricism, an attempt to bring everyone into agreement, marks an essential turning point in the history of art. It comes from the *Bauhaus Manifesto*, written in 1919 by Walter Gropius. It could just as well have come from Moscow, where, at the same period, the brothers Naum Gabo and Antoine Pevsner, both sculptors concerned about architecture, drafted the *Realist Manifesto* (1920), in which they put forward the basic principles of Constructivism. Their interests lay with construction in space, which they viewed as sculpture rather than as architecture. Their statement "We hold that space can only be modeled from the inside outwards by using its depth, and not from the outside inwards, depending on its volume," echoes

L'Esprit nouveau, a Paris review started in the same year as the result of a meeting between the artist-critic Amédée Ozenfant and the artist-architect Charles-Edouard Jeanneret, better known by his pseudonym of Le Corbusier, who wrote in the first issue: "Architecture has nothing to do with styles. The Louis XVs, XVIs, XIVs or gothic are to architecture what a feather is to a woman's head—sometimes pretty, but not always, and nothing more." The Russians expressed the same notion in point four of their manifesto, saying "We reject decorative line. We require that every line of a work of art should stress the internal lines of force of the subject." Malevich took a turn at expressing the idea in 1924, in his *Suprematist Manifesto*: "... We, Suprematists, are seeking allies in the struggle against the forms of the past...."

From that time on, a jumble of squares sprawled across the paintings of Malevich, Mondrian or Léger, and spread into the sculpture of Vantongerloo, the buildings of Gropius, Le Corbusier or Mallet-Stevens, into Rietveld's furniture and Malevich's teapot and onto the facade of the Café De Unie by J.J.P. Oud. They overflowed into the jewelry of Dunand and decorated the automobiles and dresses of Sonia Delaunay. The circle, already used in the previous decade, was split, as though to stop time, or show that nothing is ever finished, that everything may begin again. It presided over the destinies of the Bauhaus, with Joost Schmidt's poster, appeared in such contrary forces as Dadaism and Purism, with Picabia and Léger, and united Delaunay, Kandinsky and Rodchenko across geographic frontiers. Templier took it as the motif for a piece of jewelry, Legrain for a book-binding, Dunand for a screen, Fauré for a vase. It could figure in graphic art, as a poster by Jupp Wiertz and Loupot, a Prisunic dress by Popova, a stage costume by Léger, or even a folk doll painted by Souza-Cardozo, who gave one to the Delaunay couple when they passed through his country, making it impossible to say whether it was the doll discovered in Portugal with the famous circles on its dress which inspired the couple, or whether the gist of their own work inspired the doll.

Good sentiments do not always lead to art of genius. Thus, by too ardently wishing to imitate the American way of life, with its relaxed, sporty image, personified by the Yankees who came to help the Old World resolve its quarrels, artists transformed the notion of speed—particular to the decade—into a stereotype of "frozen movement." In the era of the automobile and the cinema—two of its extreme representations—movement made a notable entry into art. "When composing a poster," explains Cappiello, "all its different aspects must be pulled together to create a unified, efficient structure, the arabesque" and Klee, writing in *Das bildnerische Denken* ("Creative Confessions") (1920), stated: "The work of art starts with motion, it is itself 'arrested motion,' and it will be perceived in motion."

Cubism, Futurism, Fauvism, and the eastern opulence of the Ballets Russes had already introduced a great variety of forms in motion and colors. The passage of the American soldiers, with their apparently relaxed discipline—those ambassadors of modernity, shorthaired connoisseurs of jazz—had left its mark. They were imitated; bodies were liberated. The female body in particular was changing, asserting and refining its form. Advertising obsessively produced uniform images, influencing behavior and even fabricating stereotyped postures. The widely disseminated photograph of the

female tennis-player, Suzanne Lenglen; the dancer, Isadora Duncan, posing on the Acropolis for Steichen, the photographer; Nikolska, the Folies-Bergère dancer, striking a similar attitude for Picot, the sculptor, for his bas-relief, *La Danse*, for the pediment of the Folies-Bergère: all these are examples of the obsession with arrested motion that marked the era. Together with the breaking away from age-old shackles, the practice of sports and dancing and the new, soft, loose clothes gave way to a new uniformity. It could be found frozen on a poster, on a vase, in a fashion photograph, an engraving, in or on anything at all, like the dancer on the stage who, at the end of a figure, freezes in a studied, graceful and graphic movement, around which a circle may ideally be inscribed. On the same principle, the Germans made the first naturist film: *Paths to Strength and Beauty*, produced in 1925 by the famous

11   Amadeo de Souza-Cardozo: *Popular Song and Bird of Brazil*. 1919. Oil on canvas, 76 × 65 cm. Mrs. Souza-Cardazo Collection.

With his friends the Delaunays, Souza-Cardozo, the "Portuguese meteor" (he died in 1918 at thirty), had discovered the profound originality of popular Portuguese art and painted pictures of dolls dressed in traditional peasant cloths with circular motifs. At the time, his work was hailed as "a concise document on the Portuguese race in the twentieth century." The Spanish flu robbed us of its further development.

12   Robert Delaunay: *Electrical Merry-Go-Round*. 1922. Oil on canvas, 250 × 250 cm. Musée national d'Art moderne, Centre Georges Pompidou, Paris.

Arrested Motion

13, 15   Georges Picot: Bas-relief of *Dance* for the facade of the Folies-Bergère with one of the dancers, Nikolska, posing for the sculptor. C. 1925.

14   The extravagant leaps of Suzanne Lenglen, unbeaten queen of Wimbledon and symbol of the era of movement. Photo *c.* 1924.

13

movie-makers Ufa, and directed by Wilhelm Prager. The creatures in the film fall as often as they can into poses, arms raised, lost in wonder for the sun. Nothing could be less erotic than this pantheistic physical culture, altogether in tune with the Aryan hymns to beauty of Arnold Fanck (in his film *White Noise*, 1931) and Leni Riefenstahl (*Olympia*, 1938). "Well enough made women," Ado Kyrou confirmed, "perhaps a little on the heavy side, strolling naked, without displaying the slightest awareness of their bodies." How astonishing and sad it is to note the extent to which this era, so drawn by change, so stimulated by motion, dedicated to action and enthralled by speed, should translate these elements into such impoverished images. The gaping chasm which may open up between theory and practice is again visible in Moholy-Nagy's definition of vision in motion—to perceive objects in relation to other objects and not as isolated entities finding their balance from within themselves!

No doubt the machine, as substitute for man and landscape, was necessary to enable the Twenties artist to feel at ease. For machines also alter art. Léger, who had met Le Corbusier and Ozenfant, and instantly fell in with their movement, wrote in *L'Esprit nouveau* (No. 14): "Machines provide solutions to given problems, a lesson in method," and he added: "The mechanical element is a means, not an end. I consider it simply as plastic 'raw material,' such as the elements of a landscape or a still life.... For me, the human face, bodies, have no more importance than nails or bicycles." Words which undoubtedly masked the panic seizing artists who, as creative individuals, were aware of the dehumanization lying in wait for a world fascinated by totalitarian techniques. Their works rightly display a pessimistic vision of the future and are at the same time a satire of the Americanization of the world and of the positivist cult in science. They anticipate Huxley's *Brave New World* (1932) and Chaplin's *Modern Times* (1935) by ten years.

Severely, angrily or humorously, according to individual temperaments, each artist strove against a future that was already revealing itself—a dark, alienated future, filled with metal monsters, scientific hazards and apocalyptic discoveries. The word "robot," derived from the Czech *robotnik* (worker), was in fact coined during the period, by Karel Capek, the journalist and literary figure. There was a unanimity that traversed frontiers, in representing the new man, covered with nuts and bolts, transformed into strange machines. *Anatomy of a Young Bride* (1921) by Max Ernst corresponds to George Grosz's *Republican Automatons* (1920), which in turn calls to mind the premonitory manikins by De Chirico. *The New Man* (1920–1921) by El Lissitzky is also *Tatlin at Home* (1920) by Raoul Hausmann. The titles of the works are scarcely cryptic. *The Intransigent* (1925) by the graphic artist Adolph Mouron, otherwise known as Cassandre, its ears connected to electrical cables, shouts out the news from its loudspeaker mouth; the magical assembly of screens and spare parts that makes up Heartfield's Frankenstein-like creature wonders: *It Depends on the Purpose of the Journey* (1925). Always poetical, Klee called his man-machines *Analysis of Various Perversities* (1922). As for Gabo, his characters were constructed, like those of Pevsner or Moholy-Nagy, with materials from the new era. The bitter humor of Dadaism also contributed, with Man Ray, for example, to his *Portemanteau* (1920), half female nude, half coatrack.

16 Rudolf Belling: *Skulptur 23*. 1923.
Silvered bronze, H. 48 cm. Museum of
Modern Art, New York (A. Conger
Goodyear Fund).

17 Hannah Höch: *Beautiful Young
Girl*. 1920. Photomontage, 35 × 29 cm.
Private collection, Hamburg.

Machines gone Mad

In retrospect, we can see that the fear registering on such finely tuned gauges as artists was perfectly justified. Raoul Hausmann wrote in 1921: "It is in this space between two worlds, at the moment when we have not yet broken with the old world and are not yet capable of giving form to a new world, that satire makes its entry, the grotesque, the caricature, the clown and the doll, and other such forms of expression, whose aim is to show to what degree life has become mechanical, comparable to puppets, the apparent and real torpor is such as to enable us to guess and feel that another life exists." While the theme of the dancer frozen—like the petrified bodies uncovered from the ashes of Pompeii—calls to mind, in hindsight, the volcano brewing underneath, that of the machine and the robotization of man has continued, often tragically, up to our days. Fritz Lang's film, *Metropolis* (1926), echoed the malaise of urban civilization, clearly evoking a race of lords living in a paradise of hanging gardens, and the world of the workers, laboring underground, the alienated servants of machines. What choice was open for these human sacrifices? Either to be ground down by the state machine, or to revolt and be crushed. Whether reflections of an emerging era or prophetic visions of a future today all about us, the creative output of the 1920s was accurate enough. The geometric sets of Fritz Lang's film, the skyscrapers, the immense staircases leading to the machine room, are simply the gulags of today, or the concentration camps of yesterday, like Mauthausen, where in 1943 a gigantic stairway was hewn out of the rock and paid for in the lives of so many, broken, either by the strain or by the beatings. Those who had seen the film might well have cried "But it's Metropolis!"

Faced with the futurist projects of Sauvage, the architect, the mind turns to pyramids, and the same pyramid can be found, transformed into a tiered cake, in the Bon Marché (Parisian department store) and City of Lyons Pavilions at the 1925 Art Deco Exhibition. Catering to all tastes, it can also be admired in the baroque flight of fancy of a sequence from the film *Metropolis*, or worse yet, altered, miniaturized, as a dressing table or a perfume bottle.

The geographic disruption which brought the art capitals across the world into contact with each other—and that brought Dada, that great disclaimer of absurdity, into being, for example in the form of Apollinaire's character endowed with ubiquity, simultaneously in Zurich, Paris, Cologne, New York, or Barcelona—did not prevent national characteristics from leaving their mark on the artists' works. Can we understand the art of Brancusi, if we know nothing of the Rumanian crafts he so loved, especially the sculpted paddock posts, which are the direct ancestors of his *Endless Column*?

Similarly, the socio-political influences on art in Soviet Russia and in the Weimar Republic were far from identical. Each country was quite differently marked by World War I, depending on how much it suffered, on

DAS SCHÖNE MÄDCHEN   HANNAH HÖCH   90

Machines gone Mad

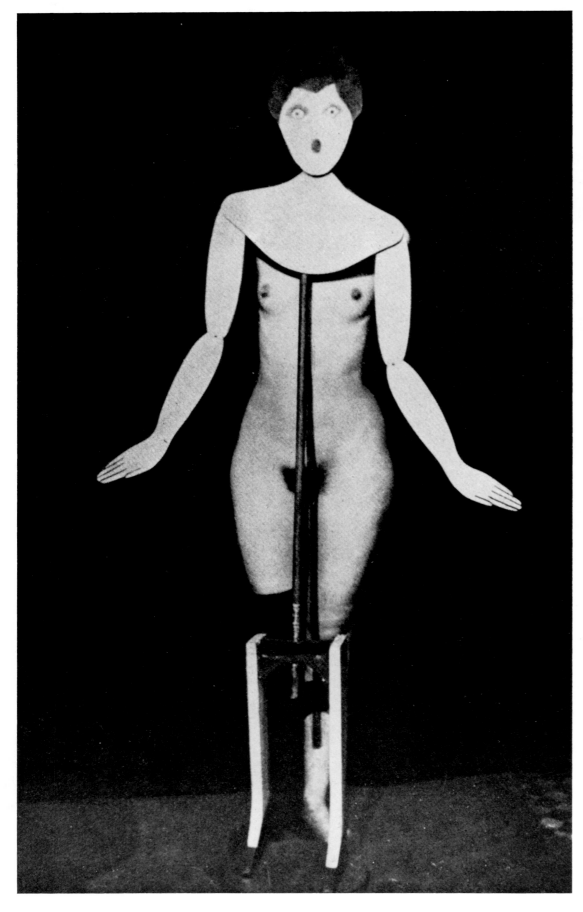

The Pyramid

20   Henri Sauvage: Project for tiered buildings beside the Seine. 1928. Gouache, 40 × 60 cm. M. Charpentier Collection, Paris.

whether it won or lost. The war was over, certainly, although it continued between Greece and Turkey—but that is not to say that perfect tranquility reigned everywhere. Italian ambition leading directly to Mussolini, occupation forces in the Saar, civil war and revolution in Russia, strikes in Great Britain, inflation in Germany preparing the way for Hitler—all contributed to the individuality of works of art from different places of origin. An artist will express himself differently, depending upon the group or school he may belong to; his own personal genre; whether times of peace or trouble, plenty or restriction prevail; whether he lives in the era of the oil lamp or that of space travel.

"The Netherlands are a major influence on De Stijl," noted Jocelyn de Noblet. The horizon in Holland is almost too perfect. Against it, a tree, a man or a building makes a 90° angle. A large part of the land of Holland was reclaimed from the sea by dykes. For an artist coming from such a country, the idea of nature is artificial. Solid land could be achieved only by containing the sea by means of horizontal and vertical lines—the precise definition of a canvas by Mondrian. The fundamental elements of De Stijl were a flat surface, a straight line and an angle. Van Doesburg initially wished to call his review *The Straight Line* and he always preferred the diagrammatic to the pictorial. De Stijl is said to have been influenced by Cubism. It was far more influenced by Holland itself. Rietveld's chair, and the facade of the Café De Unie are the direct result.

If for the Germans "rigor" rhymed with Bauhaus and "Expressionism" was synonymous with the beer drunk in Weimar—a town which in their eyes represented the capital and the army and whose true character needed to be unveiled—for the French, madly individualistic, the key word was conservatism, and even the foreigners who came to work in Paris allowed themselves to be caught up in it. Thus the Spaniard Picasso did not hesitate to abandon the Cubism of *Three Musicians* (1921) and return to neo-classical characters. The music of the Russian Stravinsky, absorbed by the French milieu he frequented, also went through a neo-classical phase. Even the supposedly avant-garde "Groupe des Six," which included Poulenc, Milhaud and Auric, appeared to reaffirm the virtues of an established musical language. The Paul Valéry of *Charmes* (1922), a fusion of classicism and symbolism, surely fits perfectly into the line stretching directly from Malherbe to Racine. As for Proust, whose work, completed in 1922, dominates the whole of modern French literature, even the title he chose—*A la recherche du temps perdu* ("Remembrance of Things Past")—suggests a considerable degree of classicism. The same typically French phenomenon is also apparent in architecture: for Le Corbusier, "the ocean liner is the first step in achieving a world organized according to the new spirit." But what Le Corbusier appreciated above all was "the order reigning aboard" and from that point it is only a short step to transforming the liner into a monastery.

But Le Corbusier should not be singled out alone. Across the world, perhaps for other reasons, the Bauhaus, Mies van der Rohe, Walter Gropius and Frank Lloyd Wright, filled with the best intentions, were drawing up plans for building complexes, for urban concentrations, for ideal and forward-looking buildings to house millions of individuals, which would lead, also through misunderstanding, to the monstrosities and built-up urban suburbs that we know today.

21 Fritz Lang: Scene from the film *Metropolis*. 1926.

22 Anonymous: Ladies' writing-desk. C. 1920–1925. Lacquered wood and parchment, 91.5 × 81 × 59 cm. Musée des Arts décoratifs, Paris.

23 Georges Chevalier: Bottle. 1925. Crystal, H. 12 cm. Musée des Arts décoratifs, Paris.

24 Louis Boileau: The "Pomone" Pavilion of the Grands Magasins du Bon Marché. 1925. Exhibition of Decorative Arts, Paris.

Painting

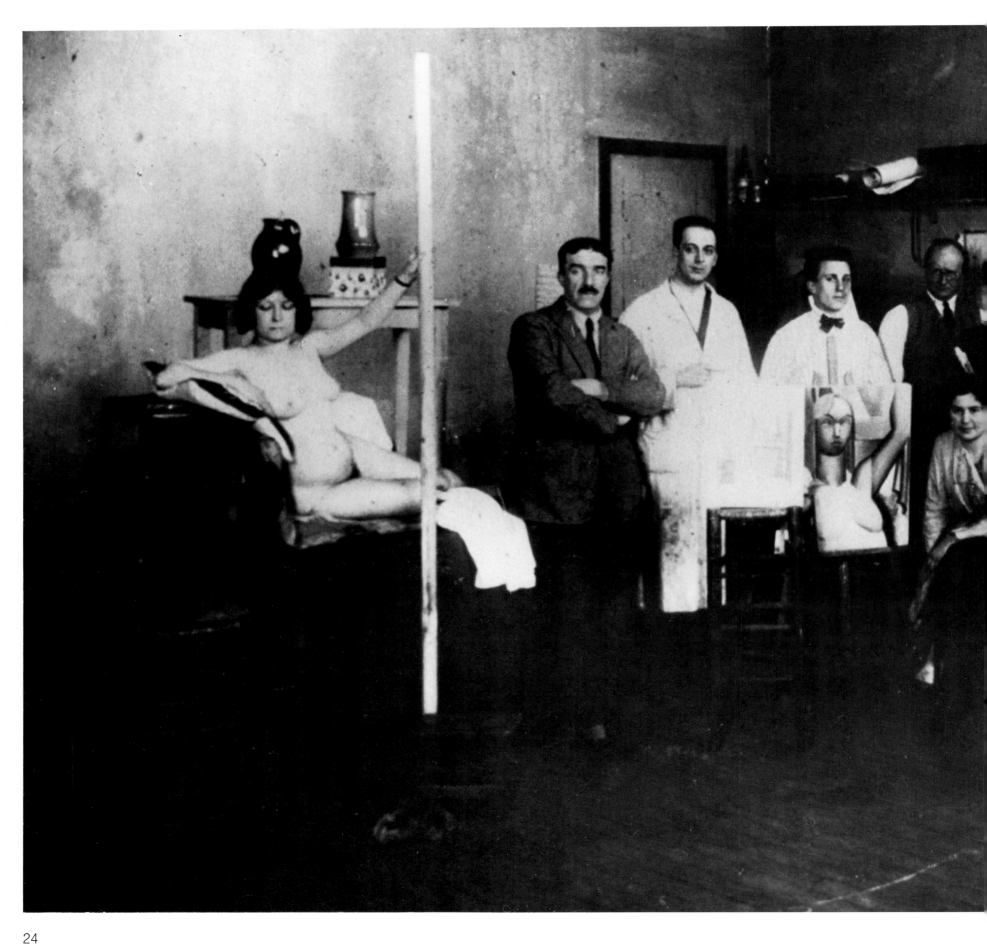

Neo-Plasticism and Esprit Nouveau

26   Fernand Léger: *Yellow Triangle*. 1926. Oil on canvas, 65 × 54 cm. Private collection.

27   Fernand Léger: *Woman with a Mirror*. 1920. Oil on canvas, 91.5 × 64.5 cm. Moderna Museet, Stockholm.

During the 1920s, the Dutch and the French were working on the problems raised and then left unresolved by Cubism.

Apollinaire remarked on Mondrian's "cerebral sensitivity," distinguishing him in this way from Picasso or Braque. His approach was indeed intellectual, even spiritual; apparent in each of his canvases is the desire to achieve a new style by going beyond objects. By unceasingly returning to familiar themes—trees, the sea, the Dutch landscape—he strove, in the course of successive versions, to reduce them to essential lines, horizontal and vertical, which were for him the sole definition of form.

"Neo-Plasticism" or "New Plastic Art" is the name given by Mondrian to his plastic designs. The theories, indeed, the system itself, were defended by the De Stijl group, which launched a review bearing the same name in

Leyden, Holland, in 1917. For the followers of this school, vertical and horizontal lines alone had to suffice as means of expression. The movement was therefore characterized by austerity and the best examples of it are Mondrian's works.

The 1920s represent another stage in the development of this conception of aesthetics: among its new manifestations are the flat technique, and the exclusive use of the three pure primary colors—blue, red and yellow—which could nonetheless be accompanied by black and white, the methodical search for the perfect square or for precise cross ruling. It was geometric abstraction, of course, but it was also, without any doubt, a spiritual quest, or, in Mondrian's own words, an attempt to harmonize "the extreme one" with "the extreme other."

In 1920 Mondrian produced a pamphlet called *Neo-Plasticism*, published in Paris by the Effort moderne gallery. It contained guidelines on how to go beyond the individual and attain the universal, so as to create a new image of the world. These same ideas recur throughout the decade and underlie creative research. The review *De Stijl*, vehicle for the ideas of the vibrant Van Doesburg and the austere Mondrian—a meeting of two of the most opposed characters possible—set the tone: "The aim of this small review is to contribute to the development of the new aesthetics. Its intention is to open the man of today to things new in the plastic arts." The idea was to bring creative artists out of their isolation, unite them and give them a voice. The various artistic fields had to communicate with each other at the same level and recognize "the principle of their fundamental equality and of a general plastic language." Individuality should disappear before "the collective realization of the new plastic consciousness."

The group was joined by painters, including the Hungarian Huszár as well as the Italian Futurist, Gino Severini; sculptors, such as the Belgian Vantongerloo; architects like Jacobus Johannes Pieter Oud and Robert Van't Hoff, both Dutch; a poet, their compatriot Anthony Kok; the famous architect Gerrit Thomas Rietveld and the painter and film director Hans Richter. De Stijl well fulfilled the criteria of the age.

A great deal was written, also. Texts by Oud, Van Doesburg and Mondrian were also published by that kindred institution, the Bauhaus. *De Stijl* was even open to the Dada movement and to the participation of Arp, Schwitters and Man Ray; then the review died a natural death in 1928.

Every school has its limits and inevitably degenerates. All the De Stijl artists had to submit to the dogma of linear right angle intersection—the new religion—and it was no doubt they who influenced Mondrian in the use of primary colors. But in painting, these principles only had a real influence on Mondrian and his few disciples and, as far as the plastic arts were concerned, on the De Stijl movement. In the same way that Monet was unquestionably alone in remaining faithful to the

Neo-Plasticism and Esprit Nouveau

Impressionist movement to the end, we can say that Mondrian was alone in remaining wholly faithful to the principles he laid down, to the extent that the term "neo-Plasticism" nowadays applies almost exclusively to his work. In the following decade, Mondrian even succeeded in making his small colored squares flash with the same restlessness as the lights of New York, mapped out in the same grid pattern as the city streets of his great adopted city.

In establishing a new plastic art, Mondrian set himself two tasks: to demolish the aesthetics inherited from the Renaissance and to construct an art of his times, a new humanism. Many of the forms that surround us in everyday life derive from his work.

While neo-Plasticism is Dutch in origin, Purism is a French movement. Two reviews following one after the other supported the theories. As early as 1915, the publication *L'Elan* stated that "Cubism is a Purist movement" and from 1920 to 1925, *L'Esprit nouveau* published Purist attempts to break free of or change avant-garde aesthetics, such as Cubism and Orphism. "Orphism" is a term said to have been invented by Apollinaire, to apply particularly to the work of the Delaunays.

Thus the search for purity in a work of art constituted the dogma of Purism. Clearly, this involved a number of prohibitions, including the forbidding of all gratuitous freedom, all fantasy and the element of chance. Its perfect authenticity was modeled on the machine. The movement had few followers and remained the affair of Ozenfant and Jeanneret, otherwise known as Le Corbusier. However, one ally of considerable weight came to their assistance: Fernand Léger. In his own words, he assembled his truly architectural pictures "study by study, piece by piece, just as motors or houses are assembled."

The meeting in 1920 of Léger and Le Corbusier is in fact of great importance. Together, they established the new relationship between painting and architecture. "How may a feeling of space be created, a breaking of

boundaries? Quite simply through color, through walls of different colors," answered Léger, explaining: "The apartment, which I shall call the 'inhabitable rectangle,' shall be transformed into the 'elastic rectangle.' A light blue wall recedes, a black wall advances, a yellow wall disappears." He was both poet and interior designer, this painter of genius. Works like *The City, Man and Machine, Woman with a Mirror*, undeniably bear the stamp of

29   Fernand Léger: *Mural Composition*. 1926. Oil on canvas, 130 × 97 cm. Private collection.

30   Piet Mondrian: *Composition*.
1930. Oil on canvas, 50.5 × 50.5 cm.
Stedelijk Van Abbemuseum, Eindhoven.

Purism

31 Le Corbusier (Charles-Edouard Jeanneret): *Still Life*. 1922. Oil on canvas, 65 × 81 cm. Musée national d'Art moderne, Centre Georges Pompidou, Paris.

32 Fernand Léger: *Still Life on Table*. 1925. Pencil drawing, 30 × 38 cm.

33 Amédée Ozenfant: *Blue Still Life on a Dark Ground*. 1922–1927. Oil on canvas.

34 Girogio Morandi: *Metaphysical Still Life*. 1920. Oil on canvas, 68 × 62 cm. Private collection, Milan.

Purism and of its manifesto, *Après le cubisme* ("After Cubism") published by Ozenfant and Le Corbusier in 1918.

This manifesto contains two major trends: austerity and decoration, as Purism aimed to be decorative in its own way. The object was to defend Cubism from the incomprehension and the misrepresentations to which it was subject; it had to be "purified" to enable it to find its strength and original direction again. A return to order and clarity, a rejection of the anecdotal, a limitation of the role of color and an absolute objectivity—such were the key notions of Purism.

The most noteworthy characteristics of Purist compositions—the majority of which were still lifes—were the strictness of the page-setting, the diminished color values and the very soft tones. But Le Corbusier was above all an architect, and Ozenfant a teacher, soon to go and teach in the United States.

The parallel works by Giorgio Morandi should also be noted. Morandi was alone among the Italian artists of the period (who were all slipping unconsciously towards the naturalism that would be brought to the fore the following decade under fascism), to avoid falling into the trap of "purely Italian art," and to keep to a representation of objects, which relates him, notwithstanding a dose of poetry, to the Purists. He did flirt briefly with metaphysical painting, whose master, De Chirico, said of him: "He looks with the eyes of a believer, and the bones within things, which, because they are immobile, are dead for us, appear to him in their most consoling aspect—in their immortal aspect. In this way he participated in the great lyricism created by the last profound European art: the metaphysics of the most ordinary objects. Habit has made us so familiar with these objects, that however aware we may be of the mystery of appearances, we see them through the eyes of a person who looks, but does not know." From 1920 on, Morandi returned to a more deeply personal art, following his own strict inclination towards a ghostly, linear style, yet retaining from metaphysical painting the contemplative flavor of the mysterious life of things.

Like that of the Purists, Morandi's art is marked by a craftsmanlike technique—to the extent of his grinding his own colors himself—by a palette which he chose to keep dull (it was said that he let dust cover the objects he used as models) and by a stock of objects which became a veritable alphabet.

With Léger, on the other hand, misty dreams are left behind, all is solid and concrete. Here we are, in the "real." And real, for Léger, consists of the everyday realities of speed, machines, color, as well as those that make up the social world of work, of life itself, with its constant bringing together of hand and tool. In the words of Pierre Abraham, he was a "herald of the people." With the 1920s, Léger's "mechanical era" began. His aim was to take account of urban and industrial civilization, characterized by speed and violence. Colors and forms rebel against unwieldy tradition: "We have finished with fog, with 'chiaroscuro,' this is the advent of the state of light." The forms are highlighted in a way similar to the works of De Stijl followers. The meeting with Le Corbusier was of critical importance, since it gave true meaning to Léger's aim of making abstract painting play a role in every possible field—initially, by obliging it to meet the requirements of architecture. His *Abstract Machines in Pure Color*, carried out between 1921 and 1925, were put to use in

Monumentality

35 Marcel Gromaire: *War*. 1925. Oil on canvas, 130 × 98.5 cm. Musée d'Art moderne de la Ville de Paris, Paris.

A loner, and on the fringe of artistic currents, Gromaire was representative of the "classical" current in French art, even though his roots were firmly embedded in Cubism and Expressionism, with Cézanne and Seurat—who provided the constructive rigor necessary to satisfy his temperament—and the French and Flemish primitives, who spoke to his need to get back to nature. Submitted to the Salon des Indépendants in 1925, *War* is his most famous painting, a simultaneously realistic and symbolic representation of soldiers in a trench. The monumental character of the work created a sensation at the time.

the 1925 International Exhibition of Modern Industrial and Decorative Arts, in the *Esprit nouveau* Pavilion by Le Corbusier and in Mallet-Stevens's *Ambassade* Pavilion. They were also used in the form of a stage set and costumes for the Ballet Suédois production by Rolf de Maré, *Skating Rink* (1922), to music by Arthur Honegger, and *La Création du monde* ("The Creation of the World"), to music by Darius Milhaud and a theme by

Blaise Cendrars. The interplay of pure colors used in each scene lent itself to a modeling of stage space by the choreography.

Léger had another passion: cinema. In 1921 he participated with Blaise Cendrars in a film by Abel Gance called *La Roue* ("The Wheel") and, together with Mallet-Stevens and the young Claude Autant-Lara, he designed the sets for the film *L'Inhumaine* ("The New

Abstraction

36   Willi Baumeister: *Figure and Segment of a Circle*. 1923. Oil and wood on canvas, 118 × 69 cm. Kunsthalle, Hamburg.

Baumeister, although his ideas were close to those of the Bauhaus, was never actually a member. He was nevertheless listed, like the members of the Bauhaus, as a "degenerate" artist by the Nazis, and dismissed from his post as teacher at the Fine Arts School of Frankfurt. His sensitivity brings him closer to Léger, Le Corbusier and Ozenfant, who recognized that his mural works of the twenties were "paintings to be integrated into the wall" and that they reflected their own interest in the machine and modern technology. They appreciated his way of abstracting and simplifying forms, without ever breaking completely with the representational and reality. They published Baumeister's works in their review *L'Esprit nouveau* and he thus became their particular link with Germany.

Enchantment") by Marcel L'Herbier, taken from a book by Pierre MacOrlan. Altogether a man of his era, Léger wanted to touch on everything and transform everything he touched. His cinematographic experience led him to some conclusions: the scenario had to be done away with, in order to leave the object alone, presented rhythmically, through editing and shifting the viewpoint. Léger was both the producer and director of the first film without a scenario *Le Ballet mécanique*

("The Mechanical Ballet") with photography by Man Ray and Dudley Murphy, and concrete music featuring electric bells by George Antheil, and, fascinated by this mobile geometry, he considered for a time devoting himself exclusively to the cinema. Luckily or unluckily, he did not do so, and in the following decade, Léger was to be found working towards an increasingly solid realism centering principally around the human face. Writing about his nudes of the 1920s, he

37 Fernand Léger: *Discs in the City.* 1920–1921. Oil on canvas, 130 × 162 cm. Private collection.

38 Frank Kupka: *Sun.* 1920. Ink and pencil on paper, 25 × 16.5 cm. Private Collection.

1920 was the key year in the transition of this artist—who was Czech in origin, but lived mostly in Paris—from figurative to abstract art. He explained: "To the objection that it is impossible to create forms and colors, my answer is that man has created the Ionic and the Doric columns and that architecture has constantly invented forms of which the various versions are well proportioned and always have a reason for being as they are.... Man gives his thoughts an exterior form by his words.... Why should he not do the same in painting and sculpture, independently of the forms and colors which surround him?"

His work centered on two principal themes, typical of the 1920s, which correspond to and even blend into each other: jazz and machinery. He suggested the syncopated rhythms of jazz by broken forms, accentuated by a bright palette dominated by red ochres, and the power of machinery by cogs and gearing, rendered in more neutral tones. In 1931, Kupka joined the Abstraction-Création group, and became a member of its directing committee.

39   Robert Delaunay: *The Poet
Philippe Soupault*. 1922. Oil on canvas,
197 × 130 cm. Musée national d'Art
moderne, Centre Georges Pompidou,
Paris.

Dada

40   Francis Picabia: *Spanish Night*.
1922. Ripolin on canvas,
186 × 150 cm. Private collection.

1920 was the year that the *Dada Almanac* appeared. It was also the year of the movement's death. Jacques Rivière published a text in the *Nouvelle Revue Française* which was at once a definition of Dada, and an obituary: "Dada managed to take hold of the being before it gave in to the system, to grasp it in all its incoherence, or rather, in its primal coherence, before the idea of contradiction appeared and forced it to contain itself, structure itself; to replace its acquired logical unity with its original, absurd unity." ("Reconnaissance de Dada".) André Gide also passed comment: "Dada is an insignificant absolute."

41   Max Ernst: *Oedipus Rex*. 1922. Oil on canvas, 93 × 102 cm. Claude Hersaint Collection, Paris.

Max Ernst was extremely versatile. He was continually on the go, changing his style, his technique, his home—even his nationality. He would invent something, then, after perfecting it, reject it. He was sceptical, doubting, ironical. Still, during the twenties, despite the fact that he remained in the background, he constituted an essential link between Dada and Surrealism. He avoided the noisy displays and the heated debates, such as the 1922 Dada Congress in Paris. He was in Saigon in 1924, the year André Breton's first *Surrealist Manifesto* appeared—it carefully avoided mentioning his name. He said himself: "I admit (...) that I kept a certain distance between myself and the Surrealists and their doctrines." This "certain distance," was, as Uwe M. Schneede points out, in fact characteristic of all his work.

announced: "With the most banal, worn-out subject, a female nude in an atelier, or a thousand others, you can usefully replace the locomotives and other modern devices that are difficult to get to pose at home. All this is simply the means: the interest lies solely in the use made of them."

"One of the results of this war is to have reduced art to bankruptcy," wrote Trotsky, momentarily turned art critic, in 1916 in Paris. Doubtless he was thinking of Dada. Dada was, in fact, an intellectual phenomenon inseparable from the First World War. In the same way that the War had destroyed everything, artists set out to destroy art. Duchamp tackled the Mona Lisa, by sticking a Daliesque moustache on her and and by informing everyone: L.H.O.O.Q. (*Elle a chaud au cul*; "she's got hot pants"). He submitted a urinal as a piece of "ready-made" sculpture, thus doing away with the concept of an *objet d'art*. Picabia designed machines that were absolutely non-operational. A writer, Arthur Cravan, asked to hold a conference on Futurism in New York, insulted the public and finished by exposing his backside, with the clear aim of mocking the views on art held by the audience. Even the name Dada is said to be the result of a pin stuck at random into a dictionary. This revolt in all its pathos reached its apogee in 1920. It spread to all countries, especially those which had most suffered the ravages of the war. Like Apollinaire's famous omnipresent character, Dada was simultaneously in

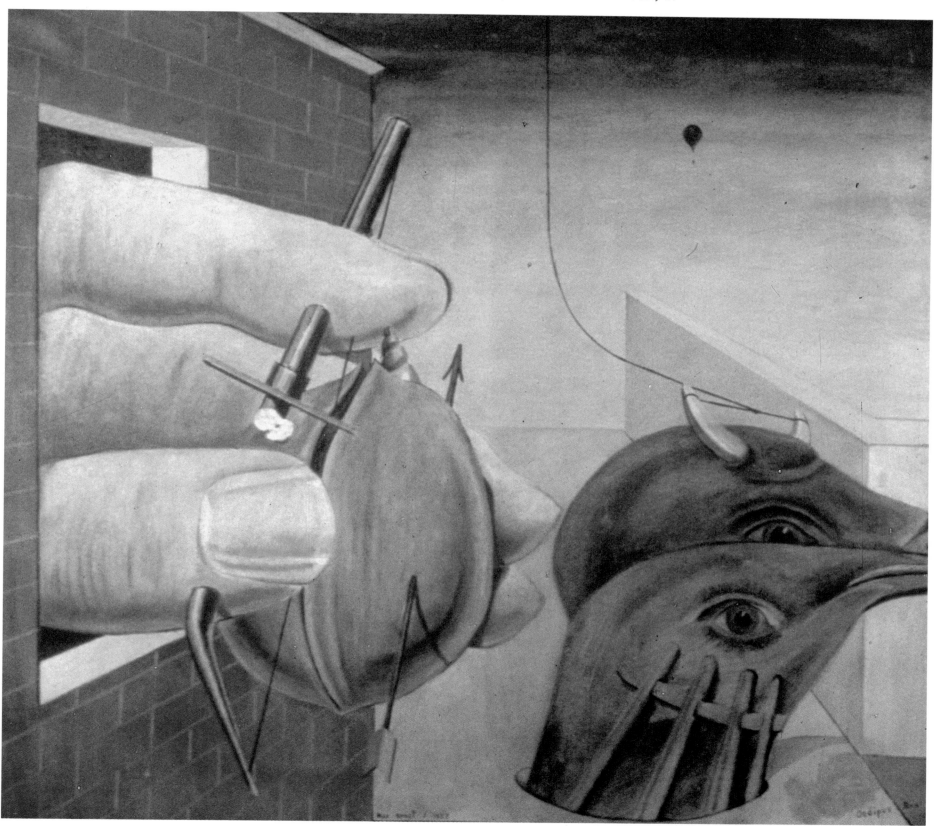

Surrealists Before Their Time

42   Max Ernst: *The Elephant Celebes*.
1921. Oil on canvas, 130 × 110 cm.
The Tate Gallery, London.

Surrealism

Spiritual zone containing traces of
resilient Cubism, with some vestiges of
a fading Symbolism. Area from which
Dada was wise enough to steer clear
as regards art, Surrealism in the 1920s
was still formulating its first hesitant
theories and attracted mostly the
artists aware of the shortcomings of
immediately previous, or even contemporary movements, such as Futurism,
and abstract art, which they considered "low-level." The closing of the
Bauhaus by the Nazis in 1933 tilted
the balance in favor of Surrealism,
creative spontaneity taking the place of
the Bauhaus's geometric rationalism. It
was at this time that such early
Surrealists as Max Ernst, Yves Tanguy,
Miró, de Chirico, Magritte, and
Duchamp were joined by new,
more orthodox recruits like Victor
Brauner, Oscar Dominguez, Meret
Oppenheim and others; even Kandinsky, who took refuge in
France, was welcomed by Breton, in
this same year of 1933, as the
Surrealists' guest of honor at the Salon
des Surindépendants. A decade
would go by before the world, including America (the Chilean Matta,
the Cuban Wilfredo Lam and the Arme-
nian Arshile Gorky, turned
American citizen), caught the Surrealist fever; the movement became
symbolic of creative freedom and was
unanimously rejected by the
triumphant totalitarian regimes of
Hitler's Germany, Mussolini's Italy
and Stalin's Russia.

Zurich, Berlin and Cologne. It even put in a brief appearance in New York. It flowed over from the capitals to be seen for a short while in the countryside, everywhere pushing nonconformity to the limits of blasphemy and obscenity. Whereas at its inception it was quite poor from a pictorial point of view, the movement was enriched by the support of artists either joining its ranks or, at least, not repudiating it. Thus the Dada gallery in Zurich presented a jumble of artists including De Chirico, Max Ernst, Feininger and Kandinsky. The Berliners (Grosz, Raoul Hausmann, Heartfield, Richter and others) used photomontage. Ernst worked with collage; Arp, cut and glued wood. Kurt Schwitters, a great trendsetter, raised any piece of rubbish to the status of a work of art in his *Merz* series, anticipating the "scrap" we know today: his technique was in turn pictorial, sculptural and even architectural. 1920 was the year when the storm broke, when the poet Tristan Tzara, having arrived in Paris, gave a definition to this extraordinary calling into question through the absurd. But Dada carried within itself the cancer which was to terminate its own short life. "Total spectacle" turns quickly to negative provocation. The 1922 Dada Salon sealed the movement's fate: Soupault exhibited a lump of tarmac entitled *Retiro City*; an empty frame, *Portrait of an Unknown*; and a mirror, *Portrait of an Imbecile*.
Nevertheless, Picabia and his "targets" remain, as does the complex case of Duchamp, the "collages" by Max Ernst, the "rayograms" by Man Ray, ridiculing the photographer's pretensions to making works of art. The end result may seem scanty, but in reality Dada opened many doors which are not all closed today. It heralded Surrealism and gave a good lesson in philosophy by defining "vacuum" as the unacknowledged center of Western values—specifically, aesthetic values.
Duchamp, who could well have been called Lewis Caroll had he been English, summarized Dada in his own way: "There is no solution because there is no problem." And vice versa, one is tempted to add.
The great artists progressed beyond Dada. They came out of the dream beyond nihilism. Thus Max Ernst moved away from Dadaist derision to the formal beauty and visual metaphysics of *The Hat Makes the Man* (1926) and *The Elephant Celebes* (1921). Unwittingly, Ernst turned Surrealist in 1923, with works that seem to have come straight out of *The Child's Brain* by De Chirico. Fairy stories and sadistic nightmares followed each other, to the extent that André Breton included Ernst among the elect in his *Manifeste du Surréalisme* ("Surrealist Manifesto") (1924).

43   Giorgio de Chirico: *Self-portrait*. 1924. Oil on canvas, 38.5 × 51 cm. The Toledo Museum of Art, Toledo.

44   Juan Miró: *Dialogue of Insects*. 1924–1925. Oil on canvas, 72.5 × 55 cm. Private collection.

45 Pablo Picasso: *Large Bather*.
1921. Oil on canvas, 180 × 98 cm.
Musée de l'Orangerie, Jean Walter
and Paul Guillaume Collection, Paris.

46 Henri Matisse: *Decorative Figure
on an Ornamental Ground*.
1925–1926. Oil on canvas,
130 × 98 cm. Musée national d'Art
moderne, Centre Georges Pompidou,
Paris.

Neo-Classicism

Whatever happened? We left Matisse and Picasso archrevolutionaries; they turn up again in the 1920s, to all appearances calmed down and disguised as bourgeois. In 1910 Matisse painted his famous *Dance*, firmly within the boundaries of Expressionism, Fauvism and abstraction. Now he was juggling with his *Odalisques* as though trying to rival the Orientalists. In 1907 Picasso invented Cubism and attempted to resolve the central paradox of painting—how to insert volume into a flat surface—with his no less famous painting *Les Demoiselles d'Avignon*. At the time everyone thought that he had painted something horrifying and mad. Braque commented that it was "like swallowing oil to spit out fire" and Derain was certain that Picasso "would be found hanged behind his painting." Yet in 1921, not only was Picasso not hanged, but he was in the process of painting designs taken from Greek vases.

The truth is that in France there is no such thing as real avant-garde. One eye is always turned to the past. Even Picasso himself fell into line, as did Diaghilev, his Russian friend. In order to design the sets and costumes for Diaghilev's ballet, *Parade*, Picasso left for Rome to attend the rehearsals. He visited Florence and Naples, and saw the sculpture and frescoes of Herculaneum and Pompeii. The experience prompted one of his about-faces, which were and would continue to be habitual, and he returned to the classicism which Apollinaire had called for already in 1918: "I would like to see you painting large pictures, like Poussin." But Picasso no more copied antique works than he had copied African art. Certainly, the subjects of *Women at the Fountain* (1921) or of the *Large Bather* (1921) are drawn from antiquity. The drawing recalls that of certain Greek vases. The women give the appearance of being cut from marble and their costumes call temple columns to mind. But while there are elements of Poussin in the works, the influence of the Ballets Russes on Picasso's painting is far clearer. "Cubism has its purposes in plastic art," Picasso declared at the time. "We see it simply as a means of expressing what we perceive mentally and intellectually, together with all the possibilities open to drawing and color, in their correct place. It has been a source of unexpected pleasure for us, a source of discovery." Thus the influence of the Ballets Russes played a role in the development of Picasso's Cubism. His still lifes became rich, sumptuous. Cocteau commented: "My dream in music would be to hear the music of Picasso's guitars." Dada, the Surrealists and the abstract artists of the period severely criticized Matisse, accusing him in the 1920s of pandering to middle-class taste by offering insipid modernist paintings, lacking visual or meta-physical depth. They had utterly failed to understand that Matisse's work is based on double meanings and implications. The artificial paradises of the "decorative figures" and other *Odalisques* are part of Matisse's magic world, with its vibrant interplay of all the plastic elements, all the colors. Can this series of *Odalisques* be

Academicism, Modernism

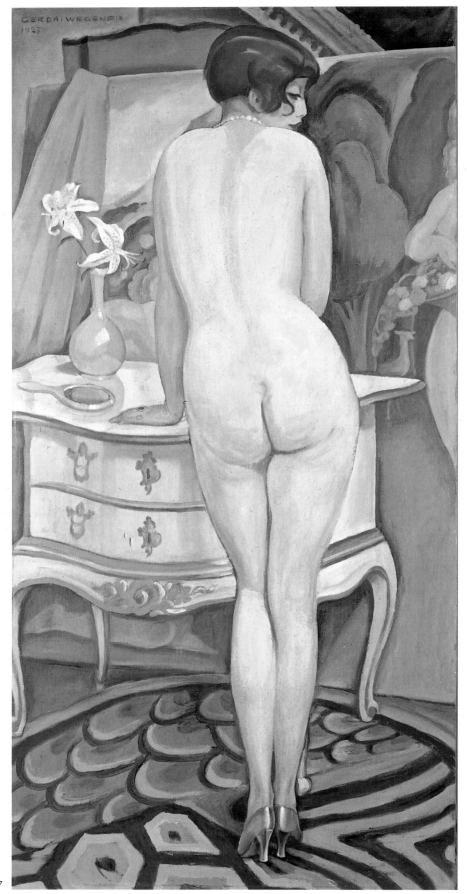

48

47

explained by the general postwar climate, the release after the horror, the rediscovery of easy living? Or was it the glorious light of the Midi, where Matisse lived, frequent visits to Renoir and Bonnard, memories of Delacroix or nostalgia for Morocco? Matisse set up his oriental decor in a corner of his atelier: a Moorish screen, some Arab hangings, a few objects. The woman is gloriously offset against this background, regal, a triumphal female arabesque. It is not clear where the rug finishes or where the paper of the hangings begins. The lemons, in spite of their position, are fully incorporated into the composition, as is the mirror, The plant is a variation on the motif of the hangings. We do not even notice the incredible vertical back of the model, so surrounded is it with curves: Matisse beguiles the spectator. There should be no mistake: the *Odalisques* are closer in spirit to Persian miniatures—despite the difference in format—than they are to Delacroix's *Women from Algiers*. Matisse is less concerned with Orientalism than with the Orient. It is as though he has entered a subtle and complex game of chess and the victorious result is the woman herself—shining out from the decor surrounding her, her body an arabesque, her costume an extravagant dance of color. In 1920 he also designed the sets and costumes for a ballet by Diaghilev, *Chant du Rossignol* ("The Song of the Nightingale") (music by Stravinsky, choreography by Léonide Massine). All in all, the war years gave both Picasso and Matisse the opportunity to take stock, especially with regard to

and Middle-Class Taste

47 Gerda Wegener: *The Lily*. 1927.
Oil on canvas, 160 × 80 cm. Galerie
Félix Marcilhac, Paris.

48 Gustave Miklos: *The First Man*.
1924. Oil on canvas, 250 × 120 cm.
Galerie Félix Marcilhac, Paris.

49 Emile Aubry: *Two Friends*. 1925.
Oil on canvas, 65 × 50 cm. Galerie
Félix Marcilhac, Paris.

50 Mario Tozzi: *After the Bath*. 1921.
Oil on canvas, 165 × 114 cm. Private
collection, Paris.

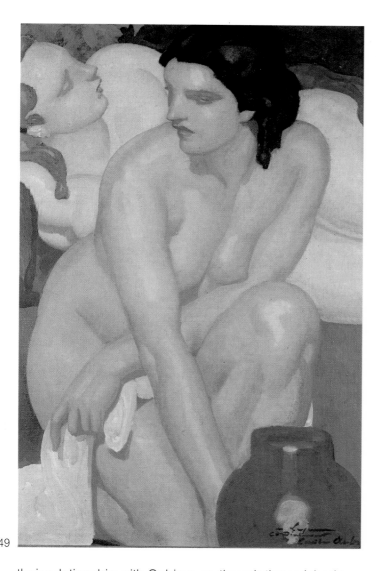

49

their relationship with Cubism, as though they wished to show their need to reconsider a good number of fundamental questions concerning the creative process. At the same time, they both presented a synthesis of the taste of the period—a mixture of the lessons of the immediate past, of the distant past and of fashionable modernism. The difference is that they did it with genius, unlike the representatives of the contemporary middle-class aesthetics.

Up with the easy life, happiness and security. The day after the war, high society, slightly disarrayed by the rise of the new rich and overwhelmed by the youth of the Roaring Twenties, felt its resistance slipping. People no longer wanted to think of the Russian Revolution, or of killing. Dada and Surrealism were rejected at one go; Impressionism was only just acceptable. Apollinaire's greatest merit, apart from the beauty of his verse, was to have been able to pin-point and express, in his highly personal manner, the poetic and artistic aspirations of his era. Of Matisse, for example, whom everyone appreciated, he wrote: "If one had to compare the work of Henri Matisse to something, that thing would have to be

50

an orange. Like an orange, the work of Matisse is a fruit of brilliant light."

René Huyghe noted that those with new fortunes, on the lookout simultaneously for showy spending and good investments, began to scent out the potential of artistic crazes and caught sight of the possibility of speculation. The merchant-prophets, struggling to gain acceptance for a rejected art—like Durand-Ruel for Impressionism or Kahnweiler for Cubism—were already being replaced by hot-headed and greedy business-men.

Influenced by them, and despite initial distaste, the middle class adopted modern art and even "played" the market, as it represented an investment which could shoot up in value. A race of artists supplied on demand, all too happy to find a place in private collections. "You like that?"—"Oh, you know, one gets used to it in the end."

Indeed, the bourgeoisie had to rally in opposition to the Bolshevik—the "man with the knife between his teeth." In today's language, it was necessary to "capitalize on" the strength and creative power of past movements while remaining "with it." Representational art need not necessarily be considered retrograde; academicism should be able to stimulate art while at the same time providing reassurance. To refer to Bonnard, Vuillard or Matisse was, after all, to draw on solid quality. Why not retain the acceptable elements of Cubism or Fauvism?

52

51

Totalitarian regimes vigorously espoused this position; in Russia, for example, the government insisted on socialist realism in painting as well as in sculpture. The same René Huyghe called this the "return to appearances," as though, after terrible trials and the long reign of death, life was once again beginning to assert its rights.

Paris remained the international capital of painting for a little while longer. The compulsive negativism of Dadaism was opposed by the "virtues" of realism. Cubism was increasingly left behind, considered too esoteric, insufficiently universal, although it was used to re-instill greater solidity to forms, to give more power to expression and inject new youth into decoration.

Thus began the official reign of the "French Artists" style, the academic revival. Modernist imitations displayed Ingres-like traces; Tozzi corresponded to Kisling. The female form was upheld against its "massacre" by Fauvism, Expressionism or Cubism. French tradition came into play; the "painting-profession," painting free of cosmopolitanism and intellectualism was championed. The word of the day at the Salons was to make "pleasant" pictures. The female nude came back into favor as the heritage of previous generations and the natural outgrowth of school teaching. After avant-garde art the Salon felt like a refuge.

Miklos, Pougheon, Emile Aubry, René Crevel and Fauconnet, among others, produced a decorative style based on a friendly compromise, which was quickly absorbed by the system and so widely disseminated as to become a new academic art. Nationalism and political concerns entered the scene. The French bourgeoisie, understandably, was against anything that smacked of Bolshevism or came from Munich! The world of "sharks, profiteers, dupes, hawkers and... sharpsters" had to be taught a lesson, or so the art critics explained under the general title of *Pictorial Madness*, in which they claimed to support "true art" against that springing from a "Bolshevist" background. "Drawing has been totally undermined, reduced to nothing more than a stupid mess, an excuse for the ignorant, the lazy and for shirkers; it is a crass fallacy to hold that distortion has the power regularly and inevitably to give strength to expression.... Only through the truth of the movement, the expression of the face, the setting and the color can we comprehend the drama, and by these means the artist must suggest it. But an Expressionist or a Surrealist finds it easier to work with caricature and ugliness. We should,

however, be at least slightly grateful to them for deigning to agree that painting may dare to strive for meaning. Is it not the current byword that 'painting today must not express feeling?' Why, one might as well study a collection of butterflies or a Turkish rug. When an art which claims to be 'living' is reduced to such poverty, it has reached rock bottom. When the Byzantine mosaic workers or the cathedral carvers distorted, they did so to suit the pillar, the wall or the lighting, and with what intelligence!"

Endless controversy threw out, arguments identical to those which have always separated the avant-gardists from official taste. But times were changing, and little by little the French artists lost official support, although they retained that of the collectors and speculators. The Musée du Luxembourg was closed in favor of the establishment of a Museum of Modern Art. State commissions remained numerous, but academic imperialism was no longer what it had been. As J.-E. Blanche wrote: "The French artists had a group spirit, they had common interests maintaining their cohesion as a social group, a charitable board, the Prix de Rome day nursery, an old soldiers' rest home. But what was this tranquil society of complacent artists? Country bumpkins come to Paris!"

The naturalist tendency displayed by the French Artists' Salon and their attempts at "modern stylization" were by no means a limited phenomenon.

51 Eugène Robert Pougheon: *Composition with Horse's Head*. 1924. Oil on canvas, 70 × 60 cm. Galerie Félix Marcilhac, Paris.

52 Gustave Miklos: *Figures and Dog*. 1921. Oil on canvas, 180 × 100 cm. Galerie Félix Marcilhac, Paris.

Keeping Up with the Times

53 René Crevel: *Bathers and Fauna*. 1925. Oil on canvas, 100 × 100 cm. Galerie Félix Marcilhac, Paris.

54 Georges Pierre Fauconnet: *Nude Man*. 1920. Tempera on canvas mixed media, 200 × 100 cm. Galerie Félix Marcilhac, Paris.

53

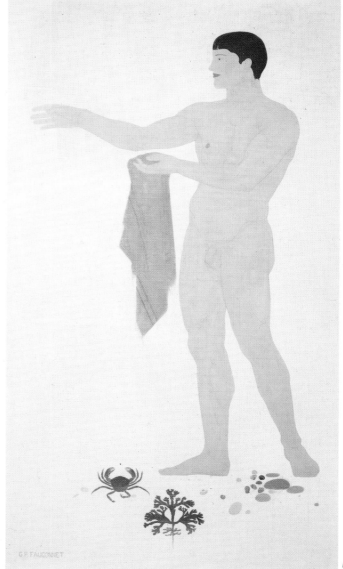

54

The Bauhaus

55 The Bauhaus teachers, period photo, from left to right: Albers, Scheper, Muche, Moholy-Nagy, Bayer, Schmidt, Gropius, Breuer, Kandinsky, Klee, Feininger, Stölzl, Schlemmer.

56 Lyonel Feininger: *Cathedral of Socialism*. 1919. Woodcut, 32 × 19 cm. Bauhaus-Archiv, West Berlin.

This plate featured on the cover of the *Bauhaus Manifesto*. Feininger was in charge of the engraving workshop there. He abandoned a musical career to take up drawing and

then—after his discovery of Cubism—painting. But engraving had a paramount influence over the spatial arrangement of his works. For him converging or parallel lines were sufficient to create volumes. The concept of the cathedral can be traced throughout the history of ideas: the importance that it had had since romanticism throughout the nineteenth century was updated in the twentieth century.
This frontispiece symbolizes the community of three related arts. Gothic is interpreted in a new way, and thus rendered in abstract forms. Franz Marc defined Cubism as a "mystical interior construction." The cathedral is a good symbol of the union—universally pursued in the 1920s—of architecture, painting and sculpture. Le Corbusier, for his part, exclaimed: "The cathedral is not a work of the plastic arts, it is a drama."

Recommended to the Archduke of Weimar by Henry van de Velde, his predecessor at the head of Decorative Arts and the Weimar Academy, in 1920 Walter Gropius had been at his post for one year. His first action had been to combine the two institutions under the name of *Staatliches Bauhaus* ("State House for Construction"). Bauhaus: the name was to remain famous, symbolizing creativity, modernism, research. The Manifesto—it had been fashionable to write manifestos since Jean Moréas's Symbolist one—set out the principles of art for an industrial civilization. It should not be thought, however, that the Bauhaus was a spontaneous phenomenon. Gropius saw himself as a successor to Ruskin and William Morris, as well as to Van de Velde and the Munich Werkbund atelier.
Since the middle of the nineteenth century, many movements had attempted to react against industrialization, arch-enemy of good taste, and against academic

57 Paul Klee: *Lightening*. 1920. Oil and watercolor on paper, 29.2 × 19.7 cm. Whereabouts unknown.

art. These groups drew their ideas from romanticism or medievalism, and their aim was to produce, for the widest possible public, objects with a high degree of artistic merit. Among them were Mackmurdo and Crane's Century Guild (1882), and Morris's Arts and Crafts Exhibition Society (1888). They were eventually swallowed up by the solely decorative Modern style. In 1900, Adolf Loos was preaching functionalist aesthetics in *Ornament und Verbrechen* ("Ornament and Crime"). In the United States, Sullivan and Wright were applying the same principles. But nothing else had the firm structure of the Bauhaus, whose influence and spirit continued to be felt long after it officially disappeared. Even today, it can still be said that our taste bears the stamp of the Bauhaus. The aim of integrating art into life, of uniting science (and the use of the machine) and aesthetics in the same creation, remains with us today. At the time, however, because of its avant-gardist teaching and its pitched battle against academic art, the Bauhaus made many enemies. Politics became involved and the movement was even taxed with "Bolshevism"—the worst possible insult—simply because it began under a socialist regime. Today in West Berlin, the Bauhaus-Archiv Museum für Gestaltung, designed by Gropius, conserves and diffuses the work of the group. While this work may not win universal approbation, it is nonetheless true that the exceptional creativity of the remarkable Bauhaus group can find a comparison only in the great flowering of the Renaissance.
The comparison also holds true for teaching at the Bauhaus, where there were no "teachers" as such, but

The Bauhaus

58   Paul Klee: *Analysis of Various Perversities*. 1922. Pen and watercolor on paper, mounted on black cardboard, 31 × 24 cm. Musée national d'Art moderne, Centre Georges Pompidou, Paris (gift of Heinz Berggruen).

Integrating
Art
into
Life

59   Wassily Kandinsky: *Study for "Green Border"*. 1920. Watercolor, 50 × 70 cm. Nina Kandinsky Collection.

The Bauhaus

The Birth of Abstract Art:

Kandinsky, like Malevich, was one of the fathers of abstract art. In 1896, in an Impressionist exhibition in Moscow, he had seen one of Monet's *Haystacks*. He tells how, on looking at this picture, he had first been struck by the drawing, which was far from exact. But then, on longer contemplation, he was more and more excited by the colors, and he started to wonder if artists did not have the right to go further still and produce compositions as free as works of music. Unwittingly, at that moment abstract art was born.

From then on, this question tormented Kandinsky. He wrote down his thoughts and these notes formed the basis of his book *Über das Geistige in der Kunst* ("Concerning the Spiritual in Art"), finished in 1910. The same year he painted his first abstract watercolor. In the chapter on forms, Kandinsky speaks of the square, the triangle and the circle as forms that may be used in abstract compositions. Kandinsky's works are in fact far more "non-figurative" than all the paintings using geometric forms produced by the Bauhaus, Constructivism, De Stijl or Esprit nouveau. Circular, triangular and square forms were not invented, but have always existed, whereas Kandinsky's non-figurative work was the product of his own imagination. When he used geometric forms, they were only part of the composition and always surrounded by totally free forms of his own creation.

Kandinsky maintained that abstract art was the most difficult art. Three elements were indispensable to avoid repetitiveness: a perfect knowledge of drawing, a sense of composition, and a poetic sensibility. Art that repeated itself became decorative and died. Thus, the master gave his pupils this advice: "If you lack these three elements, go back to nature, she will provide you with new subjects."

60 Wassily Kandinsky: *On White*. 1923. Oil on canvas, 105 × 98 cm. Nina Kandinsky Collection.

61 Wassily Kandinsky: *Well Surrounded*. 1926. Oil on canvas, 106 × 64 cm. Galerie Maeght, Paris.

rather a community of "masters" and disciples, working together to create works based on new concepts. While architecture was the point of departure for the artist-craftsmen of the Bauhaus, their research was initially based on Adolf Hölzel's theory of colors and forms. The program included, firstly, a basic course directed by Paul Klee and Johannes Itten. Two parallel courses followed, one dedicated to practical work and the other to the study of art theory; after three years these led to the pupil becoming a "journeyman" in the tradition of the trade guilds. He was subsequently entitled to exercise one of the trades, or to present himself for the "Bauhaus Journeyman" examination, leading to working with the master and completed by a training in engineering. It can be said that while the Bauhaus did not actually set out to create a style, it transformed the conception of taste, by giving it a contemporary dimension which had not hitherto existed.

It was distinct from other art schools of the period, for example, in maintaining close links with industry. In the school itself, design projects were executed for furniture, materials or lamps, which could subsequently be mass-produced by factories. The Bauhaus also played a pioneering role in the field of molded and laminated wood, and the chairs designed by Mies van der Rohe are still, sixty years after their creation, astonishingly modern and up to date.

Students worked with such materials as paper, white metal, steel, aluminium, cellophane, glass, Plexiglas and cardboard. The aim was to be able to work with the natural qualities of the materials. Gropius was an architect and a number of his colleagues came to join him. True to his program, however, he knew how to attract the active complicity of artists in all fields—painting, sculpture and graphics—and their support showed itself to be critical. After Lyonel Feininger, a founder member, the painter Georg Muche joined the team of teachers to direct the weaving workshop. Paul Klee ran the glass-painting workshop, also giving a course on the "theory of form." Oskar Schlemmer introduced the drawing and sculpture course and subsequently added advanced classes in stage design. The exiled Kandinsky arrived later, in 1922, to teach mural painting. It is inaccurate to attribute to him the Russian Constructivist influence on the Bauhaus. In fact, he had had little contact with the Russian movement; if this did have any influence at all on the Bauhaus group, it was thanks to László Moholy-Nagy and his metal-working course. Marcks directed ceramics, Feininger printing. Klee was also in charge of tapestry. Itten, a specialist in color research, taught "elementary painting." An ex-school teacher, he was utterly absorbed by children's art and encouraged his students to practice yoga, obliging them to do preliminary relaxation and concentration exercises. The Bauhaus was not the abstract application of an idea. Taking stock of the problems of the era, it found solutions to them as they appeared. Its development was based

The Bauhaus

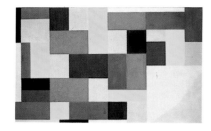

62   Theo van Doesburg: *Composition.* 1924. Oil on canvas, 52 × 21.5 cm. Private collection.

Theo van Doesburg linked the Bauhaus and De Stijl. He had in fact participated with Mondrian, Oud, Vantongerloo, Huszár and other artists in the founding of the *De Stijl* review. He was the best propagandist and most active messenger of neo-plastic painting and architecture, which was more elementary and more radical than post-Cubism in the geometric rendering of forms. He traveled a great deal. In 1920 he was in Brussels, then in Berlin. From 1921 to 1923 he stayed in Weimar, where, despite personal disagreements, his ideas had a considerable influence on the Bauhaus.

63   László Moholy-Nagy: *The Great Wheel (Large Emotion Meter).* 1920–1921. Oil on canvas, 95.5 × 75 cm. Stedelijk Van Abbemuseum, Eindhoven.

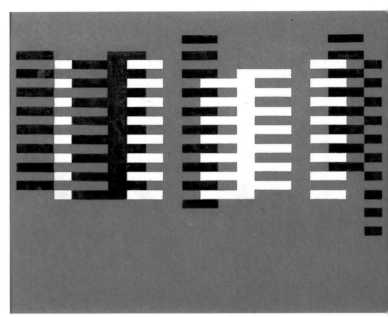

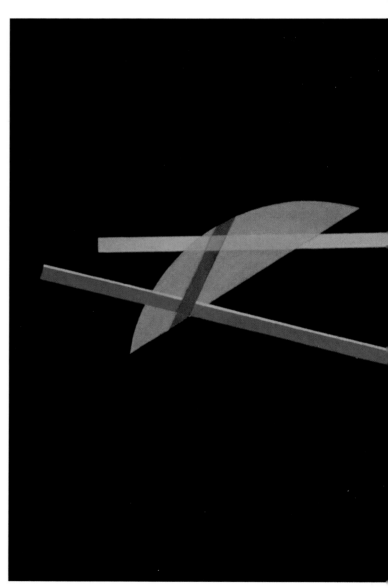

on a constant clarification of its method. The Bauhaus's significance is twofold: on the one hand, it helped rid German art of its anguished romanticism and mystic pathos; on the other hand, as the principal group workshop of the twentieth century, it takes its place in the line of movements of creative and innovative thought. The will to apply aesthetic principles was responsible, in part at least, for ushering in the desired new era following World War I. Industry in particular quickly realized the profit that could be drawn from this research: even in the case of the most banal, everyday object, good design increased sales. The International style, created in around 1920, remains one of the constants of creative output today. In the field of painting, the great merit of the Bauhaus was to assist the development of abstract art in its most positive form, above all through the publication of the writings of artists like Theo van Doesburg, Albert Gleizes, Wassily Kandinsky, Paul Klee, Kasimir Malevich and Piet Mondrian, in the *Bauhausbücher* series. The aim was not to teach an artistic style, but to impart a functional, organic whole. Klee wrote: "To grasp the function firstly, rather than the definitive form, is a beneficial necessity." Although he was constantly seeking new techniques for painting and developing new forms, Klee did not attempt to teach his inimitable and various styles. Rather, in the spirit of the Bauhaus, he strove to impart the basic concept of analysis. Similarly, Max Bill, who was his pupil, said of Kandinsky that his

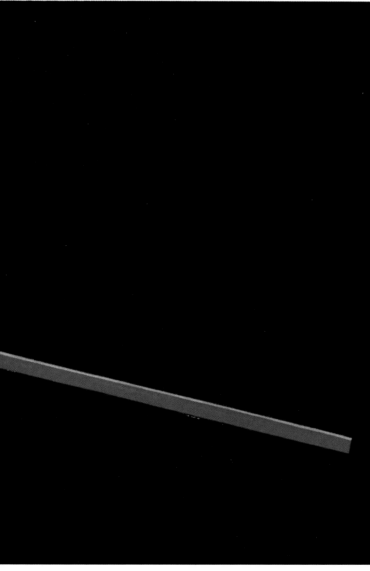

drawing classes took the form of exercises in observation rather than in art as such, their objective being a grasp of structure rather than superficial detail. Klee's creed is spelled out in the first sentence of his *Schöpferische Konfession* ("Creative Confession") (1918): "Art does not reproduce the visible, it renders visible." In his inaugural course at the Bauhaus, Klee described a disturbance in the movements of two planets, which, bursting out of their orbits, come closer and closer together and finally collide, precipitating an explosion. "What happens next?" Klee asked his pupils. "Draw that." Clearly, this was a new approach to teaching.

At the Bauhaus, Kandinsky was nicknamed the "sign-doctor." In analyzing a leap made by a dancer, for example, he gave the following outline to his pupils: dots represent the hands and the feet, a circle shows the movement of the costume, diagonals express the outspread arms and legs. He explained the arrival of abstract art in these words: "Today, in painting, a dot may sometimes say more than a human face. A vertical associated with a horizontal produces an almost dramatic sound. The contact of the acute angle of a triangle with a circle has no less effect than that of God's finger against Adam's in Michelangelo."

Moholy-Nagy was, along with Klee, Kandinsky and Gropius, one of the great artists and great teachers of the Bauhaus. He was the originator of a new kind of sculpture, one which used plastic materials for the first time; as a painter, he was the perfect example of a pure plastician. To develop his spatial and architectural vision, he eliminated the effects of style and texture and chose his colors according to their optical properties. In retrospect, the work of his pupils, which he closely guided, seems daringly prophetic, anticipatory and fantastic: reminiscent of El Lissitzky's page setting —Moholy-Nagy was simultaneously painter, sculptor, photographer, graphic designer and typographer—it foreshadows the architecture of Mies van der Rohe and opens the way for the sculpture of the second half of the century.

Josef Albers, an American painter who joined Gropius, in between his industrial prototypes, worked with stained glass. He was passionately concerned with the problems of color combined with those of basic forms. He played, with the greatest possible precision, not only with line and color, but also with different degrees of opacity and transparency. He maintained that color was the most relative of all mediums, and that man could rarely perceive its intrinsic nature. Rauschenberg was later to say that Albers was the best teacher he had ever had.

Schlemmer, many of whose paintings were destroyed by the Nazis, was extremely interested in the theater and in ballet. His pictures represent the human form as schematized lay figures, treated according to the same plastic and musical laws as a stage director would use to organize movement and rhythm on stage, giving equal importance to light and volume, to objects and space.

64 Josef Albers: *Fugue.* 1925. Ground glass, vitrified red glaze, partially sculpted, partially painted in oil, 24.5 × 66 cm. Kunstmuseum, Basle.

65 László Moholy-Nagy: *Construction.*

The Basic Forms

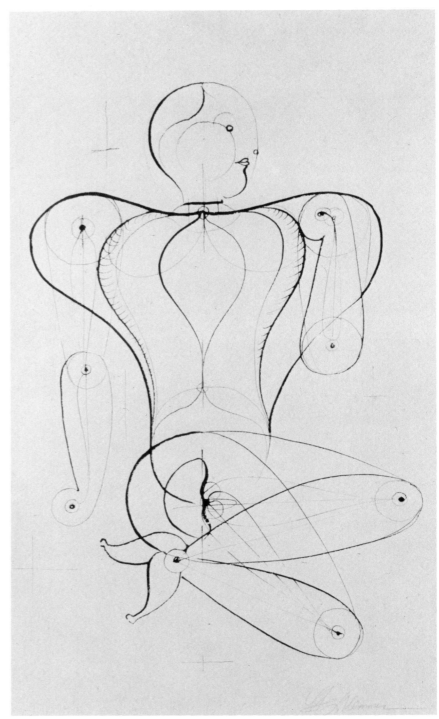

66   Ivan Puni: *The Musician*. 1921. Oil
on canvas, 144 × 98 cm. Mr. and
Mrs. Hermann Berninger Collection,
Zurich.

67   Oskar Schlemmer: *Homo Figur T*.
C. 1920–1921. Pen and ink on paper,
41.2 × 29 cm. Graphische Sammlung,
Staatsgalerie, Stuttgart.

The Bauhaus

68 Oskar Schlemmer: *4 Figures and Cube*. 1928. Oil and tempera on canvas, 250 × 160 cm. Graphische Sammlung, Staatsgalerie, Stuttgart.

69   Max Ernst: *Above the Clouds Midnight Passes.* 1920. Photographic enlargement of a collage, retouched in pencil, 73 × 55 cm. Kunsthaus, Zurich.

70   Willi Baumeister: *Head.* 1923. Photographic collage, 35 × 24.8 cm. Graphische Sammlung, Staatsgalerie, Stuttgart.

Rastadada

72 Hannah Höch: *Dada Dissects with a Kitchen Knife the Bourgeois Culture of Weimar Germany*. 1919–1920. Photomontage, 114 × 90 cm. Staatliche Museen Preussischer Kulturbesitz, National-galerie, West Berlin.

71 Francis Picabia: *Tableau Rasta-dada*. 1920. Collage on paper, 19 × 17 cm. Private collection.

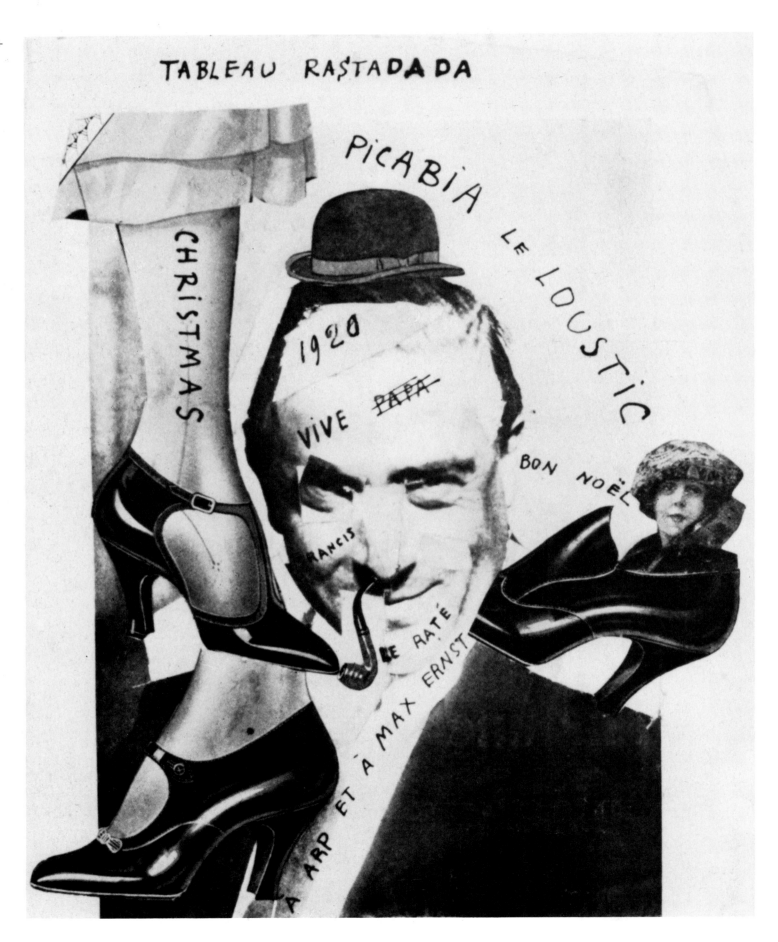

Dada Will Win!

In 1920, Dada was at its height. By 1922 it was already dead. Shocking, provoking Dadaist productions were on the increase throughout Europe.

In Paris: Tristan Tzara arrived from Zurich and such choice recruits as Aragon, Breton and Soupault—the editors of *Littérature*—joined the Paris Dada group. In February and March, there were public evenings, trips, and exhibitions. The *Great Dada Festival* took place on May 26. A manifesto was read by Ribemont-Dessaignes, Breton, Dermée, Eluard, Aragon, Tzara and others. Among the most representative painters were Duchamp, Max Ernst, Francis Picabia and Man Ray.

In Zurich: birthplace of Dada. The movement took its final bow in the form of the *Great Dada Ball* in March, and scandalized the public for a last time with an open-air salon.

In Berlin: Baader, Hausmann and Huelsenbeck, stars of the *First International Dada Fair*, continued the series of evening readings in June. Dix, Schlichter, Scholz, Ernst, Baargeld, Picabia, Grosz, Höch and others participated with their works. Hannah Höch, Raoul Hausmann and John Heartfield had developed a new photographic collage technique, allowing the contradictions and oppositions of society to be translated into artistic terms. From now on the movement was politicized, playing an active part in the revolutionary struggle. It became subject to state repression. In Cologne: One of the other two Dadaist centers, the police closed the *Pre-Spring Dada Exhibition*, but it reopened in May, accompanied by a vengeful poster proclaiming *Dada Will Win!* Activity in Cologne and Hanover was principally literary.

In New York: Marcel Duchamp, who had left the city for Paris in 1918, was welcomed there again in 1920. The result was the founding in April of the Société Anonyme, set up by Duchamp, Man Ray and Catherine Dreyer, whose major role was to present modern art in general—and especially European modern art—to the American public.

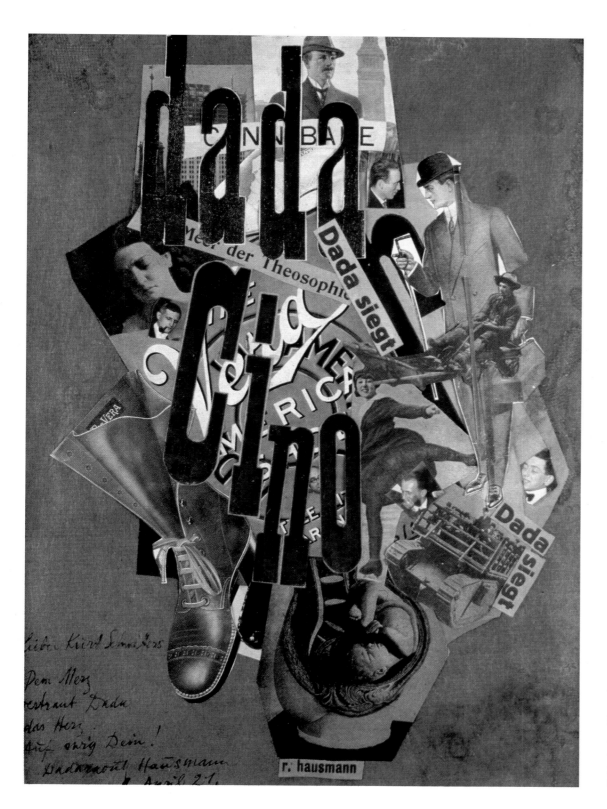

73 Raoul Hausmann: *Tatlin at Home*.
1920. Photomontage, 40 × 27.5 cm.
Moderna Museet, Stockholm.

74 Raoul Hausmann: *Dada – Cino*.
1920. Gouache on collage,
30 × 40 cm. Philippe-Guy E. Woog
Collection, Geneva.

Berlin in the Twenties

"The Capital and the Army wish themselves a prosperous new year." In a political satire review entitled *Die Pleite* ("Bankruptcy"), George Grosz denounced those responsible for the economic disaster in Germany after the war. Germany was shaken by *coups d'état*, political assassinations, general strikes and their bloody suppression. Faced with a steadily worsening economic situation and the general insufficiency of the Weimar Republic, German artists abandoned Dadaism, Cubism and Expressionism, movements directed essentially against the old society and the war. They declared themselves in favor of an art which accepted its social responsibility. Many of them, like George Grosz, John Heartfield, Wieland Herzfelde and Erwin Piscator, belonged to the Communist party, but this soon led to conflicts, since they spoke out against the bourgeois aesthetics supported by the party.

In 1920, in *Der Kunstlump* ("The Artistic Good-for-Nothing"), John Heartfield and George Grosz attacked all art which did not enter into the class struggle. Conrad Felixmüller publicly expressed his support for a revolutionary art. The November Group, in its spirit of opposition, devoted itself to acting as the instrument of the masses and to building a new society with them. Franz W. Seiwert developed, under the influence of Aleksandr Bogdanov, his idea of a proletarian culture. Otto Freundlich called for a collective art and the participation of non-artists in the creative process. Their letters and manifestos appeared in such reviews as *Die rote Fahne* ("The Red Flag"), *Die Aktion* ("Action") or *Freiheit* ("Freedom").

In line with such declarations, the painting of George Grosz, Otto Dix, Christian Schad and Hannah Höch changed. They adopted a "Verist" style, an objectivity so bare as to be an accusation. The "group of progressive artists" from Cologne developed a kind of political Constructivism. The painting of Conrad Felixmüller, Heinrich Maria Davringhausen, Georg Scholz and Rudolf Schlichter introduced the *Neue Sachlichkeit* ("New Objectivity"). In short, Germany was seething—only with Hitler's arrival did things settle down.

The expression *Neue Sachlichkeit* was coined by Gustav Hartlaub, director of the Kunsthalle in Mannheim. Around this idea, in 1925, he collected a number of artists, who otherwise had no particular connection with each other. The participants, of whom there were about thirty, had neither a common aesthetic program nor a definable style. Various influences can be detected in their works, especially traces of Dadaism and of metaphysical painting. It is, however, possible to isolate three tendencies. Firstly, a clearly satirical and political orientation, as displayed by George Grosz and Otto Dix. Secondly, a leaning towards portraiture, often with an apparent coldness of manner—Otto Dix again being an example, as well as Christian Schad.

Schad was a curious artist—the most distant, the most perfect, the most enigmatic of all the painters of the

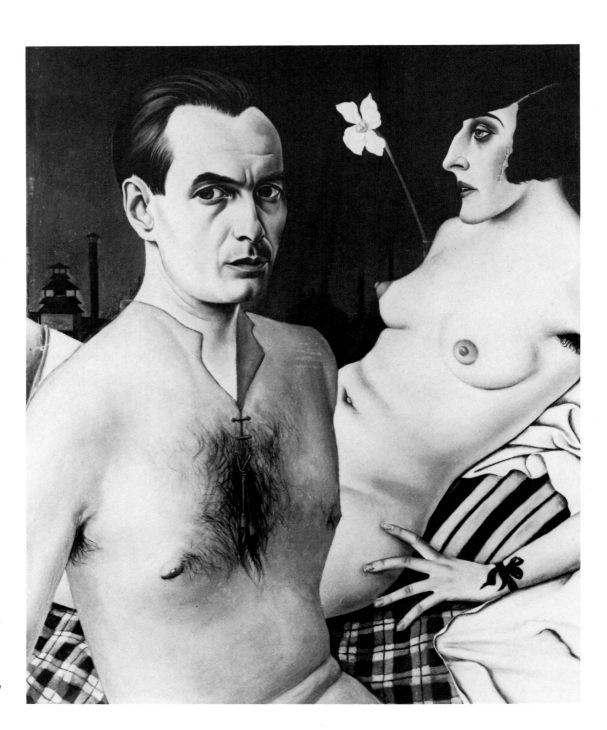

75   Christian Schad: *Self-portrait with Model*. 1927. Oil on wood, 76 × 61.5 cm. Private collection, Hamburg.

76   Christian Schad: *Nude*. 1929. Oil on wood, 55.5 × 53.8 cm. Von der Heydt-Museum, Wuppertal.

Verism

77   Otto Dix: *Three Prostitutes in the Street*. 1925. Tempera on chip-board, 95 × 100 cm. Private collection, Hamburg.

Berlin group. He observed his models with a glacial eye, and, although he claimed to be interested only in surfaces and appearances, in fact he touched the very mystery of their humanity, revealing their tragic solitude. Every one of his characters is alone, even if they are more than one—a man and a woman after making love, for example. And he presents them to us like a showman at a fair, or a detached photographer: just so many specimens—the aristocrat, the doctor or the naked woman—all equally distant, like envelopes, the very essence of mystery.

The third tendency was an attempt to give as precise and impersonal a description as possible of the industrial world, often making use of collage and photomontage. Apart from the Communists, most of the members were apolitical, though this did not prevent the Nazis from considering the productions of the *Neue Sachlichkeit* to be degenerate art; a great number of works were destroyed by them.

This was a world of bureaucrats, decorated soldiers and disabled people, where bourgeois men and women were displayed as interested only in the satisfaction of their instincts, obsessed by sex and money. The themes were to earn Grosz, in particular, many heavy fines.

The universe of Otto Dix is parallel to that of Grosz. The same bitter humor is present, the same assemblage of

78 Rudolf Schlichter: *The Rooftop Studio*. C. 1920. Pen and ink with watercolor, 45.8 × 63.8 cm. Galerie Nierendorf, Berlin.

79 George Grosz: *Model*. 1927.
Watercolor, 65.7 × 47.4 cm. Private
collection, Germany.

images lacking all traces of flattery and without the slightest poetical allusion, unlike their predecessor of the *Blaue Reiter* ("Blue Rider") group. They worked with a realism deliberately directed towards unusual subject matter which is still with us today, such as births or surgical operations.

Grosz, who spoke and published the most prolifically and who was the most frequently brought to court, announced his intentions in 1922 in *Der Mensch ist nicht gut, sondern ein Vieh* ("Man is not Good, but an Animal"). "Men have constructed an abject system. There is a high and a low. A few earn millions, while thousands of others have scarcely enough to live on.... But what is the connection of all this to 'great art?' The connection resides in the large number of artists and authors, known as "spiritualists," who continue to tolerate the system, rather than deciding to fight it. Although the time has now come to cleanse the sewers, to combat all such rotten individualism, the cultural hypocrisy and the cursed lack of love in our civilization, they are content to remain at the edge of the battlefield, cynical spectators. The reign of blessed and all-powerful private initiative has come. To help shake this belief, to show the oppressed the real face of their masters, that is my duty."

And Grosz painted works with titles such as *Metropolis, Diamond Traders, The Middle-Class Rises Up* and *Let Those Who Know How, Swim, and Those Who Are Too Heavy, Sink.*

In 1925 Grosz and Wieland Herzfelde outlined the intentions of their form of art in a text entitled *Die Kunst ist in Gefahr* ("Art is in Danger"): "We understand our new and great task as follows: to create an art with a point of view and place it at the service of the revolutionary cause. Still today, and even more than before, the affirmation of a political tendency in the field of art gives rise to indignant and scornful protests. Nobody denies, of course, that a political art has always existed and that its importance is irrefutable, but it is judged on its purely artistic and formal qualities, rather than on its polemical aspects. To judge in this way is to ignore completely that every art, of any period, has a political tendency and that it is only the character and clarity of this tendency which has altered. When, today, the friends of art try to demolish a work by attacking on principle its political leanings, or by accusing it of sensationalism, they are not dealing with the work of the artist, but stating their hostility to the idea defended by his work."

Developing an attitude in line with Marcel Duchamp's, Schwitters summarized, in a deliberately provocative formula, the simple and fruitful idea on which his own artistic theory was based: "Everything spat out by an artist is art." For his collages, which draw their technique from Cubism, and their arrangements dominated by horizontal-vertical oppositions from De Stijl, Schwitters made use of a multitude of materials, and more than anything, all sorts of refuse and discarded materials

80   *Die Pleite*, No. 6. 1920.

"I like newspapers" wrote George Grosz in 1926, "even if I maintain a critical attitude towards them. As propagators of ideas, of course, newspapers are considerably more important than books, since they have a far greater readership...."

For the cover pages that he carried out for reviews like *Die Pleite* ("Bancruptcy"), Grosz moved from art to political agitation. Taking a Spartacist stance, he waged war on capitalism, the army and social democracy, which had drained the revolution of its force. In many drawings he set forth his political beliefs by attacking personalities. In others he imagined that the revolution had already taken place: he thus expressed the hopes of those who had failed, and looked towards the future they had fought for. Here, for example, he hangs Capital and the Army. The images are almost an order to act, a call to arms.

"For me," he wrote, "art has not to do with aesthetics. Drawing is not an end in itself, it has a meaning. It is not a musical type of scribbling, to be felt and decoded by cultivated, subtle-minded beings. Drawing must once again take up a social purpose.... Graphic art can exert a considerable force against the medieval brutality, and the stupidity of men of our century, the moment it is directed with a single-minded will and a competent hand."

On the Way to "Scrap Art"

81 Franz Wilhelm Seiwert: *The Joyless Street*. 1927. Oil on canvas, 65 × 80 cm. Private collection, Hamburg.

82 Kurt Schwitters: *Victory*. 1922. Oil and collage on cardboard, 38.2 × 32 cm. Wilhelm Hack-Museum, Ludwigshafen.

With Schwitters, abstract, "scrap" art appeared. He used a Cubist technique for his collages, but he drew his inspiration mainly from refuse material, which he retouched with paint. Fragments of words finished off his works. Thus *Merz* appeared for the first time, by chance, in a 1919 work and subsequently served him as a name for his entire output and for his philosophy: "Merz is form." He even used it as the title of a review he published, which defended in turn Dada, neo-Plasticism and Russian Constructivism. He was deeply distressed at having to leave his first *Merzbau*, which was afterwards destroyed by a bombardment during the war, and was an accumulation of incongruous objects, both ordinary and unusual, a "house within a house" which represented his artistic approach: "Everything spat out by an artist is art." Time has shown us the result of this profession of faith.

(tickets, prospectuses, labels, wrapping paper), which he mixed with fragments of wood, metal, rubber and the like, often highlighting the whole with paint. A scrap of printed paper gave this group of works their title: *Merz*. "Merz is the form," he said, and went on to make Merz paintings, Merz sculptures, Merz houses, accumulations of everyday or other objects, in no way related to each other, except in the way dictated by the artist, simultaneously dwellings and monuments.

So, in the 1920s already, art could be made out of anything. Schwitters anticipated all the Pop art, Minimal art, Land art and other future happenings, as well as today's "trashcan archaeology" whose object is to preserve the detritus of civilization in Plexiglas, just as the ashes of Vesuvius preserved the empty imprint of bodies burned to cinders.

7 in

C. K.

ring)

e

s

enver

Sieg

BENGALISCHE Z

Marken sind nicht

Constructivism and Suprematism

matist "ideas" of skyscrapers or teapots than they were utilitarian objects. Malevich accompanied his famous *White on White* with this exhortation: "Throw yourselves into whiteness with me, fellow pilots, and swim into infinity. I have established the Suprematist semaphore. I have trampled the frontiers of colored skies underfoot, uprooted them, made them into a sack into which I have thrown all colors. Swim! Like an unbound sea of whiteness, infinity lies open before you."

On the other hand there was Tatlin and the Communist fanatic Rodchenko, who insisted that the artist had to turn technician and learn how to make use of modern production tools and materials, so as to direct all his energies towards benefiting the people. "Art in life" was the Constructivist slogan.

Suprematism was spiritually and aesthetically based. Constructivism sprang from the life of society itself. Aleksei Gan, one of Tatlin's disciples, stated: "We are the pioneers of intellectual-material production.... Painting, sculpture and theater are just expressions

On the one hand there was Malevich, Kandinsky and the Pevsner brothers. This group maintained that art was an essentially spiritual activity, the aim of which was to impart order to man's vision of the world. To organize life from the point of view of the artist-engineer was, according to them, to push artists down to the level of ordinary craftsmen. They held that art, by its very superfluous and non-useful nature, transcended functional craft design. Malevich's *Architectons*, *Planites* and pottery were more Supre-

of the capitalist, bourgeois aesthetic culture, satisfying the spiritual needs of consumers coming from a disorganized social order. We do not wish for abstract projects, but to take concrete problems as our point of departure, problems that the communist way of life obliges us to face."

Communism required an art for the people. If, immediately following the days of October, the avant-garde artists who came out of the Revolution, but were developing a new classicism, such as Malevich, Pevsner, Kandinsky and a few others, happened to be given important university posts in the fine arts, it was purely and simply, Gabo stated, because the academic professors were at the front (the civil war and the war with Poland were still going on), but once the military situation had changed, to the advantage of the Soviets, and the former incumbents of these posts returned to Moscow, the climate was suddenly and totally different. Lenin's easy-going tolerance was replaced by the open hostility of the Stalinist tendency which already, in 1921, was making its influence felt. One day, these "deviationist" artists found their Vkhutemas shut—and that meant leave of indeterminate duration. Almost all of them went into exile: Pevsner in France,

Gabo in America, Kandinsky to the Weimar Bauhaus. Only Malevich remained in Soviet Russia—isolated and forgotten until his death in 1935. He was buried in a coffin entirely covered with Suprematist motifs, which he had painted himself.

El Lissitzky, with his *Prouns*, in the field of typography and poster design, did his best to combine Suprematist and Constructivist principles, by trying to make "non-objectivist" abstract compositions work for Bolshevik propaganda. He even spread these simultaneously Constructivist and Suprematist ideas in the West, where he traveled widely from 1921 to 1930—a veritable ambassador of reconciled Russia. However, while he influenced the Bauhaus, in his own country he always came up against the irreducible slogan of the right-thinking doctrinaire Constructivists: "Art is dead! Art, like religion, is a dangerous weakness, an abandoning of reality...."

It was in the United States that the torch of geometric abstraction, buried with Malevich, was taken up again. The impact of *White on White*, exhibited at the Museum of Modern Art, New York, is at the origin of the entire wave of abstract geometric art which began in America in the 1960s.

86

ЛЕТЯТ НА ЗЕМЛЮ ИЗДАЛЕКА

88

87

WENDINGEN

89

It was precisely in 1920 that Soviet critics christened as "Constructivism" a movement which had started some years earlier in Moscow with the aim of forming a "synthesis of the plastic arts."

Yet, curiously, on August 5, 1920, yet another manifesto appeared, signed by Naum Gabo and Antoine Pevsner and entitled *Realist Manifesto*, which contained the essential principles of Constructivism.

Constructivism was not in fact a profession of artistic faith, but rather an idea which aimed to instill a new form of thought into modern art: in the new society, functional considerations should take precedence over aesthetic ones. In this way, painting became the poor relation of architecture, sculpture and the applied arts.

Earlier decorative movements were simply hangovers from the good old days; the utilitarian form became essential. To a certain extent, design was a direct spinoff of Constructivism, which placed materialism above the idea of artistic spirituality, mysticism and the philosophical theories dear to Kandinsky, Malevich and Mondrian. It should nevertheless be noted that Malevich's Suprematism and Mondrian's abstract geometry did find a concrete application in Constructivism.

In short, ideas proliferated in Moscow; the basic tendencies were the same, but some of the artists leaned towards the purest and most rigid materialism, others towards a degree of spirituality. Stalin would set the clocks right: fall in line or resign....

Malevich, who in this critical year of 1920 published *New Systems in Art*, was to a certain extent one of art's mystics. In his early works he was simply a painter, but he very quickly developed the consequences of Cubism—conceiving painting as an object—an idea which leads to the nonrepresentational. He developed this non-figurative, Suprematist art in the fields of sculpture, architecture and town planning.

The inventor of the unsurpassable *White On White* which, by superimposing one single color in neighboring values, explores the extreme limits both of the subject and of abstraction, was quite dogmatic when it came to the human virtues which could be expressed in art, but not with regard to the forms of expression which art should take. The importance of his painted work is considerable, and its formal inventiveness amounts to a cosmic conception of the world. Further, he claimed that "the pen is sharper than the brush" and his writings are no less important. His work gave rise to a whole aspect of contemporary art, from the Circle and Square (1930) and Abstraction-Creation (1931–1936) groups, up to the American Hard Edge and Minimal art of the 1960s, by way of Yves Klein, Vasarely and many others.

The program of the first Constructivist group was a direct reply to the realist manifesto. Vladimir Tatlin, head of the group and fierce partisan of materialism, went to the roots of Gabo and Pevsner's claims, stating that all abstract art must itself become a reality, useful to everyday life and participating in this way in the construction of a new Russia. Art, just like science and technology, was called on to support the efforts on an entire people: "The Constructivist group's aim is to give a communist expression to materialist, constructive work. (...) The specific elements of the work of the group justify, ideologically, theoretically and experimentally, the transformation of the material elements of industrial culture into volumes, planes, colors, space and light. These constitute the basis of the communist expression of

materialist construction. (...) Down with the traditions of art, long live the constructive technician."

The struggle was bitter and Kandinsky, for example, was quickly knocked out. When the Inkhuk ("Institute of Artistic Culture") was established in Moscow, the first curriculum was proposed by Kandinsky and immediately rejected by the Constructivist members who took control in his place: Rodchenko, Stepanova, Babichev and others. Naively, Kandinsky had envisaged research on the emotional effects of forms and colors. He would take up his teaching, starting in 1921 at the Bauhaus. The Constructivists preferred to follow their own project of a strictly objective and scientific analysis of art, concentrating above all on its materials.

At the Inkhuk there was also a course given for art and technical workshops, called Vkhutemas. This school was comparable to the Bauhaus, teaching architecture, painting, sculpture, ceramics, wood and metal working, textiles and typography. It was founded by a decree of Lenin in November 1920. The aim was to unite all artistic disciplines and integrate them in a general system of education and aesthetically based production: art at the service of industry. As at the Bauhaus, the artists preferred the title of "engineer"; the sculptor Naum Gabo, together with Tatlin, also a sculptor, were the main craftsmen in this school of Constructivist thought.

For Tatlin, who declared himself a Productivist—people were bold with words in 1920s Russia—the unusual became a source of creativity for objects not drawn from life, thus calling into question the "work of art" as it had previously been understood. These objects were the "counter-reliefs," designed, in truly revolutionary manner, to be suspended.

The best example is the monument for the Third International. The iron model was 25 meters high, but Tatlin had planned a final work 400 meters high, composed of three volumes suspended by steel cables—a cube, a cone and a cylinder: the elements inherited from Cézanne!

Gabo, for his part, attempted to use his sculptures to resolve the problems posed by painting: to break down the volume and give it depth, a concept utterly opposed to academicism.

"Art is dead" was the slogan of this great Russian period. On the one hand it reflected a desire for modernity in creative work, and on the other, the problems besetting the new socialist state, just after the October Revolution, in building a new society from nothing.

Ilia Ehrenburg, who was to join the movement later, provided a definition for artists: "Work, clarity, organization." We are a long way from the frenzied post-Romanticism of Marinetti and the Italian Futurists, who were quickly repudiated by the Constructivists. Indeed, the word "construction" was the key word which went against the utopian views of the Italians. Another important word was "production": "True modernity is production." So, by contrasting words, it is possible to illuminate the guiding idea behind the movement: replace "construction" with "building" in architecture, and the idea would be acceptable to Le Corbusier.

Constructivism was, in fact, not limited to the new Russia, the USSR. It found an echo in Holland with De Stijl, which also brought together artists and architects who preached strict austerity and who sought a new language in abstract geometry, all with the aim of launching a new industrial society.

Nor should it be forgotten that Moholy-Nagy, who was

86   Kasimir Malevich: *Suprematism*. 1920. Gouache on paper, 29.5 × 22.5 cm. Russian Museum, Leningrad.

87   Kasimir Malevich: *Suprematism*. 1920. Watercolor on paper, 23 × 15.5 cm. Russian Museum, Leningrad.

88   El Lissitzky: *They Came to Earth from Afar* and *The Story of Two Squares*. 1920. Preparatory sketch. Ten-page book conceived and drawn by the artist. Published in 1922.

89   El Lissitzky: *Wendingen*, cover for the Dutch revue. 1921. Color lithograph, 33 × 33 cm. Document Centre Georges Pompidou, Paris.

Following pages:

90   Kasimir Malevich: *The Red Cavalry at a Gallop*. 1918–1930. Oil on canvas, 90 × 140 cm. Russian Museum, Leningrad.

91   Kasimir Malevich: *Suprematism within a Contour. The Athletes*. 1929. Oil on canvas, 142 × 164 cm. Russian Museum, Leningrad.

92   Pavel Filonov: *The Petrograd Proletariat Formula*. Towards the end of the 1920s. Oil on canvas, 154 × 117 cm. Russian Museum, Leningrad.

Hungarian, not Russian (he accepted Gropius's invitation and taught at the Bauhaus from 1920 onwards), had discovered avant-garde Russian art during his stay in Berlin. He soon became a friend of El Lissitzky, Malevich's brilliant deputy. Painter, sculptor, photographer, graphic designer, typographer—the complete artist—he played, to a certain extent, the role of linkman between Constructivism and the Bauhaus.

From Moscow to Berlin, in Holland and France, the world resounded to these rational aesthetics, in tune with machine civilization: "The cube and the parallelepiped are the essential forms of infinite space."

Aleksei Gan went so far as to proclaim "an unconditional art war." For Constructivism, just like all other groups and movements of the Twenties, already reflected a malaise in civilization, which up to the present day has only worsened. The nineteenth century folded with World War I, and the need for a "new era" made itself felt in a more or less confused way: hence the multiplicity of attempts to create, construct and, above all, "be modern."

Malevich was the greatest of all these minor geniuses: his work would have the greatest effect, because it defended against all odds a degree of spirituality, without which art can never be anything but a poor subterfuge. He was teaching at the Vitebsk branch of the Vkhutemas—when he decided to found his own group for "new forms of art," the Unovis. His friends wore a black square on their sleeves. Those who followed him shared his views: among them were El Lissitzky and the Poles Strzemiński and Kobro. They were a minority and were looked at askance. They were already marked out as "deviationists." Malevich stated clearly, in fact, that painting was outmoded, but he was not afraid to add that their research would "open up the world of spiritual, Suprematist utilitarian and dynamic objects." Town festivals were organized and Suprematist design and decorations invented. Plans and projects were more numerous than concrete results. Malevich can be thought of as having anticipated Conceptual art.

It has to be said that the theoretical development of Constructivism was not accompanied by the great works that were hoped for. Curiously, it was in the United States that work really was done. It was only with the development of American cities that Constructivism became the style of the twentieth century, with Mies van der Rohe's design for the New York Seagram Building and the Illinois Institute of Technology. A policy alone, without the necessary financial backup, is useless.

What is important to the history of contemporary art, is the determining role played by Constructivism as a way of reasoning, once the style and the aesthetics that characterized it were outmoded. It can be said that this was the first "optimistic" school of art of this century. Repudiating the "eternal and absolute limits imposed by reality" (Gabo), Constructivism highlighted the notion of "structure," supported linguistically by Ferdinand de Saussure and ethnologically by Marcel Mauss. Constructivism has also been compared to the Gothic style, which first introduced the principle of "construction" freed from mass. Invention alone does not create style, which can exist only thanks to the intellect, the source of methods of thought. Constructivism demonstrates this, especially in the applied arts, by imparting a sense of the "functional," tending to simplify everything to the greatest extent possible. It is also to this spirit that contemporary typography owed its success, not to mention the new

photomontage techniques which were effectively invented by Constructivism.

The Russian affair ended badly, or well, depending on one's viewpoint. When the Russian authorities prohibited all art that was not utilitarian, Gabo, Pevsner, El Lissitzky, Puni, Kandinsky, and others still, left the country. Tatlin and Malevich, inimical brothers, remained. But Malevich never gave up and was reduced to silence.

The Triumph of the Concrete

Sculpture

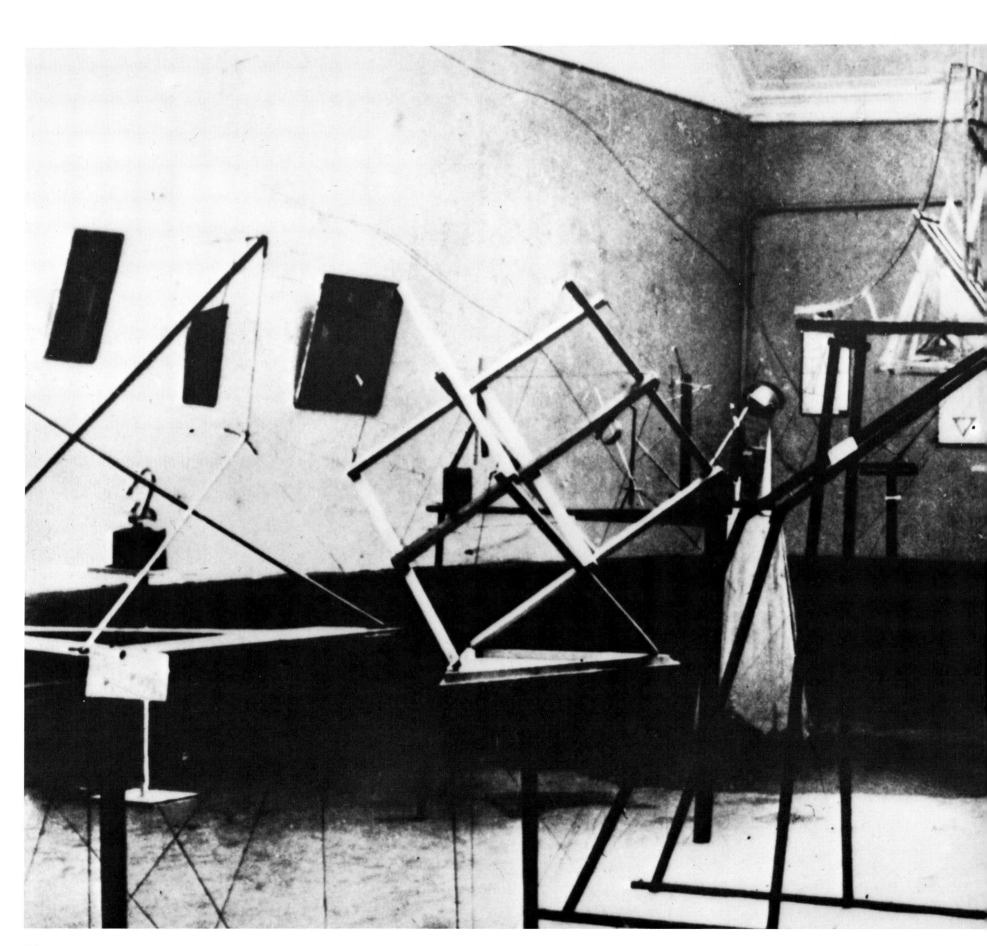

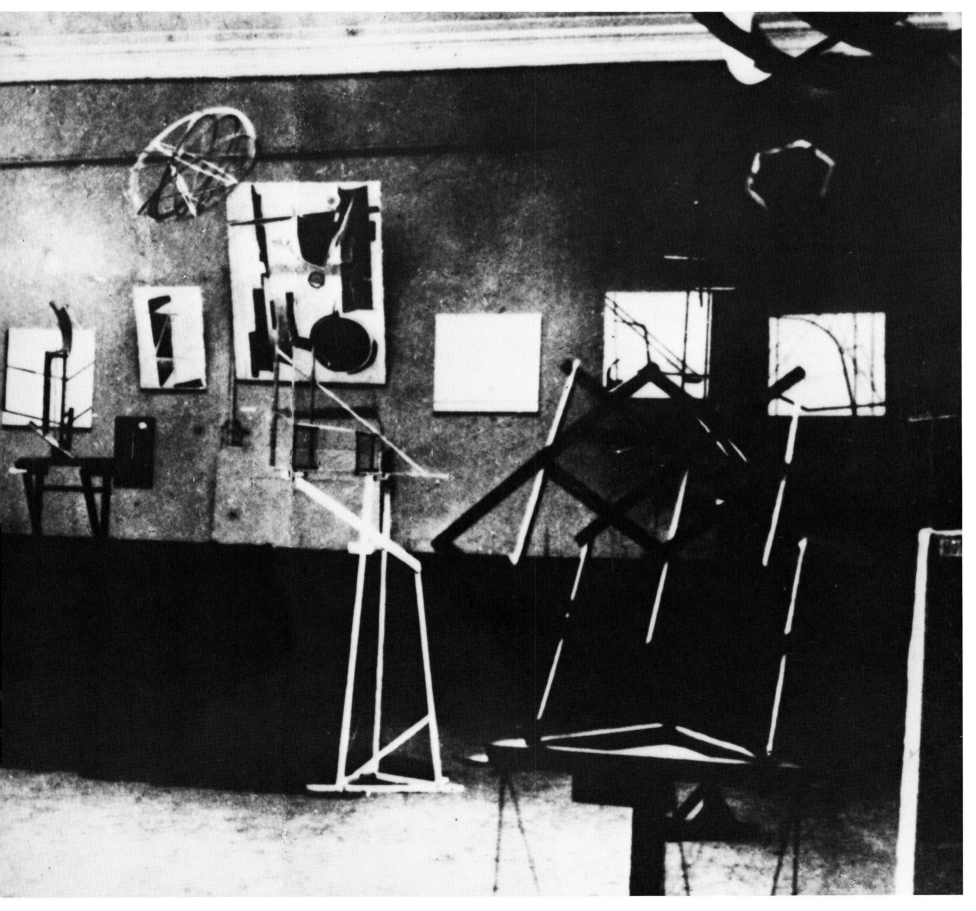

93 Stenberg brothers: *Spatial Constructions.* Obmokhu (Society of young artists) Exhibition, at the Moscow Vkhutemas, May 1920.

94 Sophie Taeuber-Arp: *Dada Head*. 1918–1919. Musée national d'Art moderne, Centre Georges Pompidou, Paris.

Sophie Taeuber-Arp was a member of the Zurich Dadaist group until 1920. She then began to limit herself to geometric forms and compositions in pure colors. Her work exemplifies the purity and the rejection of fashion that a few women sculptors proposed to their male colleagues. She thus exercised a certain influence on the work of Hans Arp, whom she married in 1921. That same year, they went to Tarrenz, in the Tyrol with several Dadaists. In 1923 they were in Hanover, with Kurt Schwitters, collaborating on *Merz*. In 1925, Arp, with El Lissitzky, published *The Isms of Art*, a kind of critical anthology of all the avant-garde movements. Sophie and Hans Arp subsequently became Surrealists.

95 Auguste Herbin: *Sculpture*. 1921. Polychrome wood, 46 × 28.8 × 29 cm. Musée national d'Art moderne, Centre Georges Pompidou, Paris.

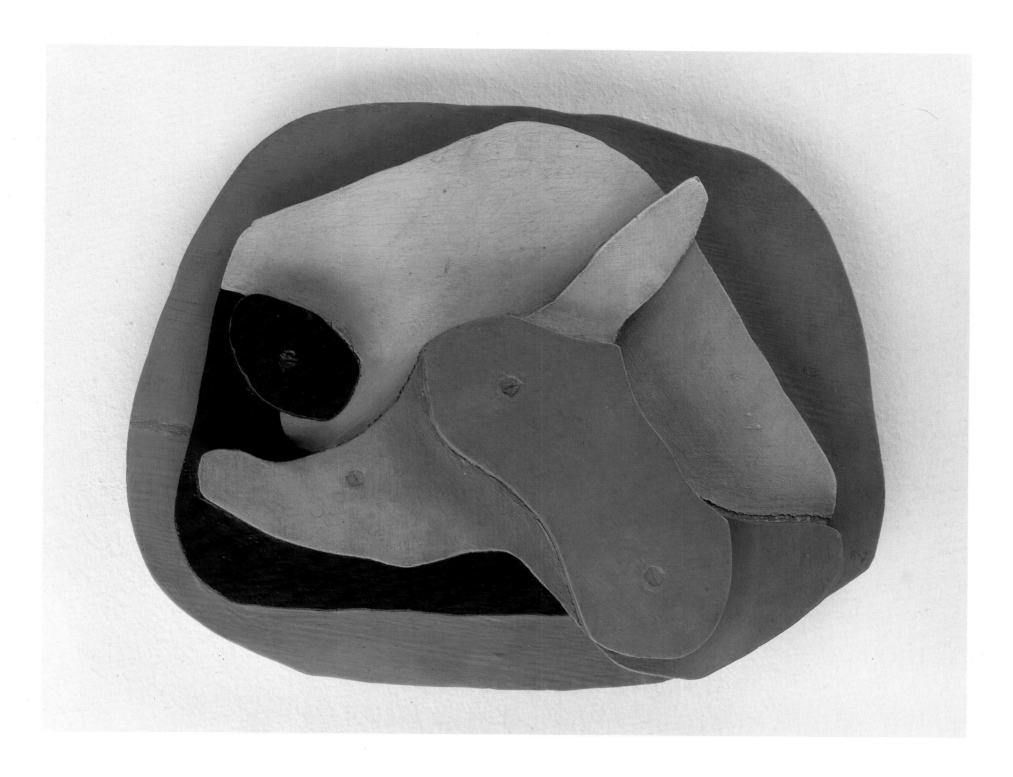

"It appears to me that the art of today advances, like a man, on two feet: a left foot which breaks new ground, a right foot which conserves. When they do not contradict each other, they are complementary, but their very contradiction is a valuable stimulus. It is perhaps the secret of the vitality of the art of the century. Sometimes these antagonisms can be found in curious balance in one artist, though this is not often the case.... May I once again draw attention here to the presence of the cry and the style which, apparently in opposition, work together as two original forces in one entity."

This text by Michel Seuphor, preface to *La Sculpture de ce siècle* ("The Sculpture of this Century"), is especially applicable to the Twenties. This era, in which reflection preceded action, let loose its cry in painting—a medium which allows a more immediate reaction—whereas in sculpture, perhaps on account of the very materials used, slowness and reflection predominated.

96   Hans Arp: *Relief*. 1916–1920. Painted wood, 42 × 60 × 11 cm. Staatliche Museen Preussischer Kulturbesitz, Nationalgalerie, West Berlin.

From Revolution to Classicism

It is thus hardly surprising that the 1920s were a remarkable period for sculpture. But which sculpture, and why? We have seen with painting that the best and the less good coexisted, and that the avant-garde nevertheless lived quite happily with middle-class taste. After all, life is a continuous series of compromises between daring and prudence.

The sculpture of the Twenties includes both the era of Brancusi and that of the war memorials raised everywhere, even in the smallest villages. Obviously, not every town had, as Mont-de-Marsan did, the good luck to have a local artist of the stature of Charles Despiau. Like painting, sculpture in the 1920s fluctuated between the application of Cubist principles to decorative sculpture (from Csaky to the Martel brothers) and the use of Constructivist elements (from Tatlin to Pevsner and Gabo). Of course, in between these two poles, which may also overlap (as in the case of Gabo), all imaginable influences and nuances may be found, from Dada (Arp, Sophie Taeuber-Arp) to the Bauhaus (Schlemmer, Moholy-Nagy) and from neo-classicism (Matisse, Pompon) to abstraction (Brancusi). Everyone was, however, in agreement with Mondrian's statement: "The surface of things gives pleasure, their interior quality makes them live."

What difference is there, for example, between a sculpture by Auguste Herbin and a relief by Hans Arp, both in painted wood? We are told that Herbin progressed along a direct path, beginning with a simplified Cubism to arrive at the most radical abstraction. Arp's path is roughly similar, since he passed from Cubism to a form of abstraction which led him into contact with Kandinsky. Yet Herbin, who was one of the first Cubists, was also one of the first French artists to practice pure abstract painting containing formal and ideological elements close to Suprematism and De Stijl. Arp, on the other hand, had a weighty past in Dada. He even married the doyenne, Sophie Taeuber, in 1921. His polychrome cut-wood sculpture, which he continued to produce throughout his life, often introducing an element of chance into the design—certain reliefs were modeled on pieces of cut-up cardboard, shaken at random and fixed wherever they stopped after sliding down a sloped surface—consists of forms which have been described as half human and half vegetable. We must suppose that their vulgarity and the arbitrary nature of the construction sprang from a desire to shock. But do not two elements come into play? Does not Herbin's sculpture also aim to shock? Surely there is humor in the work of both sculptors. In 1925, Arp figured among the painters who exhibited at the first Surrealist exhibition. Does he not answer our question by qualifying his equally important attachment to abstract art with a spoken preference for the name "concrete art," proposed by Van Doesburg, and by publishing with El Lissitzky, a small "theoretical" and ironic work, entitled *Kunstismen* ("The Isms of Art")?

articulating the different volumes between them. The effect of their Cubist trees, almost 10 meters high, illustrates clearly the technical possibilities of cement and is entirely representative of the era.

The lead the solitary Brancusi had over the sculptors of the period is astonishing and immediately apparent in the context of the works executed in the same year, 1920, by artists coming from different countries, each with differing aspirations.

Van Doesburg invented the term "concrete art" after his split with Mondrian. He intended it to designate the creation of autonomous objects, possessing their own emotional and intellectual value on the basis of their physical presence alone, and which could not be categorized as abstract art without contradiction. It is tempting to apply such a term to the manikin sculpted by Oskar Schlemmer, rather than the title of *Abstract Figure*, which he chose himself, because the work was clearly derived from his theatrical experience.

From now on it was clear that the middle class wished to avoid headaches and preferred the reliable simplicity of the stars of the Art Deco style, the twin brothers, Jan and Joël Martel. Not a trace of ambiguity in this "right-footed" sculpture. Since modernity is what they want, give them modern! Their cement Cubist trees, designed to embellish the garden conceived for the 1925 Paris Exhibition of Decorative Arts by the architect Mallet-Stevens, are in line with the "simultaneous art" applied by Sonia Delaunay to her dress models. The Martel brothers favored a nicely relaxing geometric division of space and a play of possible rhythms: a twofold solution to plastic art. They voluntarily stylized Cubism. When they sculpted characters in bas-relief, they started with a realistic representation. Then, by successive approaches, they simplified the forms to their limits, creating a minimum of softly curved, more or less geometric volumes, surrounded by sharply defined edges which constituted a group of precise force lines, perfectly

It is amusing to note that in 1920, they were all doing roughly the same sort of sculpture. Archipenko and Zadkine had come to Paris from Russia, Csaky from Hungary, Lipchitz from Poland. They arrived at the same time, with Laurens and Chauvin. They were perhaps marking time, falling back on the lessons of Cubism, whether they had been for or against it, before taking paths that would lead them further.

Sculpture is not a hasty art. It is slow, reasonable and reasoning. It has an essential, ineradicable balance, as man does. "Sculpture is not so affected by the passage of time as is painting," notes Seuphor. The distance separating the slaves on the tomb of Pope Julius II by Michelangelo from a work by Brancusi or Csaky, is less great than that separating the ceiling of the Sistine Chapel from a painting by Kandinsky.

Zadkine, at this time, swore only by Rodin: "In the entire twentieth century, there has only been one master: Rodin. He alone is great." The work of these post-Cubists in 1920 is characterized by constant references to the "fourth dimension," mentioned from 1911 on by Apollinaire, in respect of painting. Cubism was, we know, above all to do with painters, and Cubism in sculpture was simply the application of a system which would quickly lead to what Archipenko rightly referred to as "sculpto-painting."

The first to produce a real, three-dimensional Cubism in plaster and stone was Jozseph Csaky, who had come to Paris from his native Hungary at the age of twenty. With

97 Oskar Schlemmer: *Abstract Figure*. 1921–1923. Nickel-plated bronze, 105.5 × 62.5 × 21.4 cm. Bayerische Staatsgemäldesammlungen, Staatsgalerie moderner Kunst, Munich.

98 Two women wearing the "simultaneous" dresses by Sonia Delaunay, in front of the cement "Cubist" trees (H. 10 m.) by the Martel brothers, which were to adorn the garden designed by the architect Mallet-Stevens for the Tourism Pavilion at the Exhibition of Decorative Arts in Paris in 1925. Sonia Delaunay Archives, Paris.

99 *Machine-men*. 1925. Exhibition of Decorative Arts, Paris.

Post-Cubism

100   Aleksandr Archipenko: *Standing Figure*. 1920. Cast cement, H. 180 cm. Hessisches Landesmuseum, Darmstadt.

101   Ossip Zadkine: *Woman with Fan*. 1920. Bronze, 85 × 34 × 27 cm. Musée national d'Art moderne, Centre Georges Pompidou, Paris.

102   Jozseph Csaky: *Head*. 1920. White stone, H. 34 cm. National Museum, Budapest.

103   Henri Laurens: *Woman with Fruit-dish*. 1920. Stone.

104   Otto Freundlich: *Ascension*. 1929. Bronze, 225 × 107 cm. Museum Ludwig, Cologne.

105   Jacques Lipchitz: *Seated Clarinet Player*. 1920. Stone.

106   Jean Chauvin: *To the Tune of an Accordeon*. 1920 (1956). Plaster, H. 46 cm. Private collection.

him, Cubism became more human. In his own words: "Cubism attempted to create a new order, a new geometry in plastic art, but in the absence of ideology, it became a witty plastic art game, very charming, an exaggerated affectation of a fine trade." Csaky entered the Twenties giving full rein to his feelings. He distanced himself from Cubist research and found a means of expression in a new lyricism by returning to figurative art. Doubtless the Paris air had something to do with it, but also the ideas current at the time: he was concerned, as were other sculptors, that the fundamental mission of art was to exalt a collective ideology. He continued working according to the laws which governed the plastic art of his period. Strongly influenced by his Cubist experience, he sought through his own sensibility to connect with Ancient Greek and Roman art. His sculptures responded to a social need; they have a logical meaning, easy to understand and accessible to all. They are made to be contemplated and reflected on.

The vertical is inherent to the nature of these post-Cubists; columnar forms, perhaps related to Black totemic art, dominate. These sculptors quickly felt the limits of abstract art and fell into a stylistic harmony with each other. Thus the Frenchman Henri Laurens, whose first reliefs date from 1919, quietly drew on the influences of his immediate surroundings before making use of Cubist techniques. He was more interested in the contours of forms and, little by little, he came under the influence of the smooth-surfaced sculpture of Matisse and Maillol.

Cubism for the Lithuanian Jacques Lipchitz was neither a game, nor an experimental exercise, but the object of concerted research. Contrary to what has been said, he never executed any experimental Cubism under the influence of Picasso. In the Twenties, an elaboration in the size and relief of his works can be observed, reflecting the spirit rather than the letter of Cubist theories. With Lipchitz, the former volume of sculpture was replaced —not artificially, as it was with Archipenko, who literally played with cones, cylinders and spheres, but by a rhythmic and almost architectonic sense of space.

As for Ossip Zadkine, a Russian living in Paris, his work was a long way from reaching its final stage of development. He had an innate sense of wood and stone, and the figurative remained fundamental for him. While maintaining the relationships between convex and concave which sprang from Cubism, he brought a quality to his work which set him apart from the others: lyricism.

It many be surprising to study Naum Gabo in the context of these post-Cubists. This Russian settled in the United States, and his work is linked to the complex world of the Constructivists. He considered himself, with his brother Pevsner, to be anti-Brancusi, since the doctrine of the *Realist Manifesto* stipulated the abolition of full forms. He systemized the feature which had been becoming apparent over several years in the works of Tatlin and of Archipenko, another Russian settled in the United States: the "active vacuum." Nevertheless, the head by Gabo illustrated here in no way mars the collection. It plays with light. And it plays also with the air circulating freely through it. "The brothers Pevsner and Gabo," notes Seuphor, "led us from revolution to classicism...."

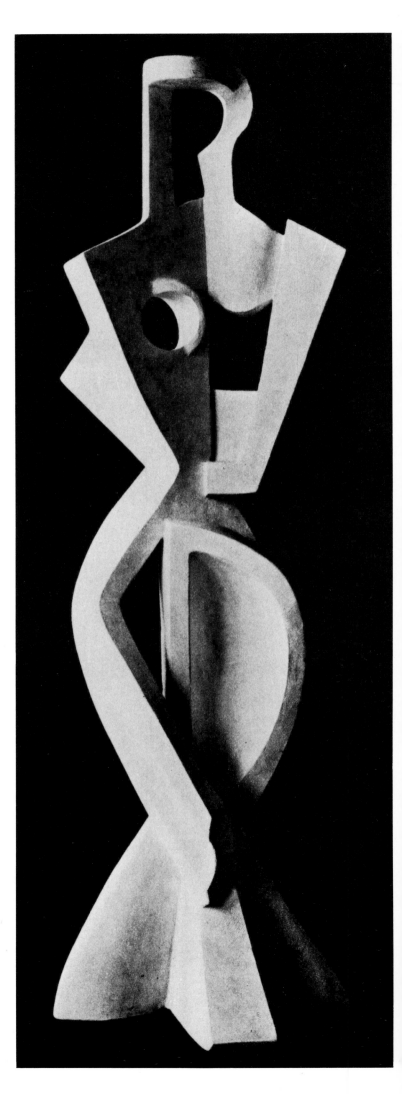

101
103
105

102
104
106

The Brancusi Era

107 Constantin Brancusi: *The New Born*. 1915–1920. 18 × 24.8 × 17 cm. Musée national d'Art moderne, Centre Georges Pompidou, Paris.

108 View of the interior of Brancusi's atelier, with, from left to right, *Plato, Mlle Pogany II* and *The Golden Bird*. 1920. Photo taken by the artist himself, who did not trust other photographers to portray his sculpture as he intended.

Brancusi wanted his atelier to be considered as a temple from which one came out strengthened. His major pieces were enthroned there. "He even had some-where," Michel Seuphor, who met him in 1923, recounts, "the parts to make an authentic Hindu temple, which was meant to measure ten meters square and only admit one person at a time. He had done the drawing at the request of a great Indian lord, but political events obstructed its realization."

In this temple, Brancusi worked indefatigably on his great creation, *The Egg*. It was the round form which interested him, in fact. It appears in *The Beginning of the World, Child's Head, Mademoiselle Pogany, The New Born*, and even in the elongated parabola of *Bird in Space*, each and every one of these works explores the ovoid or the oblong—the creations of a titan who would be a jeweler! In 1920, Brancusi exhibited *Mademoiselle X* at the Paris Salon. The work raised a storm of protest. Matisse, always sharp-tongued, is said to have exclaimed "Why that's the phallus" on seeing the work. The still all-powerful supporters of academicism seized the occasion to denounce the work as offensive to public morals and demanded that the police remove it from the gallery. It was a major clash between the partisans of a new art and the academics. In fact, with this work, just as with all the others he had been laboring on for years, this peasant from the Carpathians, who had arrived in Paris in 1904, was in the process of utterly transforming the very idea of sculpture. Brancusi, was definitely a "left foot." "It is not the exterior form that is real," he said, "but the essence of things. With this truth as a point of departure, it is impossible for anyone to express something real by imitating the exterior surface of things." This formula is clearly close to Mondrian's declaration. Michel Seuphor—is it possible to speak of Mondrian without quoting him?—drew an accurate parallel between the two artists, both solitary, both bachelors, as much artisans as creative artists, both seeking, unceasingly, the most elemental form.

"It appears logical to me," says Seuphor in substance, "that the sculptor should find it with the help of curves, and the painter with the help of straight lines, since the first has to deal with three-dimensional space to create an object, while the second divides up a rectangular surface plane."

It can also be noted that Brancusi and Mondrian both owe their fame to America, despite the fact that most of their work was carried out in Paris. Paris, in fact, did not treat them as well as New York did—though it has to be said that the American customs officers refused entry to *Bird in Space* for an exhibition, as a work of art, claiming that it had to be taxed according to weight like an ordinary lump of copper. The lawsuit between Brancusi and the Customs Office lasted two years and finally ended in his victory. Today we would consider it to be wonderful free publicity. It was by dying in New York in 1944 that Mondrian secured publicity in the major

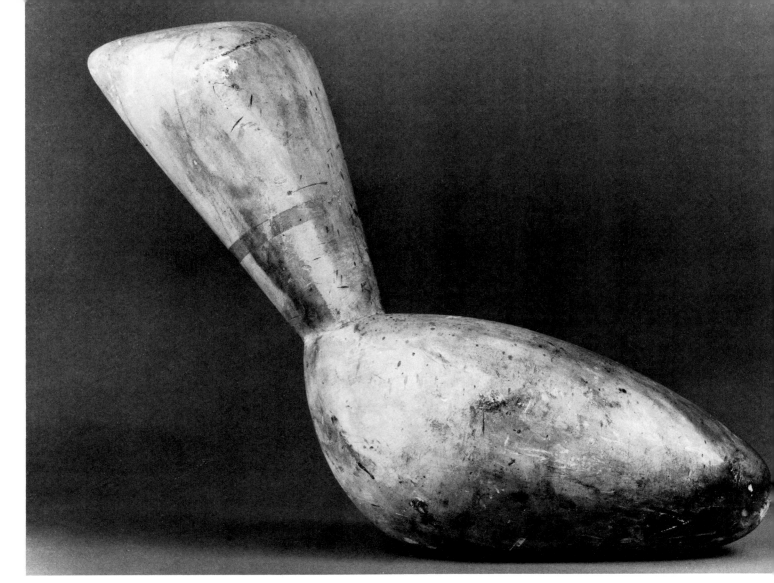

109   Constantin Brancusi: *Leda*. 1920.
Marble. Musée national d'Art moderne,
Centre Georges Pompidou, Paris.

110   Constantin Brancusi: *The Beginning of the World*. 1920s. Marble,
17.5 × 32 × 24 cm. Musée national
d'Art moderne, Centre Georges
Pompidou, Paris.

papers; Brancusi got his on disembarking there in 1926. Like his famous *Endless Column*, Brancusi has neither beginning nor end. To search for his ancestors would be in vain. No sooner had he begun his search than he attained its object. No doubt the basic simplicity is as much derived from Black art as from traditional Rumanian craftsmanship. His sculpture is quite simply a meditation on form itself. And the form is the egg, or, in its other aspect, the six-sided cube. Such works, through their elemental nature, their quiet daring, defy the anguished research both of their period and of our own. They require no commentary; they are not so much lessons as presences.

The shadow of Rodin was still cast over the world of sculpture throughout the first quarter of the twentieth century. His influence remained considerable and it may be that even today, despite the ups and downs in the representation of forms, he is still a point of reference. To an extent, Brancusi marked a turning point in the history of sculpture. The vocation came to him when he was constructing a violin with the most elementary of tools, by dint of patience and obstinacy. And it would be impossible to understand these "idols of a new age" which he spent long days polishing, without some knowledge of the objects of Rumanian craftsmanship he accumulated in his studio. The famous *Endless Column* resembles the carved supports of the entry gates to the gardens in his country. And surely the feature which characterizes him more than any other is his love for materials. He often tackled the same subject in turn in marble, stone and bronze. The result was that between 1912 and 1940, he executed twenty-four versions in different materials of the sculpture entitled *Maiastra*. Brancusi's work is indeed rare. It centers around two or three themes which he never tired of returning to, although each version is an achievement in itself. "The work of art requires great patience and above all absolute commitment." More than anything else, he worked without haste, according to his own inner clock. In an era when everybody courted extravagance, and where speed dominated, he understood that the only luxury was to take one's time.

He pushed spareness further than the Cubists and, without any knowledge of the intellectual aspects of the movement, he referred naturally to their cosmic symbolism, anticipating on his own the twenty-first century, which, as Malraux said, would be spiritual, or would not be at all.

Better than the rest, the Americans felt it right away: Carl Sandburg said of Brancusi that he probed unfathomable depths and discovered the very essence of form.

Brancusi was not alone. It is often forgotten that Matisse was one of the giants of sculpture of the period. Like Picasso, he occasionally abandoned his brushes to attack three-dimensional art. The question whether he contributed to the development of modern sculpture is often debated. One thing is certain: he was the master of

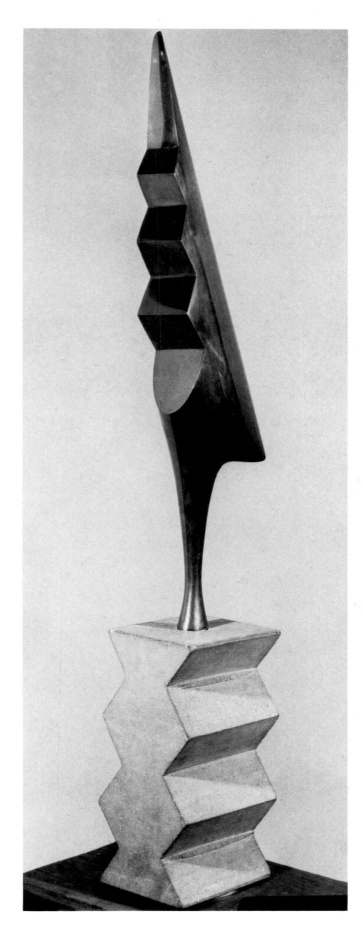

111 Constantin Brancusi: *The Rooster*. 1924. Bronze, 103 × 21 × 11 cm. Musée national d'Art moderne, Centre Georges Pompidou, Paris.

Smoothness and Curves

112 Henri Matisse: *Torso*. 1920–1925. Bronze, H. 20 cm. Private collection.

"A human body is a piece of architecture made of forms that are jointed and support one another, comparable to a building of which all the different parts play a role in the whole." This observation by Matisse well defines his sculpture, which he used as a means of deepening his study of the human body and as an indispensable complement to his research into space and surface in painting. If he mocked Brancusi and his "phallus," it was because Brancusi's preoccupations were very different from his own, which were, rather, linked to European classicism. It is nonetheless true that Matisse, with Picasso, belongs to the line of painter-sculptors of whom Rodin said: "A painter who knows how to draw knows how to sculpt"—a line which stretches from Renoir, Daumier, Degas, Gaugin and Modigliani, to Miró, Ernst, de Chirico, Magnelli, Derain, Braque, Dali, Delaunay or Léger, and which contributed decisively to the freeing of forms and matter.

114 Aristide Maillol: *Woman Holding her Foot.* 1920. Bronze, H. 20 cm. Private collection.

In 1920 Maillol was pursuing his research in pure plastic art, with the sole aim of perfecting the linking of volumes. He tirelessly smoothed and curved his full female bodies in order to allow the light to play on the surfaces. He had no time for fashion and, as a result, was the most classical sculptor of modern times in the field of figurative art; his work has therefore exercised a great influence throughout the whole world. He added French grace to Greek sobriety. His work is colored with a calm dignity, a moving sense of balance. He has achieved timelessness.

113 François Pompon: *Large Panther.* 1929. Bronze, H. 24 cm. Musée des Beaux-Arts, Dijon.

115 François Pompon: *Crowned Crane.* 1926. Bronze, H. 108 cm. Musée des Beaux-Arts, Dijon.

116 Gaston Lachaise: *Woman Walking.* 1922. Gilded bronze, H. 33 cm. Hirschhorn Museum and Sculpture Garden, Smithsonian Institution, Washington, D.C.

117 Aleksandr Archipenko: *Woman.* 1923. Construction in painted relief, wood, and copper, H. 140 cm. Hirschhorn Museum and Sculpture Garden, Smithsonian Institution, Washington, D.C.

Back to Style

118   Jean Lambert-Rucki and Jean
Dunand: *Prayer*. 1926. Lacquered
wood and eggshell, H. 75 cm. Galerie
Félix Marcilhac, Paris.

119   Jan and Joël Martel: *Dance*.
1925. Lacquer ware, 90 × 45 cm.
Galerie Félix Marcilhac, Paris.

Audacity, but with Prudence

"distortion." He was the first painter after Degas, Daumier, Renoir and Gauguin to leave an important body of sculpture in which he made use of expressive distortion—a practice which dated from the extra vertebrae which Ingres slipped into his *Odalisque*, and was already to be found in Matisse's painting; it would henceforward become characteristic of contemporary plastic art. Maillol quoted one of Matisse's flashes of wit one day, in which he described the *Venus de Milo* as a "forward young woman"; and this was not meant disparagingly, since it applied perfectly to his own figures, who were prey to their natural exuberance. To his pupils, Matisse explained (and this commentary was just as applicable to sculpture as to painting): "The arms are like rolls of clay, but the forearms are also like ropes, because they may be twisted... the basin fits into the thighs and calls to mind an amphora. Fit the pieces into each other and build your figure as a carpenter builds a house." Or again: "In this African posing you can see a cathedral—that is to say, a superb, majestic, solid construction, the result of assembling numerous elements—and there is also a lobster to be seen in him, because of the perfect articulation of the muscle joints, whose play and tension bring to mind the precise overlappings of a carapace. However, from time to time, it is essential that you recall that he is a Black man and not lose sight of him, and yourself with him, in your construction."

If Matisse ridiculed Brancusi and his "phallus," it was because Brancusi's concerns were far removed from his own, which were linked to European classicism, especially as regards his character studies. Along with Picasso, Matisse belongs to the line of painter-sculptors of whom Rodin said: "a painter who knows how to draw also knows how to sculpt" and who contributed decisively, with Miró, Ernst, De Chirico, Magnelli, Derain, Braque, Dalí, Delaunay or Léger, to the liberation of forms and matter.

Bourdelle, a pupil of Rodin, was the most fashionable. His famous *Heracles* of 1910 raised him to fame and flooded him with orders for busts of famous people. Then there was Maillol, who in 1920 was continuing with his studies in pure plastic art, with the sole aim of perfecting the linking of volumes. The inventor of the robust, buxom female body, he, too, liked light to slide over the curves of the volumes. He was also adept at

120–121 Some examples of "bourgeois aesthetics" that one might encounter on visiting the gardens of the 1925 International Exhibition of Decorative Arts in Paris.

122 Henri Laurens in his studio.
1920s.

123 Céline Lepage: *Algerian Woman*.
1925. Wood, H. 32 cm. Isabelle Poulain
Collection, Paris.

smooth surfaces even if in this year his career was coming to a close, rather than beginning. Marcel Gimont is in the line of Maillol, while Paul Landowsky's work smacks more of "official sculpture."

There was the astounding François Pompon, as well, triumphing in 1922 with *The Polar Bear*, exhibited at the Autumn Salon. "I like sculpture with neither holes nor shadows" said Pompon, whose attractive name would remain linked with animal art. Bored with working on Rodin's tortured forms in the master's atelier, this Burgundian peasant spent his time making funeral monuments and polishing an astonishing menagerie of little animals, whose conception owed something to Egyptian aesthetics. They are not stylized; on the contrary, there is an inclination to stress the essential forms and modulations through which the movement is expressed. He was accused of making his animals hairless, just as Brancusi's *Maiastra*, that fabulous bird from popular Rumanian folklore, was entirely free of what might normally be described as feathers, wings, feet and head, in order to endow it with the magic character appropriate to the legend which had inspired it. Like Brancusi, Pompon polished the surface, stretched the forms to impart greater feeling to the volumes; in his own words: "It is movement which determines form," or "lyricism in sculpture must be contained, and strictly logical, like that of architecture," or lastly, "to capture the spirit of a form, it must be well observed from a distance and then rendered after the elimination of all useless details."

This was also the period when metal engulfed sculpture: Gargallo, Gonzalez and Calder used it regularly. Not only metal, but also plastic in the work of Pevsner and Gabo, and all sorts of materials such as glass, string and wire used with wood, were transformed into objects by the hands of Giacometti, Picasso, Miró, Bellmer, Hausmann and others.

But the one who went the furthest and to whom justice should now be paid was Moholy-Nagy, who, in 1922, achieved Malevich's wish by dictating three pictures by telephone. He had arranged the project with the foreman of a sign-making factory, making use of a color index and paper catalogues. The result was three pictures of different sizes, which demonstrated, through alterations of space and density, the importance of the structure and its emotional impact.

Aleksandr Rodchenko had in 1920 already undertaken mobile and suspended constructions, with a view to introducing movement and time into sculpture. The impulse behind the desire to move on to works of art in three dimensions was not so much a need to be free of the constraints imposed by the artist's easel, as an urge to work in space: this urge soon spread to include urban space. The Constructivists wanted to leave their mark on towns. To these three dimensions was added a fourth: time, which Rodchenko and Gabo introduced into their works by virtue of either incidental or induced movement.

124   Raoul Hausmann: *Mechanical Head*. 1921. Wood, leather and metal, H. 32.5 cm. Musée national d'Art moderne, Centre Georges Pompidou, Paris.

125   Dadaist Exhibition in Paris in 1921.

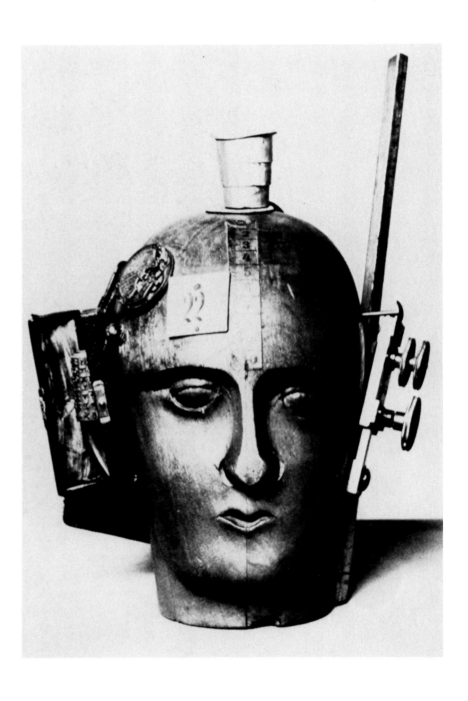

Moholy-Nagy's "bizarre mechanisms," executed from 1923 on, under the title *Lichtrequisit*, went further still, inventing "kinetic art"—a type of animated sculpture which reflected rays of light projected onto its mobile chrome surfaces. Moholy-Nagy described this development: "From a block like the pyramids, one passes through modeled sculpture (in positive and negative volumes) to arrive at perforation, suspension and finally kinetic sculpture." He added: "We must replace the static principle of classical art with the dynamic principle of universal life." The spectator is trapped before the work of art, since his own vision is included as a creative element. With Moholy-Nagy, sculpture took on a new dimension: it became both movement and light and broached scenographic fields.

The triumph therefore went ultimately to the Bauhaus, with the synthesis of movement, light, color and form, thanks to the use of electricity. Nevertheless, it was Moscow that was responsible for having passed from figurative sculpture with abstract elements to pure abstraction, with Tatlin and his famous suspended reliefs. In the middle, France, as always, digested these developments, swallowing Cubism and resurrecting smooth forms.

Kinetic Art

126 László Moholy-Nagy: *Light-Space Modulator*. 1922–1930. Metal, wood and glass, H. 151 cm. Busch-Reisinger Museum, Harvard University, Cambridge, Mass.

127 Aleksandr Rodchenko: *Hanging Construction*. 1920. Metal. The Museum of Modern Art, New York.

Architecture

128 Inauguration of the 1925 International Exhibition of Decorative Arts in Paris.

The Art Deco Exhibition and the International Compromise

129 Louis Boileau: The Porte d'Orsay with the giant banner announcing the Exhibition. On the back there was a painting symbolizing decorative art, whose author, the painter Vogué, subsequently remained in total obscurity.

The history of architecture in the 1920s scarcely began to take shape until around 1925, a key year. 1920 was still too close to World War I. But paradoxically—or, on the contrary, perhaps naturally—the two nations which were the first to symbolize the emergence of a new functionalist architecture were the two countries particularly affected by the disasters of the war: the newly formed USSR and Weimar Republic.

The architecture of the Weimar Republic has often been overestimated to the detriment of the Soviet architecture contemporary to it. In reality, both developed during the same period (1919–1933) and both were shattered by the same tyranny, under two different forms. But by dint of the emigration of the leading lights of German architecture to the United States after the Nazis, and as a result of the silence and the pure and simple disappearance of creative architects under Stalinism, German architecture has become more widely known. The Bauhaus was opened in the Weimar Republic by Gropius in 1919 and, in the next year, the Vkhutemas Faculty of Architecture opened in Soviet Russia. These two schools were to offer the most advanced architectural training in the world. Modern architecture began in Russia in 1920, with the industrialization of the country. Over a period of ten years it produced a mass of buildings or theoretic studies which have no equivalent elsewhere. But the construction techniques, which fell short of the intellectual creativity of the architects, and the disastrous economic state of the country, prevented the large-scale realization of

130 Henri Favier and André Ventre: The Porte d'Honneur linking the Grand and Petit Palais. The theme of the falling jet of water crowning the pillars reappeared on Brandt's grills and on Lalique's molded glass.

103

131 Tony Garnier: The Rhône et Loire Pavilion at the 1925 International Exhibition of Decorative Arts in Paris.

The Art Deco Exhibition

many of these initiatives. Engaged in civil war until 1920, when General Wrangel's counter-revolutionary army was defeated, the USSR produced an avant-garde "Constructivist" architecture, in which artists and sculptors played a major role, until 1930. This was in fact a general phenomenon throughout Europe, as painting and sculpture had, almost everywhere, a ten-year advance on architecture.

Some sort of artistic event was needed to show that France had won the war, still existed and was about to spring back into vigorous action. The 1925 Art Deco Exhibition, first thought of twenty years earlier, was both a political and an artistic windfall. Yet, there also, a chasm yawned between the plans and the concrete results. As ever, the eternal struggle between the old and new, between conservative administration and avant-garde creativity, reared its head.

In 1925, one could believe in an extension of the new ways of creating and of feeling—in the "melting-pot" that brought together the ideas of the Bauhaus, De Stijl or Constructivism. All too soon a resistance made its presence felt, which, although wearing the guise of modernism, in fact sought to impede anything which seemed to lead towards an "international art"; and the

stronger the opposition to this art, the more rigorously its protagonists tried to impose it.

The Art Deco Exhibition was thus a test-phenomenon: a kind of revenge of the middle class against Dada and Cubism, while at the same time a recognition of their existence and a genuine show of support for modernism. F. Mathey has highlighted the double nature of this support in all fields and especially in architecture.

As R. Huyghe also notes, it was a sign of the luxury of the post-war Roaring Twenties, of the sentiment of victory—albeit expensively bought—of the place regained by France in a world supposedly at peace, if one ignored the problem of Germany and the new Soviet universe.

Zola can never be quoted often enough when he said that Paris is a "stomach" which digests all the various artistic trends, grinds them up, mixes them, liquefies them and finally reconstitutes them in a homogenized form, acceptable and easy to assimilate by all. Obviously, this type of commonsense leveling does not necessarily mix well with genius and the resulting union often results in some curious cross-breeds.

Paris acted as a permanent link between the prewar heritage and the "new gospel" that was spreading

throughout the world, transmitted by the avant-gardists and their manifestos. There was, for example, a resurgence of the Modern style, less forgotten than one might think, remodeled by the after-effects of a Cubism adapted by the Munich and Scandinavian styles, which had recently been discovered in France. The result was that it was possible to speak paradoxically of a "geometric spineless style"—another example of the French Cartesian mentality!

The title "decorative arts" is revealing in itself: it implies a desire for a unifying style. And surely it is also a kind of compromise between the purism of the Cubist spirit, in the manner of Loos, and the old, turn-of-the-century decoration, rehashed by a new system. "Firstly, I should like to know who yoked the two words 'decorative' and 'art' together. It is an aberration," Auguste Perret declared to the journalist Marie Dormoy. "Where there is true art, there is no need for decoration."

It was therefore more a marriage for the sake of convenience than for love. Things had to be "modern," which meant simplifying the lines; they also had to appear "rich," through the use of costly materials. In many respects, the 1925 Exhibition expressed a certain display of wealth; it was also an attempt at a

compromise to vie with the Bauhaus, the new spirit and, above all, the "Bolshevik or Munich styles" aimed at the people, which the bourgeoisie lumped together in their disapproval, mocking the intentional sparseness of the Esprit nouveau Pavilion and Melnikov's USSR Pavilion. Down with poverty-stricken art; up with a "French" style, the manifestation of rebirth of the nation, prosperous and powerful. The rather confused aims of this choice remained to be clearly defined.

The Exhibition was strongly criticized, in one way or the other, depending on whether one was of a revolutionary or a reactionary turn of mind; but everybody flocked to it. It had something for everyone, entrancing both Parisians and country people who came up to Paris for the occasion. They all remembered it as a place to stroll about, as a center of attraction in all senses of the term; it was both a festival and a place to become acquainted with the diverse aspects of contemporary art.

Whatever the reactions of the public, the press, professionals, architects and decorators, whether they were involved, or not, in its realization; whatever it contested or lacked, the 1925 Exhibition was a considerable event in this politically troubled period separating the two world wars. It came at a significant

132 Pierre Patout: The Ruhlmann Pavilion at the 1925 International Exhibition of Decorative Arts in Paris.

The door was the work of Edgar Brandt, the bas relief by Joseph Bernard, the stone group "to the glory of Jean Goujon" by Jeanniot. A note of false luxury dominated this pavilion, baptized by Ruhlmann, in homage to the "power of money," the "Private House of a Rich Collector," bearing witness to a cynical turn of mind, or a rare obliviousness.

133 A. Laprade: the "Studium" Pavilion of the Grands Magasins du Louvre at the 1925 International Exhibition of Decorative Arts in Paris.

134 Konstantin Melnikov: The USSR Pavilion at the 1925 International Exhibition of Decorative Arts in Paris, built by Paris carpenters, in wood and glass, from the architect's plans and under his direction.

moment: the confrontation of two civilizations—the one carried over from before 1914, which had apparently passed through the war without greatly changing, attached to the bourgeois system, to the constraining, technically and stylistically limiting side of tradition, rather than to its dynamic side; the other turned towards the future, towards a new art of living.

Yvonne Brunhammer, high priestess of the period, both its guardian and its defender in the Paris Musée des Arts décoratifs—she organized an anniversary exhibition of the 1925 Exhibition in 1977—draws the moral better than anyone. There were two opposed conceptions: on the one hand, decorative art in the traditional sense of the term, an elite art, where a unique work is the rule; on the other, industrial art, or art with a view to industrialization, aimed at the greatest number of people, using forms designed by the best creative artists.

By its very contradictions, the Exhibition was in fact a quite precise reflection of the prodigious creativity of the

period. It is right that "1925" should have become the symbol for all the tendencies, from 1909 to 1930, which came together to form the style of the era. The 1925 Exhibition represented the balance sheet: it coincided with the ultimate point of the Art Deco style—the moment where, already carrying the seeds of its destruction, a reaction was set in motion.

This explanation applies to all the trends in architecture at this important moment. On the one hand there were the architects who upheld the Art Deco style, who wished, at all costs, to unite modernism and tradition—the great formula of the Exhibition; they in fact managed to massacre tradition and retain only the superficial elements of the modern. On the other hand there were the architects who supported the International style, defined by Gropius in 1924 and represented in France by Le Corbusier. Detractors of this style wasted no time in labeling it as the "German" or "Bolshevik" style. Against this background, notes Michel Ragon, the architects and artists of De Stijl and the Bauhaus

seemed very puritanical with their cubes. Moreover, the Exhibition refused to display in Paris the two most avant-garde movements in the world (if one discounts Russian Constructivism, which was, miraculously, represented): neither De Stijl nor the Bauhaus were represented at the Exhibition of Decorative Arts and that alone is sufficient to indicate its partisan nature and general level.

The symbol of the Exhibition was not Le Corbusier's skyscraper projects, but the four great concrete towers, with verandas at their tops, built by Plumet. Most of the French innovators were there, however, since apart from Mallet-Stevens and Le Corbusier, there were Auguste Perret (a theater), Tony Garnier (the Lyons Pavilion) and Sauvage and Wybo (the Primavera Pavilion, Printemps department store).

The Austrian Pavilion was the work of Josef Hoffmann, and the Russian one was by Melnikov. This "Bolshevik Pavilion," as it came to be known, with its great stairway and wall of glass, was one of the big attractions. It was thought of as a sort of curiosity, while in fact its architecture was the most forward-looking at the Exhibition. Le Corbusier presented a Pavilion-Manifesto called *L'Esprit nouveau*. Relegated to the Cours-la-Reine, between the two wings of the Grand Palais, it took the form of a villa that could be dismantled. The "Voisin plan for Paris" was there, with its skyscrapers. It was in fact Gabriel Voisin, the automobile and airplane builder, who financed the building of Le Corbusier's Pavilion, together with Henri Frugès, the industrial tycoon who commissioned Le Corbusier to build the workers' living complex at Pessac in the same year of 1925. Voisin and Frugès were more patrons than sleeping partners to Le Corbusier. Nevertheless, he attached the following provocative slogan to the pediment of his pavilion: "Heavy industry is taking over construction."

In spite of its shortcomings and its weaknesses, the great merit of the 1925 Exhibition of Decorative Arts was that it allowed the innovators represented there to gain awareness of their role, to take stock and, ultimately, to unite. At the time of the Exhibition, the Librairie des Arts décoratifs published a volume entitled *Le Style moderne. Contribution de la France* ("Modern Style. The Contribution of France"), which provides us with a preliminary inventory. Like the Exhibition, which was meant to be visited as much on the outside as on the inside, this publication had the advantage of mixing various forms of the plastic arts. Included were the Orly warehouses and the bridges by the engineer Freyssinet, as well as the dining room table and chairs by the painter Robert Delaunay. Also featured were Sauvage's house in rue Vavin and a golfing outfit by Jean Patou. There were also examples of Tony Garnier's and of Le Corbusier's architecture, as well as a tomboy hairstyle by Antoine; a standard villa and a piece of bathroom furniture by André Lurçat; a signal box for the Compagnie des chemins de fer du Nord; Mallet-Stevens's facade for an Alfa Romeo showroom and a seaside villa, as well as a Gabriel Voisin automobile and the bridge of a Compagnie transatlantique ocean liner; an entrance hall to a public building and a smoking car by Francis Jourdan; sash windows and balconies by Pol Abraham and a lavatory by Pierre Chareau.

In the preface to this work, Van de Velde recalled: "The resolution which we took all of thirty years ago: first to change our own immediate surroundings and then the face of the world, by not tolerating a single object, a

single building—be it warehouse, monument or palace —which to our eyes did not appear as it should be, but expressing adequately and perfectly, truth and sincerity...." After pointing out that he found it impossible to reconcile the Art Nouveau style with a rational conception of objects, he stressed that this rational conception led inevitably to "the most rudimentary and primitive forms of objects long since invented and known....

135 Ludwig Mies van der Rohe: Project for a glass skyscraper. Charcoal, brown chalk and pencil on paper, 138.5 × 83.2 cm. The Museum of Modern Art, New York (donated by George Danforth).

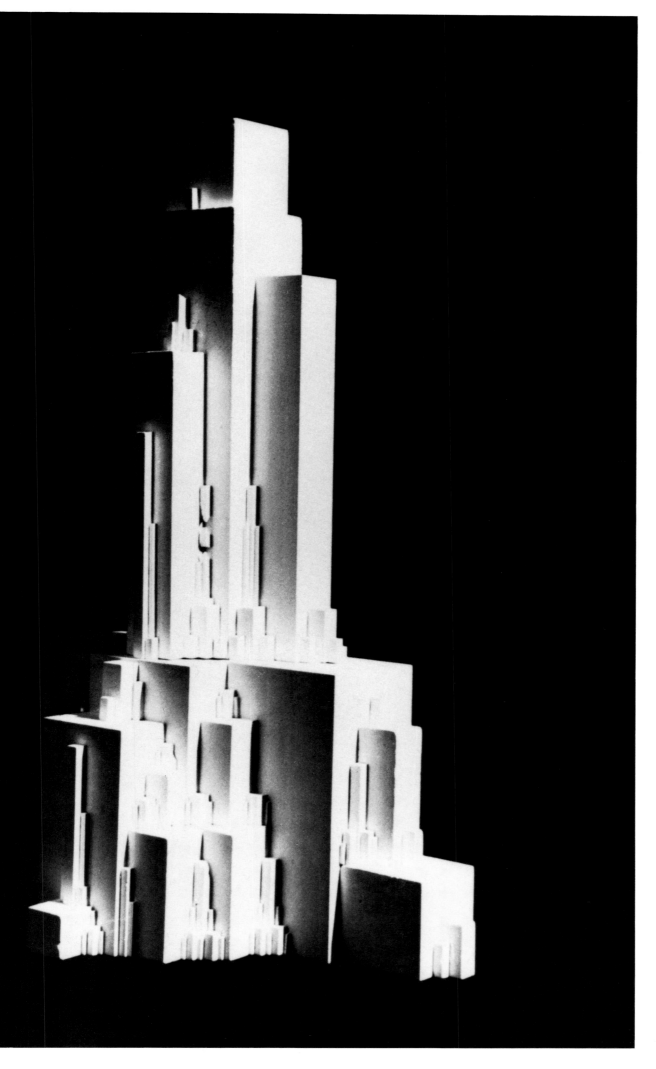

The
Skyscraper
Age

136   Kasimir Malevich: *Gota Architecton.* 1923. Plaster.

The Skyscraper Age

Time is of no importance, the most ancient forms are born again modern.... Rational conception is the inextinguishable and eternally fresh source of an entire spectrum, ranging from the tools fashioned in Paleolithic times to wood and metal agricultural instruments, musical instruments, armor, vehicles, boats and mills, right up to the electric lightbulb, machines, automobiles, airplanes."

the delight of periods before ours: those of the Baroque, the Renaissance, les Grands Louis, etc. This is what the public understands by modern forms, since when it is confronted with a 'pure new form,' it never fails to cry out against the ugliness or the barbarism.... All of you who have applied the discipline of rational conception to produce furniture, objects and houses have been denounced as barbarians."

It was, in fact, the term *barbare*—barbarian—that the president of the Salon des Artistes français regularly used to denote the "moderns."

Painting has always preceded architecture. It is impossible to overstate the importance of its experimental role in this domain. Generally speaking, painting anticipates and prepares the way for the architectural event. It reveals, elaborates and imagines the space which man will sooner or later employ to construct his dwellings, his gathering places or rest areas, his places for work, leisure, meditation or contemplation.

In other words, as Robert L. Delevoy notes in his book *Dimensions du XXᵉ siècle* ("Dimensions of the Twentieth

137   Fritz Höger: Chile House, Hamburg. 1923–1924.

138   Bruno Taut, Walter Günther and Kurt Schulz: Project for the *Tribune* Tower, Chicago. 1922. Private collection, Germany.

Van de Velde also warned his young French colleagues (he was sixty-two at the time) against the trap of modernism: "If someone among you advises you to seek 'modern form' otherwise than by applying the laws which since time immemorial have determined the existence and appearance of form, it can but lead to some new depravity, to which the term 'modern' will only apply to distinguish it from other aberrations which were

trend in twentieth-century art, yet its hold over Picasso is more often referred to than its equally marked influence over the strictly regulated "arrangements" of Léger, La Fresnaye, Mondrian and Schlemmer. The idea that it may have affected architectural research may well illuminate the position of both Seurat and architecture in the historical continuum.

It has been said many times that Seurat was above all a man of technique, the inventor of Divisionism. But he

139 Ludwig Mies van der Rohe: Project for a skyscraper. Model. 1920–1922.

Century"), painting, as a cultural act, should be considered as a special way of translating visual, spatial, linear and structural conceptions, which architecture subsequently attempts to take up, taxed with the additional constraints imposed by sociological and technological necessities.

This is clear if one considers, for example, that Malevich's *Architectons* or *Planites*, which led to the New York skyscrapers a decade later, themselves stem directly from Constructivism (one of the models or works of sculpture clearly anticipates the shape of the New York Rockefeller Center). Equally, it is possible to consider Mies van der Rohe's architecture as the absolute result of the combined speculations of De Stijl and the Bauhaus, while the painting of Fautrier and Rauschenberg no doubt anticipates an architecture as yet undreamed of.

Mondrian was aware of this when he stated: "As long as no entirely new architecture exists, painting must do what architecture does not yet do."

Robert L. Delevoy astutely cites the work of Seurat as an example of a speculative and experimental model for architects. It is well known that it set the tone for a major

knew how to exploit his discovery with the intelligence of a great plastician. Seurat's Divisionism led him to create a plastic space arranged with an implacable geometric severity, free from all anecdotal incident, from the sentimental or picturesque, from all decorative detail. The process is one of radical purification. Elements are taken from reality, rendered partially unreal, rigorously schema-

140 One of many projects for the Empire State Building. 1926. Model. The famous skyscraper was finally constructed from different plans, from 1929 to 1931.

111

tized and reassembled in groups where, in spite of their apparent autonomy, they function with the precision of a watch movement, the divisions of the planes of light acting as an organizing factor and increasing the efficiency of the structure to the highest degree. It is an image of an order based on measure and calculation—a poetic interpretation of the requirements of Constructivism. It is also the expression of a perfectly achieved economy, and more—an art founded on a rational and scientific ideal.

It was precisely these guiding themes that brought into being a new architectural consciousness: static vision, clarification of planes, refining of volumes, ordering of functions, incorporation of light, technological requirements, rejection of ornamentation, purity of profile, silence of facings. As Delevoy goes on to point out, it should also be noted that if this architecture, at the same time as aiming at modernity, continued to reflect basically "classical" outlines—the closed, rigid and rectangular forms common from the Renaissance onwards—it was to a large extent because Seurat himself retained the essential geometry of cubic space: the very geometry which Cézanne was simultaneously calling into question. It was no mere accident that the first number of *L'Esprit nouveau*, the famous pioneering publication founded on Le Corbusier's initiative in 1920 to defend "a spirit of construction and synthesis, order and conscious will," with the intention of "presenting and commenting clearly on the works, research and ideas presently guiding our civilization," should include a warm eulogy of Seurat by Bissière. The work of the artist whom H. Read called "the Piero della Francesca of the modern movement" initiated, according to a 1920s Parisian paper, a reaction against the "imbecilic mania for the outmoded, the infatuation for Louis XV style absorbing our millionaires' budgets."

Nor was it a coincidence that Van de Velde was a particular admirer of Seurat: the "paring away" he called

for in a pamphlet is exactly the same as that practised by the inventor of Divisionism. "We will see nothing rises up until the total destruction of all that exists at present," and also: "My generation was submitted to the nightmare of growing up among dimwitted beings who played with architectural elements as children do with building blocks, putting columns on top of arches, cornices on pediments, without any logic. They were obstinate as only fools can be obstinate, and, in the excess of their mania, they larded surfaces with all the ornaments currently in vogue: naked women and flowers! A horror of this practice and fear of such a future for ourselves has caused us to come out into the streets to call for reason, so that we may be delivered."

Le Corbusier wrote later on: "We waste money and human lives in making ornaments. There is the real evil, the crime which nobody has the right to pass by unseeing."

From now on, the absence of ornament was the sign of purity of thought, a quality which Loos, the fiery polemicist, whom Karl Kraus baptized "the clean-sweep architect," attributed to peasants and engineers. Thus the foundations were laid for a way of thought which was, through the doctrine of De Stijl, the Bauhaus and Esprit nouveau, to influence the entire half-century: to construct without decoration was to construct like an engineer and, consequently, to adapt architecture to the requirements of the machine era.

It was thus only in the mid-1920s that the radical changes in the architecture of the first half of the twentieth century began to be apparent—changes that stemmed from the use of new materials (concrete, glass, steel) and the progressive mastery of new techniques. It was not enough, from 1900 on, to say: "we must create space and not design facades," it was also necessary to strive for a universality of language, brought about by the industrial nature of the materials and the extension of means of communication. Neither was it enough to claim

141 Arnold Ronnebeck: *The City of the Future*. 1925. Drawing.

142 Iakov Chernikhov: *Composition of Various Architectural Forms*. 1930. Private collection, Moscow.

Building Like an Engineer

The Utopians

143 Konstantin Melnikov: Project for a monument to Christopher Columbus. *Santo Domingo*. 1929. Pencil and sepia, 45.7 × 65 cm. Melnikov Collection.

144 Georgii Krutikov: Aerial town, apartment building. 1928. Private collection, Moscow.

kinship within Austrian, French, German or Dutch Purism, or to base the movement on the theoretical reflection developed simultaneously in France and the United States. One had to attempt to raise the theory of plastic art to the level and imaginary potential of scientific discovery, such as was evident in the work of Planck and Einstein.

To take up the delayed-action parallel with painting again, it must be admitted that, apart from Wright's and Gropius's pilot projects, nothing constructed before 1920 sprang from forward-looking fashion, and the rare significant buildings (those of Perret, Van de Velde and Loos) belong to the post-Impressionist tradition.

The birth of Cubist painting in France, followed by its almost immediate spreading to Holland (De Stijl) and to Russia (Suprematism, Constructivism), was needed

before painting was sufficiently assimilated to be translated in terms of construction in space, using solid materials.

The Schröder House in Utrecht (Rietveld, 1924), the Bauhaus buildings in Dessau (Gropius, 1925-1926), Lovell Health House in Los Angeles (Neutra, 1927-1929), the Savoye Villa in Poissy (Le Corbusier, 1928), the large Schocken shops in Stuttgart (Mendelsohn, 1928), the Van Nelle factory in Rotterdam (Brinkmann and Van der Vlugt, 1929-1930), the German Pavilion at the Barcelona Exhibition (Mies van der Rohe, 1929) are the first examples of the new poetics at work: inspired by Cubism, it introduced time into space, developed the plan as an organic whole from a central idea, and transformed the building into a structure without perspective, to be viewed from all directions.

The skyscraper technique, characterized by a curtain-wall stretched over a metal frame, has existed since 1833, since George W. Snow made the first one in Chicago, using an ultra-lightweight, thin, precise steel structure for the framework, clothed in wood, for buildings that could subsequently be extended upwards.

Similarly, in 1885, William Le Baron Jenney, of Chicago, invented the true skyscraper by building the Home Insurance Building on a revolutionary system the implications of which are still not exhausted: vertical stone pillars, encasing iron columns, which, connected to horizontal cross-beams also in iron, form the real load-bearing framework of the structure. The traditional building system of a continuous, load-bearing wall is replaced by a lightly covered metal cage, resting on support points, which may, in principle, be extended horizontally and vertically ad infinitum.

However, it was not until 1921 that these discoveries were rethought in terms of modern living and working conditions, when Mies van der Rohe carried out his first project of a skyscraper made entirely of steel and glass. At the same period the most famous of American architects, Frank Lloyd Wright, was also rethinking the problems of architecture: his 1920 project for a dwelling consisted of a series of linked apartments, attached to a cross-shaped central core of retaining walls made of reinforced concrete.

Mies van der Rohe was seeking "greater perfection." In his own words, he described his architecture as "skin and bones" and his motto was "spareness is richness." One cannot help thinking of Mondrian. Both he and van der Rohe share a common severity, both seek the absolute, the same purism, the same lyricism of the right angle.

What Delevoy called the poetics of this new architecture came, to a large degree, from the drawing boards, the handyman's workshop, and the "laboratories of the solitary illuminati," that is, from the innumerable projects, sketches, models developed simultaneously in the USSR (by Malevich, El Lissitzky, Tatlin, Leonidov, Vesnin); in Germany (by Bruno and Max Taut, Finsterlin, Scharoun, Luckhardt, Kohtz, Gropius, Mies van der Rohe); in Austria (by Kiesler); in Holland (by Rietveld, Van Eesteren, Van Doesburg, Vantongerloo); in France (by Tony Garnier, Le Corbusier, Mallet-Stevens); in Italy (by Sant'Elia, Virgilio Marchi); and in the United States (by Buckminster Fuller, Burnham). Everywhere, impatient, experimental, utopian research proclaimed the need to overthrow the conformism of academic art—to think freely, unfettered by traditional practices, local constraints and out-of-date regulations. There were totally new buildings to be imagined, urban areas and often urban complexes to be created, the formal and aesthetic potential of new materials to be investigated. Each and every one—painters, sculptors and architects—was utterly convinced that his or her mission was to meet the requirements imposed by social dynamics, to make use of the increased production capacity, of the technical, economic, scientific and demographic data springing from a new civilization—the civilization of the masses—of communication by waves, of the social sciences and of socio-cultural amenities.

The entire meaning of the architecture of the Twenties is derived from the utopian ideals on which it was based. It was the publication and dissemination of these utopias, even before their construction—whether they were signed

The Utopians

Taut or Melnikov, Le Corbusier or Mies van der Rohe, Gropius or Krutikov, Finsterlin or Luckhardt, Fuller or Leonidov—which revealed the ideas, the hypotheses, visions and prowess of these "twentieth-century Piranèses."

The glass, steel and concrete face that they gave to this utopia came well and truly into being, and in grandiose terms, when the Rockefeller Center elevated it to the level of mythology; it appeared as a "machine-house" (an expression invented by Sant'Elia, changed later by Le Corbusier to "inhabitable machine"), when Rietveld and Wright took it up each in his own way, respectively, in Utrecht and at Bear Run. These buildings are less in opposition to rational architecture and organic architecture than is generally claimed: both Schröder's house and Waterfall House are equally rooted in Cubism and both, unfettered by frontal perspective, display a freedom of planning and a tendency towards a multidirectional occupation of space.

The twentieth-century Piranèses often adopted a messianic tone. Thus, Walter Gropius, eight years after designing his first masterpiece, the Fagus factories, proclaimed: "Our work consists of nothing but fragments... but there is a consolation: the idea—the forming of a bold, impassioned and utopian idea of architecture, that will be carried out by a lucky era. Artists, pedantry has perverted right thinking and erected walls between the arts: destroy them, and become builders, all of you. Painters and sculptors, smash down the barriers separating you from architecture and seek with us the ultimate artistic goal: the conception which will bring into being the cathedral of the future—a cathedral which will include architecture, sculpture and painting.

Today, there is as yet no architecture. We are only the precursors of those to come, who will deserve the name of architect, for that name means: master of the art that transforms the desert into gardens and raises wonders to the skies."

For years, German avant-garde architecture, deprived of the opportunity to construct because of the defeat in war and the resulting inflation, was deliberately utopian. The movement published a correspondence containing articles and copies of projects and sketches; Gropius signed his articles *Mass* (Measure) and Bruno Taut *Glas* (Glass). An exhibition of utopian projects was even organized "for the proletariat," in the workers' quarters of Berlin.

Everybody called for the "right to utopia." Hermann Obrist wrote: "And now a last word: up with utopia! After all, it is

145 Wassily Luckhardt: *Glass Festival Hall*. 1919. Watercolor on cardboard, 87.5 × 113 cm. Akademie der Künste, Abteilung Baukunst, West Berlin.

the only thing we have left. Let us live in Utopia, draw up plans, castles in Spain. Let us make believe and prepare for the new era which will come in thirty years.... Since nothing will be achieved in my field, architecture, during my lifetime, I have altogether abandoned it, and sculpture as well, and I secretly design fanciful works (paintings and drawings), which, in my opinion, go considerably further than Expressionism...."

There came a moment, towards 1923, when, for some architects like Gropius, the utopian period ended and they began to build some works. The Bauhaus then entered eagerly into battle with those who obstinately continued to declare themselves Utopians. As Michel Ragon notes, there was a difficult frontier to cross, between utopia and reality—a frontier that was arbitrarily closed, at a certain moment, by those who were tired of utopia. This would happen in the USSR in the 1930s. It was decided that utopia and the era of realizations was over.

Among the Utopians, there were some in revolt already—against the "functional nightmare," against Kafkaesque bureaucrats. Naturally, they preferred the fascination of the grotto, the cavern and the labyrinth to the "glass house." Hans Poelzig and Hans Luckhardt decorated their concert halls with stalactites and stalagmites. The "sculptors," in reply to the Bauhaus theories, introduced what we today call "architecture-sculpture." The Casa Nova by Hermann Finsterlin (1919-1920) is a kind of Baroque sculpture that prefigures Etienne-Martin's current *Demeures* ("Residences"). Kiesler's Endless House (1924-1926) is a violent protest against the tyranny of the right angle. In another connection, Erich Mendelsohn, with his Einstein Observatory in Potsdam (1921), and Fritz Höger, with his Chile House in Hamburg (1923), asserted the right of architecture to be "emotional" and, indeed, symbolic. Chile House took the form of the prow of a ship; the Einstein Tower is an astonishing demonstration of the possibilities of modern lyricism in architecture. By virtue of its form and its internal dynamism, this astrophysical observatory comes close to the work of the Futurist sculptor Boccioni.

As Michel Ragon also notes, the work of Erich Mendelsohn—who formed a link between Germany and the United States, being born in West Prussia in 1887 and dying in San Francisco in 1953—is very unjustly underestimated, as is that of Poelzig, Finsterlin and Kiesler, who are, in fact, all highly important. Mendelsohn and Poelzig made noted debuts at the same time as Gropius. Poelzig employed glass surfaces in horizontal bands from 1911 on, and gave his water castle at Posen a visible steel frame. Mendelsohn began his architectural career in 1912. Both were devoted to the world of theater and shows. In 1920, Poelzig was able to

146 Hermann Finsterlin: *Glass Dream*. 1920. Watercolor. 18.8 × 29 cm. Staatsgalerie, Stuttgart.

147 Max Taut: *The Marble Cathedral*. 1921. Taut Legacy, Berlin.

148 Walter Gropius: *Total Theater Project*. 1927.

The Utopians

give full rein to his visionary impulses, when Paul Wegener asked him to design the sets for his film *The Golem*.

But it was Mendelsohn who was the most prolific Expressionist architect. It could be said that he was the only one who built in any quantity, although he submitted a large number of projects which were considered utopian and which remained at the design stage. On the eve of the decade, he exhibited a series of architectural drawings at Paul Cassirer's, in Berlin, entitled *Architecture in Steel and Concrete*. They were drawings of religious buildings, observatories, silos and factories, and they displayed such imagination of form that Henry van de Velde saw Mendelsohn as his true disciple. Frank Lloyd Wright also attributed some importance to the projects and achievements of Mendelsohn.

The Einstein Observatory was planned to be constructed in concrete. The aerodynamic aspect of the building was

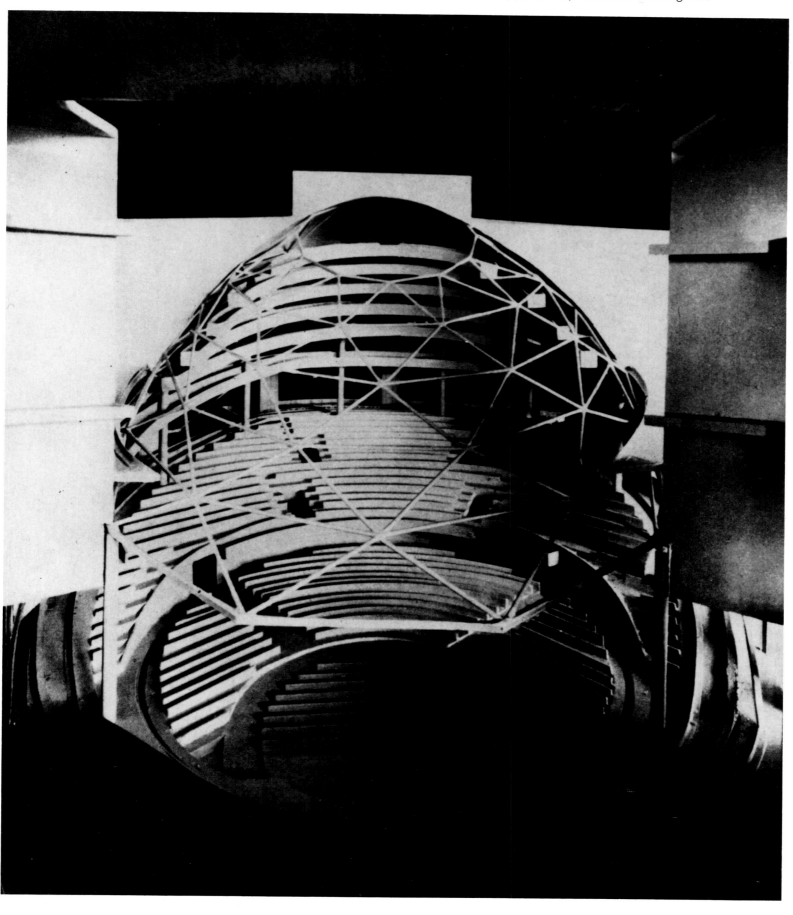

not only intended to heighten its emotive quality, but also to demonstrate the structural properties of reinforced concrete, rid of the already clumsy verticals and horizontals of academicism. Shuttering problems caused concrete to be abandoned and the Einstein Tower was built in plastered bricks. Unfortunately, Mendelsohn's emigration to the United States proved fatal to him, just as it did to Gropius. In exile, neither of them constructed such powerful and original works as under the Weimar Republic.

Finsterlin and Kiesler, on the other hand, built almost nothing at all. Finsterlin began by studying chemistry with Bayer, physics with Röntgen, Indian philosophy, then painting at the Munich Academy. Deliberately anti-rationalist, his project for a "house of meditation," a kind of sculpture in marble and smoked quartz, dates from 1920; his pamphlet attacking the right angle from 1925; his first private show in Stuttgart from 1928. In close and sometimes animated contact with Rudolf Steiner and Gaudí, Finsterlin remained an architect without works. He collaborated regularly with Bruno Taut and in Taut's review *Frühlicht* ("Dawn Light"), in 1921, he pleaded the cause of a tactile architecture. At the same time, however,

he put forward the idea of built-in furniture, which was utterly foreign to the Bauhaus theories.

"The relationships between town, house, furniture and vase represent only a tiny part of the formal tangle of the universe: the one is the inevitable result of the other. Traditional furniture looks like foreign bodies in modern rooms. Has the obligatory system of six walls never irritated you—have you never felt the need for spaces attuned to the vibrations of your soul? The furniture of the new rooms will be part of the architecture—it will be inseparable... here and there walls will swell to form cupboards... welcoming hollows will provide resting places for tired bodies, the foot will pass over transparent floors, carved in bas relief to soften the harshness of the necessary horizontal... at each step, the bare foot will tread a sculptured ground...."

We know that some of Kandinsky's theories were influenced by another Utopian—Rudolf Steiner. Steiner (1861–1925) was not only a theoretician but also a practitioner, building the Goetheanum near Basle for his community. The philosophical aims and architectural forms of this building were in absolute opposition to those of Gropius's Bauhaus, which was built at the same time. The Bauhaus was rationalist and the Goetheanum spiritualist, Gropius functionalist and Steiner set against anything utilitarian. But the two communities had fundamentally the same desire to form a synthesis —called by Steiner a "reconciliation of the arts"—and they shared a common fascination with Goethe.

With utopia, all these architects struggled against what they called "the prison-cube, universal panacea." In opposition to the theories of Le Corbusier, Frederick Kiesler affirmed: "The house is not a machine, nor the machine a work of art. The house is a living organism and not a mere arrangement of dead materials: it lives as a whole and in its details. The house is an epidermis for the human body."

Michel Ragon, specialist on the subject of hanging towns, says that in 1925 Kiesler planned a project for a spatial town, which he exhibited at the Grand Palais. This idea of a hanging town has today become one of the guiding ideas for the future. At the time, however, it seemed so crazy that even Le Corbusier asked Kiesler

149   Erich Mendelsohn: Einstein
Observatory at Potsdam. 1917–1921.

150   Azéma, Max Edrei, Hardy:
Douaumont Ossuary, near Verdun.
1920–1932. Postcard.

151   Walter Gropius: Monument to
the March Dead, Weimar. 1921–1922.

New Monuments

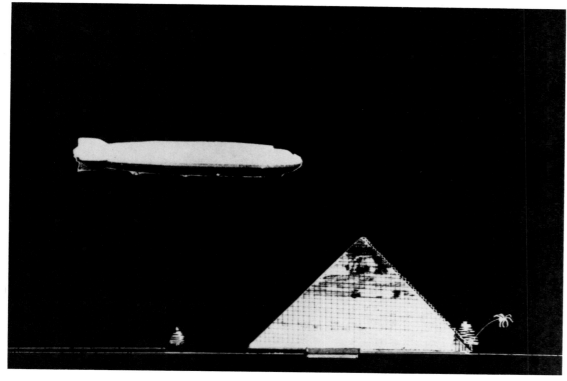

ironically if he meant to hang his spatial town from zeppelins. Still, shortly afterwards Le Corbusier himself adopted the idea of a town raised on stilts.

At the same time, Soviet architects were dreaming of a socialist architecture. They drew on the writings of Marx and Engels, with their strict suppression of the distinction between town and country. In the absence of materials and means, spatial urban projects were drawn up more to respond to the problem of how to inhabit space than to the needs of the individual. Among the garden-cities, the shared houses, rocket towns, appeared an obsession with monuments, as a sign of the times, as a present and real indication of the power of the great Russian people. Had not Lenin himself suggested that towns should raise monuments to all the heroes of the Revolution? The list of heroes to be thus honored included Belinsky and Chernyshevskii, but also Mussorgskii, Courbet... and Cézanne. Surely Tatlin's monument, to the Third Communist International, is also a monument, albeit in the form of a project, symbolizing the architecture that sprang from the October Revolution. The project did not progress beyond the maquette stage, which people were content to carry in the parades, and perhaps that was all for the best. In fact, the model, more than the tower, had it been constructed, became a symbol of the utopia these artists dreamed of achieving. It showed their limitless ambition. For, although ready to abandon their easels, which they now considered to be anachronistic, these artists were inflamed with the idea of taking an active part in the construction and organization of the new world, but were not in the least prepared for the role of engineers. Technical difficulties, the lack of raw materials, monopolized by industry, rendered increasingly difficult the realization of projects by Melnikov, Ginsburg, Vesnin, Krutikov and others.

In his book *La ville radieuse* ("The Radiant City"), Le Corbusier said later, "One fine day, authority—the door of reason through which good and fanciful dreams have to pass—announced in the USSR: 'That's enough now, stop the fun and games.'" As we know, authority at the time was called Stalin. Architects, like everyone else, would have no more fun and games for a long time to come.

152   Ivan Leonidov: Project for the Palace of Culture, Proletarskii area, Moscow. 1930. Sports Pavilion. White gouache and collage on black paper, 34.9 × 33.2 cm. A. Shchusev Museum of Architecture, Moscow.
A pyramid and a palm tree, or Egypt come to Moscow. The Utopists were daunted by nothing.

153 Herbert Bayer: Project for a newspaper kiosk. 1924. Distemper and collage on paper, 64.5 × 34.5 cm. Bauhaus-Archiv, West Berlin.

154 J.J.P. Oud: Facade of the Café De Unie in Rotterdam. 1925.

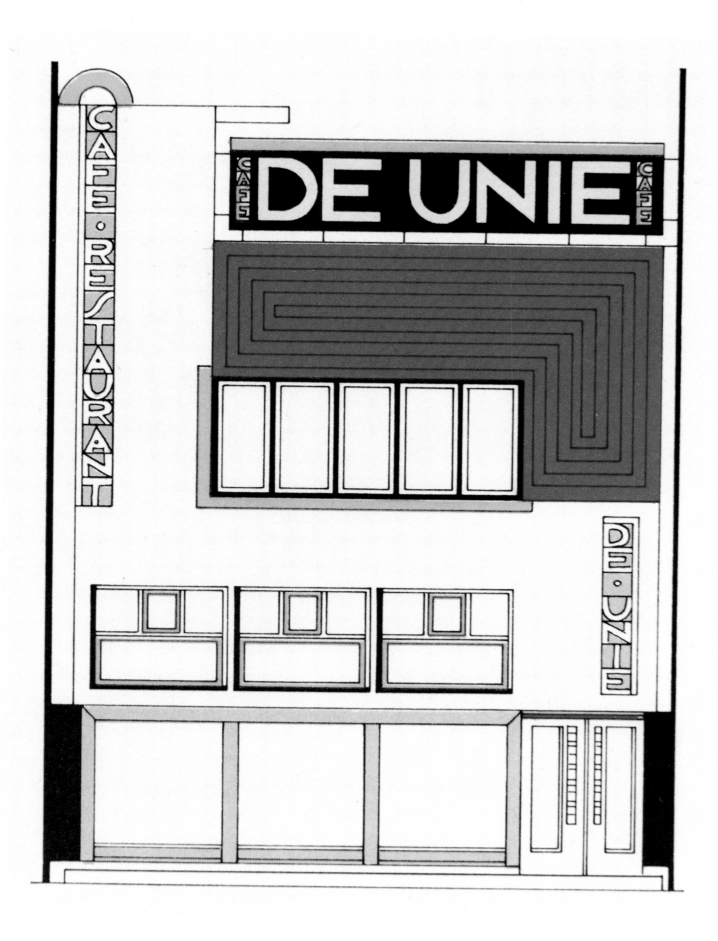

For De Stijl, architecture was the synthesis of all the arts and ought to spring quite simply from life itself. Oud professed that the exterior aspect of a building should imply its interior architecture. The facade of the Café De Unie by Oud, like Bayer's kiosk, is clearly the work of a graphic artist in the spirit of the covers for the *De Stijl* review, adopted by the periodical in 1921, under the heading of "new typography." This term in fact covers modern graphic art as taught in Switzerland today. The origins of this new typography are various. It appeared simultaneously in Russia, Germany and Holland after the First World War, around 1917. Van Doesburg and the Russian Constructivist El Lissitzky practiced it before Moholy-Nagy introduced it to the Bauhaus in 1923. The Dadaists and the Italian Futurists were probably the first to use it, beginning in 1914.

155 Ivan Golosov: Zuiev Club in Moscow. 1926–1927.

156 Konstantin Melnikov: Rusakov Club in Moscow. 1927–1929.

The creation of apartment complexes in Austria was a phenomenon with a great and often sad future. Christened *Hof*, these were three-or four-story buildings constructed around a closed courtyard. Each *Hof* contained living accommodation for a thousand families, rented out at a minimum rate which covered only maintenance costs. This major policy for popular living quarters was adopted by the socialist municipality of Vienna in 1920, thus prefiguring the West's housing policies following the Second World War.

In 1920 the Spanish engineer Artura Soria y Mata died. Born in 1844, he was the first to practice modern town planning. It was in fact in 1882 that Soria y Mata published the sketch of his linear city in the Madrid newspaper, *El Progreso*. Soria y Mata put forward the idea of "linear cities," urbanized ribbon developments. "A single road, fifty meters wide and of unlimited length—that will be the town of the future; it could stretch from Cadiz to St. Petersburg, from Peking to Brussels," he stated. Soria y Mata's idea was taken up successfully in the USSR, in particular with the construction of Stalingrad, and also, more recently, by the Japanese.

In his plan for the reconstruction of Saint-Dié, Le Corbusier also adopted the idea of a linear plan for a city, this time along a highway. The trend for ribbon development along highways is now well and truly with us, even if its purely speculative nature is far removed from Soria y Mata's idea.

There are only two real examples of Le Corbusier's urban theories: the garden city of Pessac and the Chandigarh plan. Nevertheless, these theories dominate the whole between-the-wars urban utopian current. This is explained by the fact that Le Corbusier's thought was in fact a synthesis of all progressive urban ideas from Fourier to Gropius. He succeeded in presenting these ideas as daring, vivid plans, and he was, moreover, the first person to publish a series of books, in a style accessible to a wide public, amounting to a sort of "bible," for the use of future generations.

Le Corbusier's first plan for a "contemporary town of three million inhabitants" (1922) completely overturned the idea of the town center that was being constructed in Europe at the time. Le Corbusier's center was composed of twenty skyscrapers, sixty stories high, on a cruciform plan. Each of these could contain 10,000 to 50,000 employees. While the plan anticipated the current trend towards the construction of business centers made up of office towers, it nonetheless drew heavily on what already existed in Manhattan at the time and, more precisely, as Le Corbusier never denied, on Auguste Perret's idea for city-towers. The same year as Le Corbusier, Perret published a project for city-towers to take the place of the old fortifications around Paris. These towers were also sixty stories high and were designed to house 40,000 persons each.

In 1925, Le Corbusier returned to his idea and transformed it into the "Voisin Plan for Paris." This called for eighteen two-hundred-meter towers, designed as offices, right in the center of Paris, facing the Ile Saint-Louis. The predictable furor ensued. From that moment on, government and public alike viewed Le Corbusier as a blindly progressive destroyer of the past. These two plans contained the basis for what Le Corbusier called the "Radiant City" in 1930. This was a plan which contained the notion of joint dwellings and service establishments. It was Fourier's old phalansterian idea, an idea which incidentally was widely applied in the USSR at the same period, under the name of "common houses." Le Corbusier's Radiant City falls into the Babel-like utopian current which ran through Europe in the twenties, beginning with Sant'Elia's Citta Nuova. At the same time as the United States was building slightly apologetic skyscrapers that often tried to resemble medieval cathedrals, Europe, from Berlin to Moscow, was dreaming up Babylonian cities, vastly grander than the most grandiose dreams of the Chicago school.

While Mies van der Rohe was drawing up his projects for transparent steel and glass skyscrapers (1919-1921), and Kiesler, as we have seen, was designing a "space city" (1925), raised up at different levels, leaving the natural ground for parks, grassland and canals, Mart Stam was proposing the construction of aerial carriageways over the buildings of Amsterdam (1922-1924). This idea was related to Kiesler's, since one entered the latter's "spatial town" by the rooftops; it was also connected to Perret's "bridge-skyscraper," linking sixty-five-story high-rise blocks half way up with arched bridges, and to a project by Daniel H. Burnham for a "skyscraper bridge" for the banks of Lake Michigan in Chicago, with each pile of the bridge containing twenty-five stories of offices. The European visionaries were unable to give a form to their dream until the United States, after 1930, opened up again to modern architecture.

Le Corbusier fastened onto the theory of the "machine-man," so dear to Descartes and the philosophers of the Age of Enlightenment. It was an idea which led him inevitably, as it did Sant'Elia, to the notion of the "inhabitable machine," the ideal habitat for the "machine-man." "A house is a machine to live in," he wrote. "Baths, sunlight, hot and cold water, the desired temperature, food conservation, hygiene, beauty, in proportion. An armchair is a machine for sitting in, etc." Curiously, this particularly rationalist era was scandalized by the idea of a machine to live in, but at the same time blithely conformed to the positivist and Cartesian credo! Although Gropius was considerably less concerned with urbanization than Le Corbusier and wrote little on the subject, he did apply the same principles as those of the Radiant City to his "lamelliform" buildings. Instead of adopting a system of construction by blocks, Gropius specified a system of rows of buildings at right angles to the street. Each building had to be separated by gardens. On their rooftops, Gropius also stipulated

Cities of the Future

day-care facilities for small children and his ideal was to achieve what were known as "common houses" in the USSR. Both Gropius and Le Corbusier tended towards the same phalansterian ideal. Gropius, however, was less radical. He admitted that there should be a mixture of high and low buildings, depending on the various requirements, since he recognized that "the low house, surrounded by a garden, offers greater peace, isolation and possibilities for relaxation." He deserves thanks for this good thought!

If apartment complexes have become omnipresent since the Second World War, they appeared revolutionary when their models were built in the twenties. A great number were constructed, in Germany in particular, until the economic crisis of the 1930s. Gropius built several in the suburbs of Berlin. In the Frankfurt suburbs, Ernst May constructed 15,000 homes with interior fittings for 50,000 people. These accommodations, grouped in units for 1,200 to 1,500 people, included both rows of single-family houses and collective buildings. Built of standardized materials, with a common usage of concrete slabs, flat roofs and the adoption of geometric volumes, their form is precisely that taken up again and systematized after 1950. Ernst May also designed the furniture and fittings for these buildings, which were provided with a collective central heating system, common laundries and kindergartens. The great interest elicited by the buildings in Frankfurt caused May to be called to the USSR in 1930.

But the alignment of May's and Gropius's buildings, to ensure solar exposure, led to the monotony which we know only too well. This monotony became altogether sinister when May applied the system to whole towns in the USSR—not unlike what has been done throughout the world since the Second World War.

While Germany, Austria and the USSR (the plan for the construction of electricity power stations, voted by the Soviet parliament in 1920, established gigantic

157   P. Portaluppi: Study for the Alabanuel area of Milan. 1920.

126

158   Le Corbusier (Charles-Edouard Jeanneret): *Paris in the year 2000 (The Future City)*. Project submitted to the Autumn Salon in 1922. Fondation Le Corbusier, Paris.

industrial undertakings in non-urbanized regions, which involved the construction of workers' cities, then of new towns), were the most important areas of construction of large, working-class living complexes between the two world wars, we should not forget Holland, where in 1925 J.J.P. Oud applied the principles of green zones and shared amenities to Kiefhoek, his complex in Rotterdam.

France's situation in the 1920s was paradoxical. On the one hand, its antiquated political structures and its anemic industry placed it low on the scale of progressiveness, in comparison to the Weimar Republic, the USSR, Sweden or Holland. On the other hand, the genius of a Le Corbusier, the innovations in technology and the plastic arts of Beaudoin and Lods, Mallet-Stevens, Lurçat, Perret, Tony Garnier, Freyssinet and others placed it at the highest level of avant-garde architecture. French architecture between the wars, Michel Ragon underlines, was as inventive as it was underemployed, as hard-hitting as it was held in check. France did undertake town-planning, however, in Morocco, where Lyautey called upon the town planner Henri Prost, who built modern Western towns there until 1922, including Rabat, which was inaugurated in 1920. From 1919 on, in the *A.B.C. of Communism*, a kind of guide for the use of militants, Bukharin and Preobrazhenskii were concerned with the "new constructions which have to satisfy the needs of a communist society." But at the onset of the revolution, these two theoreticians

were still uncertain as to which sort of habitat would be the best: either large blocks, with shared services—especially restaurants—as advocated by Fourier, or "small, well-laid-out workers' houses." This hesitation led to many future debates. However, Bukharin and Preobrazhenskii took a firm position on the association of industry and agriculture and the uprooting of city-dwellers, stuck in joyless towns, "deprived of pure air, cut off from nature and destined for an early death."

Numerous architects shared this preoccupation with "small separate houses." Of course, in capitalist countries, the prototypes were for the use of the wealthy, but all architects subscribed to the notion of developing factory-made, prefabricated structures which could be erected without the use of mortar, at the building site. It was these individual housing units which were intended to lead to the utopia of houses "built like an automobile." It is parodoxical, to say the least, to see Le Corbusier, Gropius, Mallet-Stevens, Rietveld, Oud, Dudok and others, whose dream was to build for the masses, whose ideal housing drew its inspiration from the café, the railway carriage and the ship's cabin, and whose ideology, like that of all the other avant-garde architects, was anti-bourgeois, having nothing but bourgeois clients and ultimately continuing, albeit in modern forms, the architectural traditions of the bourgeois villa—the principal object of nineteenth-century architecture. Some masterpieces resulted, whether it was the Savoye Villa in Poissy by Le Corbusier, Mallet-Stevens's house in

Residential Units

159 Emil Fahrenkamp: Shell Building in Berlin-Tiergarten. 1929–1931.

Paris for Mr. Dreyfus, or Dr. Schröder's house by Rietveld. Like Gropius with his "Variations" (1921), they were all seeking the same type of prefabricated, Cubist houses, joined by repetition or by coupling cell-units.

The most perfect practitioner in the field of Cubist architecture, the most admired and, like Le Corbusier, also the most criticized, was Mallet-Stevens; work bearing his personal stamp did not appear until 1923, with the house he built for the de Noailles in Hyères. At the 1925 Exhibition of Decorative Arts, his importance was highlighted by his participation in numerous sections—altogether in the tradition of the era: architecture, furniture, cinema. His sets for Marcel L'Herbier's films, especially for *L'Inhumaine*, assured him an important place in the field of cinematography. In the same year of 1925, he finished two new villas: one in Ville-d'Avray for Mr. Augier-Prouvost and the other in

Méry for Paul Poiret, the famous dress designer. In 1926-1927 his talent blossomed in a whole series of private houses at Auteuil, which represent a unique Cubist group. With its broken lines, walls of glass and horizontal windows, this masterly composition can still be admired, sadly spoiled by later additions carried out by the different owners, in the street that bears the architect's name and which with time has become a veritable museum in his honor. Mallet-Stevens was to have more ambitious projects, but they remained at the design stage: a plan for the layout of the Porte Maillot, a project for Le Bourget airport and an Olympic stadium, to name a few. But he undoubtedly remains the French artist who comes closest, with his simplicity, his severe and elegant aesthetics and his use of dynamic forms, to De Stijl and Adolf Loos. We should also note in passing that Adolf Loos, who lived in Paris from 1923 to 1928,

128

also built individual villas, in particular a house for Tristan Tzara, in 1926, and a project for Josephine Baker. He exercised considerable influence over the best French architects of the era.

It was only in the following decade that the architects' projects for entirely prefabricated, low-cost housing became possible, thanks in particular to the work of Freyssinet, the engineer, who adopted the totally new technique of vibrated concrete for prefabrication.

During the Twenties, the aesthetic influence of painting and of the plastic arts on architecture can be clearly seen, following on from Cézanne, Seurat and Cubism. Throughout the same period, the technical influence of engineering was also to make itself felt in its turn. It was the combination of these two influences that produced the "International style." But a third influence, and by no means the least important, should not be forgotten—it was ideological in nature: socialism.

160 Karl Schneider: buildings in Hamburg. 1929.

161   Robert Mallet-Stevens: Mr.
Dreyfus's house in Paris. 1926–1927.

162   Gerrit Thomas Rietveld:
Dr. Schröder's house in Utrecht. 1924.

Machines to Live in

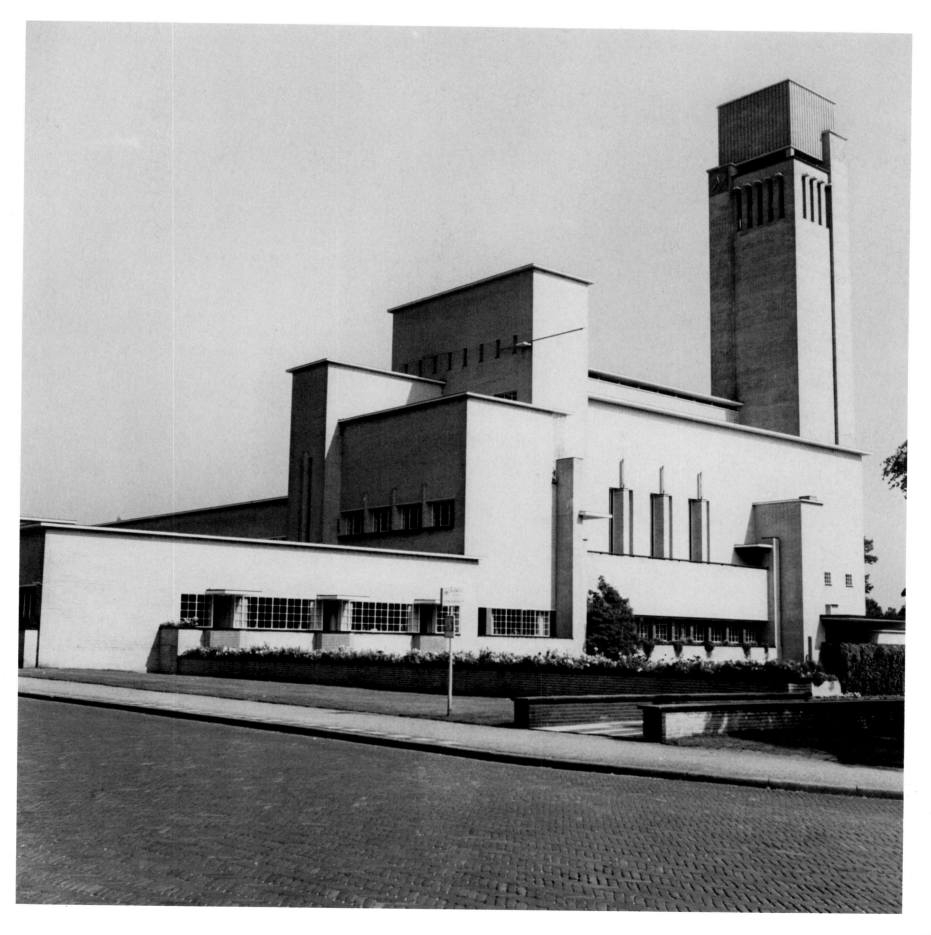

165   Willem Marinus Dudok: Hilver-
sum Town Hall, Holland. 1928–1930.

Design

Forerunners and Traditionalists

167 Gerrit Thomas Rietveld: Chair. 1923.

168 Gerrit Thomas Rietveld: Side-board. 1920.

In 1920, no one knew—and for a very good reason!—the definition that Thomas Maldonaldo would give to the word design in the following decade. Maldonaldo was a director of the Ulm school (heir to the Bauhaus), and one of the theorists of modern design: "Design is a creative activity that consists of determining the formal properties of objects which are to be produced industrially. By 'formal properties' is meant not simply the exterior characteristics, but above all the structural relationships which give an object (or system of objects) a coherent unity."

Despite the fact that his definition remains slightly vague, this was the era in which the notion of design won ground; promising contradictions began to appear, which, when genuine, all had one thing in common: a repudiation of the ornamentation and trivial decoration so beloved by Art Nouveau, or, more particularly, the spineless style.

It was not by chance that Ozenfant and Le Corbusier resuscitated in 1920, in the second number of their review *L'Esprit nouveau*, Adolf Loos's manifesto, first

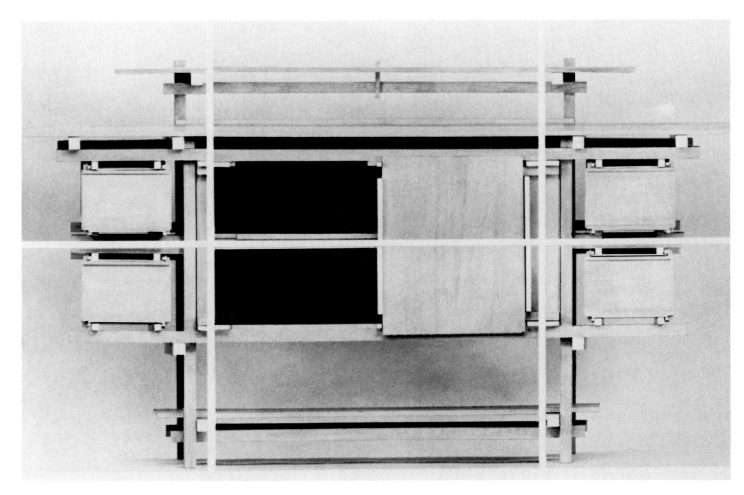

published in 1908, under the explosive title of *Ornament and Crime*. This manifesto spoke out violently against the excesses of Jugendstil and called for functional creations and geometric forms: "I have formulated and proclaimed the following law: Ornament disappears from everyday objects in proportion to the development of culture... today's man, according to his inclination, uses or rejects the ornamentation of old or exotic cultures. He

Jocelyn de Noblet in his book *Design*, this work, taking certain Hegelian ideas on form as its point of departure, was the first attempt at the elaboration of a new theory of form: *Gestalttheorie* ("Gestalt Theory"). The following are the essential laws, as set out by the French philosopher Paul Guillaume in 1925:
1. A form is something other and more than the sum of its parts.

does not invent new ornamentation. He reserves his inventive faculty and concentrates it on other objects." There were those who adhered completely to Loos's revolt, thinking, like him, that ornament hid shoddiness and that when an object was beautiful, it did not require ornament. Le Corbusier, Rietveld, Chareau or Francis Jourdain were examples of this school of thought. And there were those who simply noted the stylization of the decoration, and rejected it, retaining the other aspects of Art Nouveau.

It must be said that the avant-garde in its geometric phase, having assimilated Fauvism and Cubism, scarcely ever turned its decisions into concrete results: the Bauhaus, from the outset, remained Expressionist by temperament and retained a craftsmanlike approach, while the Vkhutemas became better known for its projects than for its actual achievements.

In 1890, a Viennese philosopher, von Ehrenfels, had published a book on *The Qualities of Form*. Quoted by

2. A part in a whole is not the same as that part isolated or in another whole.
3. Psychological facts are forms; that is, organic units which are individual and limited within the spatial field of perception and representation.
4. Every form is a function of several variables and not the sum of several elements.
5. Forms are transposable; that is, certain properties are retained in changes affecting all their parts in a certain way.

It can be said that the *Gestalt* theory altered the content of basic teaching and had as strong an influence on the Bauhaus as on the Vkhutemas. Furthermore, the basic design courses in every school throughout the world are more or less derived from the *Gestalt* theory.

In the field of design as elsewhere, the 1920s were characterized by the same tendency to move forward, one foot after the other. The left foot, here, was involved in theoretical research: it went by the name of Bauhaus,

Vkhutemas, De Stijl or Esprit nouveau. It continually attempted to elaborate a universal theory of design and interspersed its research with prototypes which formed the basis of design for the following decades. It resulted just as much from the development of an instinctive design—the result of an effort to change on the part of the craftsmen themselves—as from the drawing boards of artists, architects and soon engineers, who took an interest on their own initiative, in the formal problems posed by mass production.

There was also the right foot: the little, obscure men, such as Süe and Mare and Maurice Dufrênes, who produced and marketed, through large shops like the Primavera Studio of the Grands Magasins du Printemps, mass-produced goods which were relatively popular, but were, in fact, outmoded and pandered to the poor taste of the public. These traditionalists (strongly marked by nationalism: Süe and Mare executed the cenotaph of the Arc de Triomphe, a kind of cream cake, stuffed with

Winged Victories, which the victorious troops filed past) chose to perpetuate the Louis-Philippe style, since it was the last true French style to have existed and because it answered "needs which are still ours," in the opinion of André Mare. "Its forms are so rational," Léon Deshairs wrote in 1920 regarding this Louis-Philippe style in an article entitled "Our Enquiry into Modern Furniture, the French Arts Company," in *Art et Décoration*, "that today's coachbuilder uses it unwittingly in the design of a bucket seat. We are not restarting it; we are not continuing it out of sheer obstinacy; we find that it presents simple solutions, and, through it, we connect with all our glorious past. We are not practicing an art of fashion." This statement reveals the distance separating the satiated, flabby belly of a rich country, France, and the intellectual movements and dreams of countries like Russia and Germany, embryonic, riven by inflation and revolution. Group work, for the French traditionalists, signified above all breaking with the deadly individualism of the Art

170   Kandinsky's dining room. Furniture designed following the artist's advice by Marcel Breuer in Dessau. 1926. On the wall at the right, a painting by Kandinsky dating from 1904, Morocco. On the left, an abstract painting from 1929.

171   On the left, neo-plastic furniture in painted wood: table, armchair, standard lamp by Félix del Marle, 1926, under a painting by Mondrian. On the right, the famous Red-Blue Chair in painted beechwood by Gerrit Thomas Rietveld, created in 1917, next to a Kandinsky. Mr. and Mrs. Robert Walker Collection, Paris.

172 André Groult: Chairs in ebony and tinted tortoiseshell painted by Marie Laurencin and executed by Adolphe Chanaux. 1924.

173 Paul Iribe: Curved easy chair in carved wood. 1925.

174 Marcel Coard: Brazilian rosewood couch, sides in cane and ivory, square feet. The original mohair coverings have been replaced with leather. Commissioned by Jacques Doucet in 1930.

175 André Groult: Table and bombée chest of drawers in shagreen. Painting by Marie Laurencin. The chest of drawers featured in Madame's bedroom in the French Embassy Pavilion at the 1925 Exhibition of Decorative Arts.

**Almost
Indecently
Curved**

176 René Herbst: Furniture presented at the 1921 Autumn Salon.

The Traditionalists

Nouveau artists. They considered that an artist like Guimard had shown himself intolerably presumptuous in wishing, on his own, to meet every need. It has to be said that the "Louis-Philippards" of decoration were sowing in particularly favorable soil and, with their little geometric roses, inspired by Paul Iribe, they encountered little difficulty in pleasing the fiercely individualistic French, who took the flood of Art Deco objects to their hearts, but who always rejected the Bauhaus and despised mass-produced objects.

Iribe's rose, more or less geometric and variously adapted by numerous traditionalist decorators, including Ruhlmann, Mare, Groult, and others, assumed a significance beyond its superficial geometric aspect. Just as today, under Mitterrand, the rose in the clenched fist has become a symbol of the new face of socialism, Iribe had already used it (in the earlier era) as a nationalist symbol, against Germany, in 1915. A precursor of the ecologists, he raised it against the cube and the machine of the 1920s: "For thousands upon thousands of men,

the flower is as necessary as steel. Are we to sacrifice the flower on the altar of the cube and the machine?" Whether it was a question of unobtainable prototypes, even if they were aimed at the general public, or objects to suit middle-class taste, the result was the same: the artistic output of the 1920s remained elitist; despite the wish to be decorative and accessible to all, it was really meant only for the most privileged.

The person who launched this new art of living, before the war, was Jacques Doucet, the dress designer, who parted company with his eighteenth-century furniture to live in a modern interior. Paul Iribe designed this interior. At the beginning of the decade, Jeanne Lanvin commissioned Armand Rateau to create her apartment, whose famous blue bedroom was to pass into history. At the same time, Ruhlmann—more of a traditionalist—was working for David-Weill, Süe and Mare for Jane Renouard, Mallet-Stevens designed the singer Damia's house, and all the Parisian "gentry" dreamed of was modern art.

There were also all the new rich wanting to assert themselves and gain a place in the limelight. That explains the luxury of the Twenties and Thirties. In furniture, existing forms were reinterpreted—no new ones were made, especially at first. What was important was the simplification of the lines and the quality of the materials. Spareness was essential, as interior designers finally began dealing with environments in spaces of new proportions. No more accumulations of esoteric objects, no more stifling interiors with heavy opaque hangings, no more kitsch. This was the age of sport, the automobile, the open air—at least for those who had the means.

Louis XVI secretaires were quickly covered in sharkskin, the Louis-Philippe style was accentuated with strips of inlaid ivory, rare woods were used, such as amboyna, sycamore, palm, Brazilian rosewood or Macassar ebony. Semiprecious stones were employed to set off these skillful pieces of marquetry and the parchment previously dear to Bugatti turned up again. A certain taste for the exotic governed the creations: it was the era of Black art which inspired Eileen Gray, who, followed by Jean Dunand, precipitated a return to lacquered furniture and screens.

The 1920s were ruled, not always very happily, by imagination. In all areas of design and decoration, this outburst of novelty came both as a reaction to the outmoded exuberance of 1900 and, perhaps more importantly, as a response to the aridity of the products of the German school, the Werkbund. Invited by the French interior designers, those whom the critics referred to as the "Munich group" had answered the call of Hermann Muthesius and had founded the Werkbund—the "work-group"—in 1907: "... wishing to dignify industrial labor by ensuring the concerted action of art, industry and crafts, through education, publicity and the assertion of a common will." The bases of an essential current underlying the twentieth century, which led to the Bauhaus and influenced the Vkhutemas, are contained in these few words.

177 Léon Jallot: Interior decoration for the Salon des artistes décorateurs. Paris, 1927. Sofa and stool in red and white lacquer, screen in red, silver and gold lacquer, carpet in white, red, black and silver wool. Period document. Hervé Poulain Collection.

Geometrical Interior Design

178 Jacques-Emile Ruhlmann: Project for an alcove. C. 1920.

179 Francis Jourdain: Interior decoration. C. 1925–1930. Gouache on canson paper, 25 × 33 cm. Musée des Arts décoratifs, Paris.

Nature was still present, no longer in the forms themselves (as in the lily-shaped turn-of-the-century tables), but in the details of the decoration. Material and wallpapers were composed entirely of stylized, geometric flowers, which like Paul Iribe's famous rose, spread everywhere: carved on furniture as a decorative motif, drawn on the lamps executed by Dufy for the great silk manufacturers of Lyons, and forged on balconies as baskets of geometric fruit.

This sort of design, which can seem cold, was nonetheless comfortable, and full of color. For example, the interior decoration carried out by Paul Poiret in his Ateliers Martine, which he created on his three barges *Amour, Délices* and *Orgues*, show that the famous couturier had a sense of comfort. Couches, poufs and cushions welcomed the visitor.

When, thanks to industrialization, design came down into the streets, the forms remained, but the quality suffered, and the colors became gaudy. Here the appalling, mass-produced cozy-corners come to mind, omnipresent in low-cost apartments and, indeed, essential for organizing particularly small rooms.

If imagination was the keynote with regard to creating, it disappeared when it was a question of installing furniture. A survey of period photographs of such suites reveals a surprising lack of variety. Whether by Leleu or Lucie Renaudot, the dining room—that sacrosanct bourgeois invention of the nineteenth century—was always organized in the same way. Exactly in the center of the smooth, geometric sideboard would be displayed a sculpture by Despiau, or a superb *objet d'art* with rounded contours. In the middle of the room: the table, surrounded by its chairs; also in the middle, the chandelier, set off by wrought iron brackets symmetric with a window, ocean liner style!

Decoration during the Twenties was unashamedly exotic. It was the period when the Colonial Exhibition was being prepared and a Colonial Society of French Artists was even established, which, thanks to grants, sent painters overseas. What they returned with from their voyages was not always exemplary. However, exotic influences could result in beautiful products, such as the screens and panels by Jean Dunand who drew his inspiration from flora and fauna.

Ceramics, very much in vogue at the time, were also happily influenced by exoticism: geometric designs inspired by batiks animate the work of Linossier; animals abound, as in the example of Lalique's snake vase. Here we should also note the work of Jean Mayodon, with its strong Persian influence. These craftsmen or artists were numerous and their work was often of high quality. But Maurice Marinot, who worked with glass, remains the greatest of them. What is apparent in all artistic output in the field of bourgeois design, is nevertheless a unity which, while it may be slightly monotonous, would be expressed in the next decade with great success, for example, in the fitting out of the liner *Normandie* in 1935. With the famous 1925 Art Deco Exhibition, the art of compromise appeared in all its glory. "By choosing an embassy, rather than a People's meeting-house as the theme," Waldemar George wrote at the time in *L'Amour de l'art* ("Love of Art"), the Société des Artistes décorateurs (Society of Decorative Artists) set the tone for the work of our architects, our furnishers and our ornamenters. These architects and furnishers are not simply reactionary because of their devotion to the power of money, but also because of their failure to understand the imperatives of modern life...."
Georges Le Fèvre gave an account of his visit to the Exhibition: "Of all our 'decorative artists,' André Groult is unquestionably one of the most precious. By that I mean that he likes to work with rich materials. His pieces of furniture are the work of a veritable goldsmith—bulky jewels for boudoir or alcove.
Like many of his colleagues, he exhibits his works more or less everywhere, wherever there is a stand and... an opportunity, but, also like them, he has his battlefield.
It is in the embassy, at the Exhibition of Decorative Arts, the bedroom of the ambassadress.
I suppose, he says, not without candor, that the latter is very rich.
And consequently, sharkskin, lapis lazuli, amazonite, ivory, ebony, pink horn and quartz are Groult's favorite 'materials.' He supervises the placing of his creations with small gestures. A phlegmatic man, with a high forehead, Chinese eyes and an English smile, he caresses sensuously the curves of a chiffonnier in sharkskin, inlaid with ivory.
Curved, he repeats in a whisper, almost indecently curved...."
One incidental fact which particularly interested the press illuminates the struggle between the reactionaries and the innovators. Mallet-Stevens, in his luminous, open hall, had placed one of Fernand Léger's abstract-geometric compositions and a high narrow panel by Robert Delaunay, *Paris, the Woman and the Tower*, a version of

The "Ocean Liner Style"

the *Eiffel Tower* series. "During an unofficial visit," Charensol recounts in *L'Art vivant* ("Living Art"), "Mr. Paul Léon, Director of the Beaux-Arts, made one or two remarks concerning these panels, which did not appear to him to suit the style of the embassy. Messieurs Delaunay, Léger and Lurçat, who happened to be present, mentioned to Mr. Paul Léon that the authors of the works had a considerable standing, both in France and abroad, and that their influence on the art movement was so great that most of the constructions of the Decorative Arts Exhibition had been inspired by their works.

Mr. Paul Léon did not accept the arguments, and shortly afterwards Mr. Mallet-Stevens received an order to remove, within twenty-four hours, the panels which had so displeased the Director of the Beaux-Arts."

Among those disappointed by the Exhibition, those who were hoping for a meeting of decorative art and industry, and were equally interested in the setting out of a kitchen or a bathroom as of a living room, Francis Jourdain stands out as a pioneer. He was the first to concern himself with "the organization of increasingly constricted space" imposed by the new conditions of existence. His aim was to imagine a habitat in line with economic necessities for the new society that was emerging, by using all the possibilities offered by industry.

"Nowadays," he wrote at the time, "luxury at home looks more like a display of useful things. The taste for bric-à-brac, the interest in the object for its own sake, leads most of us to consider a piece of furniture as a decorative element. We purchase a pedestal table or a chest of drawers less for the purpose they may serve than for the happy effect they may have on the arrangement of an interior.

This is a regrettable mistake. It is possible to arrange a room very luxuriously by defurnishing rather than by

182 Léon Jallot: Lacquered cabinet, table and three-paneled green, gold, yellow and maroon screen, each panel measuring 170 × 60 cm. Exhibited at the Salon de la Société des Artistes décorateurs (Society of Decorative Artists Salon) in 1929. The group was split, but has been reunited, thanks to the patience and care of Mr. Hervé Poulain, the present owner. On the wall, the self-portrait of Tamara de Lempicka (see Plate 1); also, clock by Baccarat and carpet by Francis Bacon.

furnishing. The great interior designer of the future will be the one who limits himself to strictly necessary elements, arranging them in the correct proportion and perfect balance, so as to avoid leaving a single 'hole' or gap in their grouping, and in such a way that no part of the room for which they are intended will seem bare." Determined to offer inexpensive furniture to a working-class clientele, Francis Jourdain produced geometric forms, without ornament, made from solid wood, with wickerwork rather than upholstery. He was interested in

all aspects of interior design, turning his hand to the design of nursery furniture, cardboard toys, knot-stitch rugs. But neither industry, appalled at the idea of having to renew its models, nor the consumer, attached to his "bric-à-brac decoration," followed him. Still, new ideas were gaining ground, and Francis Jourdain's designs were in complete contrast to those of the contemporary masters, Groult, Süe and Maré, Marjorelle or Ruhlmann. The simplicity and sobriety of his art permitted neither Oriental exuberance, even in details,

183 Louis Süe and André Mare:
(Compagnie des Arts français): Dining-
room furniture. C. 1925. Musée des
Arts décoratifs, Paris.

nor the cherishing of one-of-a-kind pieces by the great
cabinet-makers, inaccessible to the general public.
Standardization can save us from artistry," he said, while
at the same time designing a prototype railway carriage
for the Paris-Orléans line—an exercise which he viewed
simultaneously as an attempt at creating an inhabitable
cell and at standardization. Francis Jourdain was the
ideologist of decoration, in the same way as were Van
der Velde or Loos in the field of architecture, by opposing
the academicism of the Beaux-Arts. In 1929, he
published an anthology, *Intérieurs* ("Interiors"), with
illustrations of works by Mallet-Stevens, Chareau, Le
Corbusier, Rietveld.
Seeing his hopes of producing for the general public
dissolve with the 1929 economic crisis, he launched the
production—out of the ordinary at the time—of garden
furniture and aquariums. He also successfully introduced
the fashion for home bars and home gymnasiums.
Thus, apart from Francis Jourdain, the architects and
decorators known as "modern" or rather "traditionalist,"

were scarcely, or not at all, concerned with the needs
springing from economic and social conditions after
1914.
This was not the case with the "forerunners," who were
concerned with the furniture so familiar to us today—the
chairs that enable us to work at the office, to lunch or to
relax in front of the television.
When, in 1924, the doors of the first Bauhaus were
forced to close for lack of funds—the institution would
move to Dessau, reopening the following year—the
balance sheet of the Weimar period was far from
negative: Marcel Breuer had executed his first chairs in
wood, prefiguring those in steel he would carry out at
Dessau. Their stylistic ancestry can however be traced to
certain chairs made by Rietveld in 1917. Marianne
Brandt and Wilhelm Wagenfeld, in the metal workshop,
had put forward some very new forms for teapots,
chocolate pots, round containers for infusing tea, an
office lamp, electric lighting systems, and so forth. All of
these items were of high quality and aimed at industrial

production. From 1923 on, Moholy-Nagy's preliminary course on forms in motion had contributed to reorienting Bauhaus research in new directions: as a result, the study of the use of glass in the metal workshop enabled Wagenfeld to produce his "Moholy" office light and to design a family of objects, including the famous Pyrex teapot, which he continued to produce for the rest of his life. Wagenfeld, like a good pupil of the Bauhaus, had learned the importance of the message contained in the object, the purity of form that lets purpose and function shine through, without the distraction of superfluous decoration.

Like the other students, he adopted the moral imparted by Bauhaus teaching: an artist accepts responsibility

184   Maurice Dufrêne: Chest of drawers. 1925. 139 × 143 × 53 cm. Presented at the Pavilion de la Maîtrise, Exhibition of Decorative Arts, 1925. Musée des Arts décoratifs, Paris.

185   Pierre Legrain: "African" style chair in palmwood veneer and lacquer. Stretched parchment seat. From the bathroom of Jacques Doucet's Neuilly studio. C. 1925–1928. Musée des Arts décoratifs, Paris.

186   Clément Rousseau: Chair. C. 1921. Ebony, shagreen and ivory, 90 × 42 × 42 cm. Musée des Arts décoratifs, Paris.

187
189

188
190

150

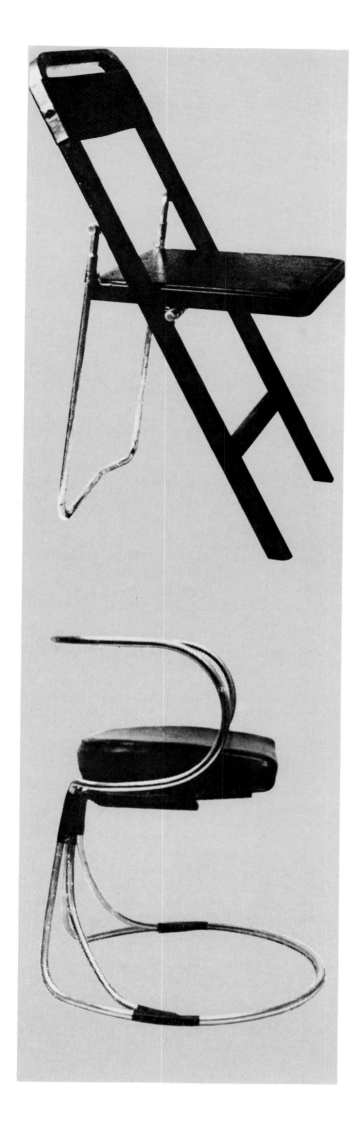

towards the public when he designs the objects which fill their lives. Wagenfeld wrote afterwards: "I have long considered my collaboration with industry as an artistic mission which can exert a major influence on society. The possibilities offered by this mission, the difficulties that may obstruct it and the means of mastering such difficulties—these are the only things which interest me. With this aim, I work with factory managers, tradesmen, technicians and other persons participating in the making and selling of products."

Marcel Breuer's research into metal furniture was contemporary with that of Mies van der Rohe and Mart Stam, and it is hard to ascertain who influenced whom. Breuer claimed that the idea of a tubular structure came to him on a bicycle ride, watching the handlebars of his bicycle! He wanted his furniture to be mass-produced and consequently he concentrated on depersonalizing it, so that it could fit into any environment. Thonet and Standard Möbel were the first to consider mass production of this metal furniture, in 1928. Knoll International are currently producing and selling Breuer's and Mies van der Rohe's chairs. The Bauhaus's influence was considerable, but it should be pointed out that it was not until a large number of teachers, architects, designers and students of the Bauhaus sought refuge in America, far from the Nazis—on April 11, 1933, the Gestapo invaded the Bauhaus premises in Berlin and arrested the students—that they were really able to put their theories into practice.

As distinct from the Bauhaus, which to a large extent remained a school of applied art where the teaching of architecture was officially introduced only in 1927, architecture courses began immediately on the opening of the Moscow Vkhutemas faculty in 1920. The preliminary course attacked the problems relative to the perception of forms, volumes and colors, by using the principles of the psychology of form.

On many points, however, the method was very similar to the Bauhaus's, especially as regards the establishment of a preliminary course, compulsory for all disciplines. There was certainly a great deal of direct or indirect contact between the two schools, if only through the intermediary of the German communists and El Lissitzky. Although the Vkhutemas was chiefly concerned with architecture, Vladimir Tatlin produced a tubular chair with a molded seat in 1927 and a low-burning stove in 1919. Rodchenko and his wife Varvara Stepanova designed an admirably functional work suit, which prefigured ready-to-wear clothes; they also designed the interior and the chairs for the Soviet Pavilion for the 1925 Exhibition of Decorative Arts. In around 1920 Malevich carried out some projects for cups and teapots for the Leningrad State Pottery. The metal-working department of the Vkhutemas was directed by Rodchenko from 1920 to 1927 and during this period his students designed and perfected clothes and furniture for a variety of uses, in each case destined for industrial production.

But it was on mass culture that these creative young people wished to have an effect. They developed their visionary ideas to a considerable degree and often saw rightly. In 1929, the celebrated architect Ivan Leonidov produced a project for a workers' club, including audio-visual teaching by means of television. As Le Corbusier often repeated, "Utopia is nothing other than the reality of tomorrow...."

"Unity in plurality" was the Dutch architect H.P. Berlage's definition of style. For Theo van Doesburg, "every

187 Le Corbusier, Pierre Jeanneret, Charlotte Perriand: Armchair with reclining backrest, chromed tubular steel structure, backrest and seat in ponyskin, armrests in black leather. Created in 1928, reproduced by Cassina since 1965. Musée des Arts décoratifs, Paris.

188 Le Corbusier, Pierre Jeanneret, Charlotte Perriand: Comfortable armchair in painted tube with leather cushions. Prototype 1928. Charlotte Perriand Collection.

189 Marcel Breuer: "Wassily" armchair. 1925. Produced in 1926 by Standard Möbel in Berlin. Bauhaus-Archiv, West Berlin.

190 André Lurçat: Chair in wood and chromed tubular steel. 1924.

191 Zemlianitsyn: Folding chair in wood and metal. Vkhutein. 1927.

192 Vladimir Tatlin: Chair, structure in bentwood, fittings in leather. 1923.

Contemporary Chairs

Л Парелю

193 Nikolai Suetin: Project for Suprematist plates. 1922–1924. Charcoal on paper, 19 × 27 cm. Galerie Chauvelin, Paris.

Industry and Design

emotion, be it sad or happy, implies a disruption of harmony and balance between man and the universe." Rietveld's "red-blue" armchair of 1917 and the Café De Unie by J.J.P. Oud in 1925 are good illustrations of the theories on which the spirit of De Stijl was based. Of all the avant-garde movements between the wars, De Stijl is the one whose creations remained the most faithful to its philosophy.

"The new way of living is stronger than art; we must not waste our time. We must create new forms, appropriate to the way modern life operates," professed Van Doesburg, who passed on the spirit of De Stijl both through his theories and the force of his personality. Rietveld's work perhaps provides the best illustration of this. Rietveld wanted his zigzag chair to be made in a single piece, but this was technically impossible at the time. It was only thirty-six years later that Verner Panton achieved his forerunner's objective by using molded plastic. The red-blue chair can be viewed as De Stijl's link with the past, while the zigzag chair looks to the future. De Stijl was animated by a spirit of research—it was a creative laboratory in perpetual transformation. This is what differentiates it from the more rigid Bauhaus and brings it closer to Russian Constructivism and Italian Futurism.

The ocean liner, the airplane and the automobile were the principal objects to capture Le Corbusier's

imagination: "These are the signs of the new times." He drew a conclusion about the perfection of technical forms: "One must attempt to establish standards to approach the problem of perfection." Later, he would contend that "a house is a machine for living in, an armchair a machine for sitting on."

Of them all, Le Corbusier expressed himself the best. He replaced the word "furniture"—which connoted "accumulated traditions and outworn uses"—with the word "equipment," and gave an example of it in the arrangement of the Esprit nouveau Pavilion: "Equipment is the classification—after careful analysis of the problem—of the various elements necessary for domestic operations. The innumerable pieces of furniture masquerading under various forms and names are replaced by standard cabinets built into the walls or fixed to them, placed in each area of the apartment where a precise daily operation is carried out, with interiors equipped to fulfill their exact role.... They are no longer made from wood, but from metal, in the same workshops where until now office furniture has been made. These cabinets alone constitute the furniture of the house, leaving a maximum amount of space in the room. Research into chairs and tables is leading to entirely new designs, from a functional, not a decorative point of view. Changing customs have removed the 'label'; it is possible to sit in many different ways, and the new forms

of chairs must take these different ways into account. Their tubular and sheet metal construction will enable them to be made without difficulty; traditional wooden construction is too limited.

Equip the house? One had to think about it."

A range was drawn up by Le Corbusier, Pierre Jeanneret and Charlotte Perriand in 1928-1929, produced by Thonet and presented at the 1929 Autumn Salon. The famous chaise-longue was there, the armchair with the folding seat and the comfortable armchairs reproduced today by Cassina in Italy, under the name of Le Corbusier alone. Produced industrially, this functional and ultimately highly sophisticated equipment was completely free of ornamentation. The chairs are now classics of contemporary furniture.

In this way, the "forerunners" of design, whether they were Purists, Constructivists or belonged to the Bauhaus, prepared the furniture of the future—that is, of today. Among the most forward-looking designs were those of Rietveld and Le Corbusier, the "Wassily" armchair designed by Marcel Breuer in 1925, as well as the cantilever chair produced by Thonet for the first time in 1928, which is still in production today.

Political circumstances—Hitler on the one hand and Stalin on the other— which obliged teachers and students to leave their countries, incontestably widened the influence of the Bauhaus and the Vkhutemas

throughout the world. One exception however, was France, and this, notes Yvonne Brunhammer, was for ideological as well as for nationalistic reasons: French sensualism accommodated such severity with difficulty. While the first Werkbund Exhibition in Paris in 1910 had thrown the ranks of the decorators into excited disarray, twenty years later the new presentation at the Salon des Artistes décorateurs (Decorative Artists' Salon), was relatively well received. The creations of Gropius, Breuer, Wagenfeld and others no longer had the air of insolent novelty that their predecessors had had!

But in 1930, as in 1920, there was still a choice, and that is precisely why this recent period holds such charm and attraction. There was a choice between the functional universe within everyone's reach, or at least, most people's—proposed by the Bauhaus and the Esprit nouveau—and the privilege of obtaining a unique piece of furniture, an object to be acquired and kept like a painting—of the type that still achieves extraordinary prices at today's auction sales at Christie's or Sotheby's. Yvonne Brunhammer draws this lesson as a sort of conclusion: more than sixty years have passed since the 1925 Exhibition, with its various successes and failures. Little by little it is losing its quasi-religious air, long perpetuated by those who made and lived it. However, it is not by accident that, living today as we do in the universe proposed by Le Corbusier and his friends, we

194 Nikolai Suetin: Decoration for a china jug. 1923. Model produced by the State Potteries and presented at the 1925 Exhibition of Decorative Arts in the USSR Pavilion. N. Manoukian Collection, Paris.

195 Marc Poirier: Ceramic vase. C. 1925.

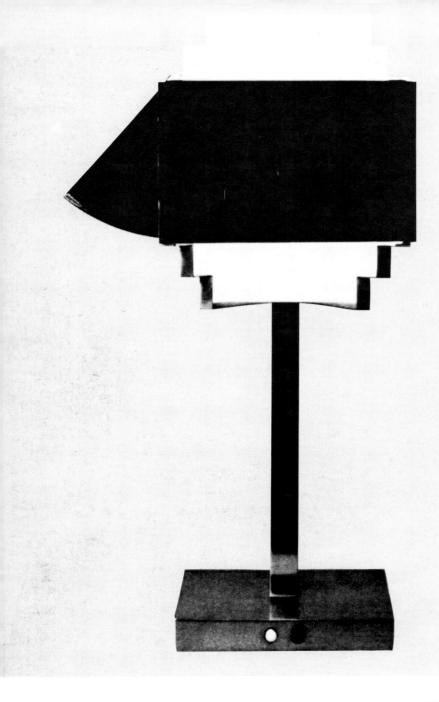 

196 Jean Perzel: Shuttered office lamp. Polished steel and glass. 1926. Mr. and Mrs. Donald Karshan Collection, Paris.

197 K.J. Jucker and Wilhelm Wagenfeld: Bauhaus office lamp. 1923–1924. Chrome and opalin glass, H. 36.2 cm. Busch-Reisinger Museum, Harvard University (gift of Walter Gropius), Cambridge, Mass.

The Bauhaus Legacy

look with nostalgia towards Süe and Mare, Ruhlmann, Rateau and Jacques Doucet's team.

An immigrant living in low-rent accommodation can hardly compete with Cleopatra dissolving her legendary pearls in vinegar as the stuff of dreams. There is the worker scrimping and saving to go on vacation and there is the designer Patou, commissioning Süe and Mare to build him a sumptuous villa near a casino, so much the easier for him to leave enormous sums of money on the green baize—with a smile, of course. When he traveled, he habitually took two limousines: one white, driven by a black chauffeur for sunny days, the other black, with a white chauffeur for rainy days. Charlie Chaplin was among Patou's guests at his great villa, and one stormy night he mimed an entire bullfight, to calm the nerves of the oh-so-frightened "beautiful people." That was the 1920s: a mixture of eccentric follies and day-to-day monotony; the eternal duality of dream and reality. A duality that made itself felt in the world of design as elsewhere: according to the principles of the Bauhaus, for example, one could as justifiably produce a design for a typewriter as for a telephone, a perfume bottle or a clock.

Even jewelry design wavered between the traditional use of noble materials and the introduction of substances

previously unthought of, underlining the distinction between two approaches to the trade. The first consists of creating an ornamental effect by using only precious stones and employing metal for strictly practical aims, while the second makes use of metals, precious or otherwise, for their own aesthetic value.

If there is one index of social distinction, it is the jewel: creative design, plastic beauty, craftsmanship, rarity, and an easily readable gauge of the owner's bank balance are all contained in its tiny facets. Whether a caprice, institutional present, amulet or financial asset, the jewel is never innocent. In a society where social status conferred by high birth is being replaced by that accompanying financial success, jewelry denotes affluence—to be attained by men and displayed by women through their dress and appearance. Thus, on the respectable woman, a jewel indicates the measure of her husband's success, while on the woman of easy virtue it suggests the degree of her lover's passion. Was this institutional code to be called into question? At the time, classical jewelry was indeed in conflict with avant-garde jewelry on many points: they had different motives, techniques and aims. In retrospect, however, a common style can be discerned across the range of an output reflecting the trends and contradictions of an

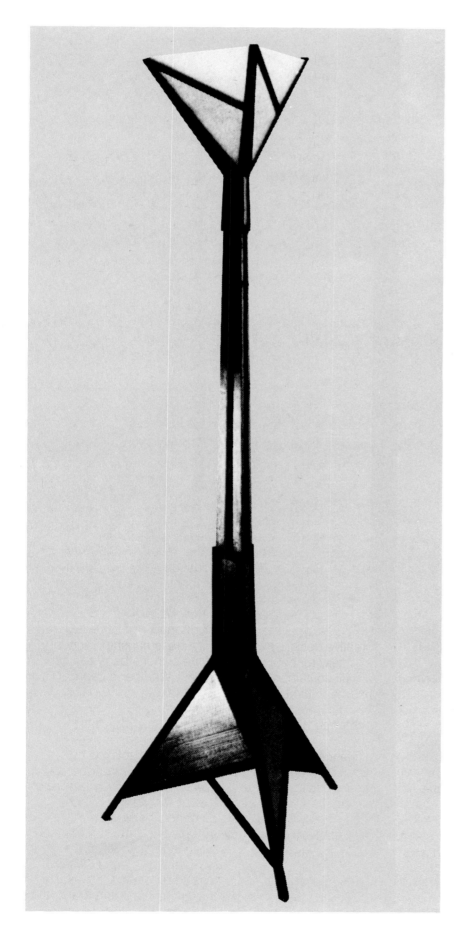

eminently creative era. The acute renewal of interest in recent years for 1920s jewelry underlines how well the artists and craftsmen of the period were able to find the right balance between the appetite for frivolity of a de luxe clientele, and the obstruseness of the most contemporary art.

Thus the creations of Dunand, Templier, Goulden, Fouquet, Sandoz, Cassandre, Miklos, Lambert-Rucki, Boivin, to name but a few, brought together the influences of Cubism, the Ballets Russes, Abstraction and Black art, creating, with the help of technical advances, a particular language of contemporary jewelry. Indeed, the technical aspect was paramount: new cuts for stones—in tables, bars, prisms, trapeziums, obtaining infinitely diverse defractions of light; the use of hard stones such as onyx, lapis-lazuli, malachite, turquoise, amber, coral, jade; the discovery of platinum, which because of its high resistance, allowed mountings to be considerably lightened, invisible behind the sheer brilliance of the stones; pearl-oyster farming, perfected by a certain Mr. Mikimoto, allowing an increase of these biological aberrations; satin finish, hammer-finish, gold or silver patina to vary the appearance; finally, the new materials, with magical, science fiction-type names like "Galalith," "Aladdinite," "Kiloid," "Ameroid,"

The One-of-a-kind Piece

"Bakelite"—these ancestors of our plastics—brought with them a considerable novelty and infinitely increased decorative possibilities. Initially they were used as substitutes for rarer materials, subsequently for their own beauty.

All these innovations attracted a new, rejuvenated clientele, eager to break the links that still bound it to a civilization whose values had been called into question by world war.

200   Jean Goulden: "Cubist" clock in silver-plated bronze and chased enamel, with projecting semicircles. 1929. Sydney and Frances Lewes Collection, Richmond.

201   Baguès: "Plume" chandelier. 1925. Gilded metal and glass beads, H. 100 cm. Galerie Félix Marcilhac, Paris.

203 Gustave Miklos: Project for a rug for Jacques Doucet. 1929.
Gouache, 180 × 80 cm. Galerie Félix Marcilhac, Paris.

202 Cassandre: Study for a clasp for Georges Fouquet. 1924–1925.
Pencil, gouache and watercolor on gray paper, 28.3 × 19.6 cm.
Musée des Arts décoratifs, Paris.

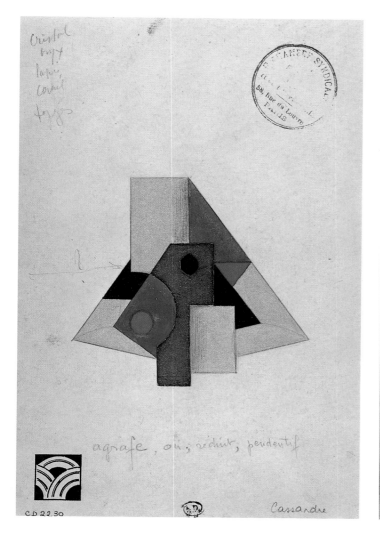

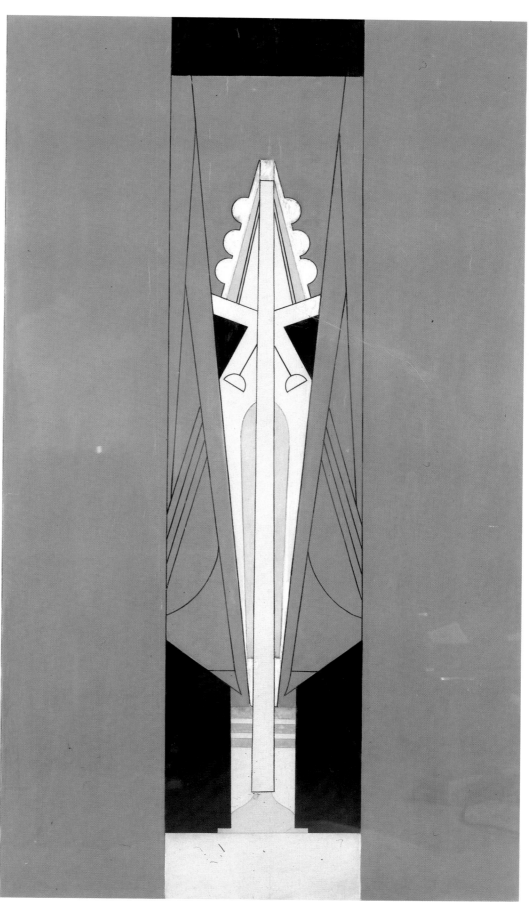

204 Remington typewriter. Great Britain. 1920.

205 Pick and Johnston: Logo for the London Underground. 1920.

206 Telephone. Germany. 1920.

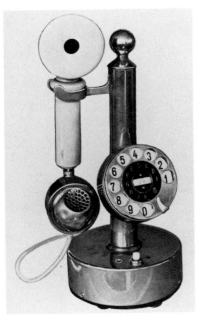

The applied arts of the period, in all their industrial forms, blithely mixed circled and squares, verticals and horizontals. They had learned their Cubist lessons, via De Stijl, the Bauhaus and Constructivism.

The Avant-garde Becomes Mainstream

Example of design: This object is made up of a series of containers divided into quarters disposed in a circle around a central axis; the straight edge of each quarter lies along this central axis, while the curved edges, turned to the exterior, form a globe or sort of sphere. These four quarters are enclosed in a very particular wrapping. Like most commercial wrappings, this one is disposable, What is the object in question? An orange (Bruno Munari).

207   Jean Dunand: Bracelet in silver, red and black lacquer detail. C. 1925. Private collection.

208   Raymond Templier: Brooch of platinum, diamonds, galalith, and enamel. 1925. Musée des Arts décoratifs, Paris.

209   Even perfume bottles adopted the cube (Chanel), or the sphere (Lanvin), in contrast with the delicateness generally favored by the perfume manufacturers. 1920.

Woman and the Automobile

210 René Vincent: *Elégante au volant*
("Elegant Woman at the Wheel").
C. 1925. Watercolor with gouache,
31 × 27.5 cm. Private collection, Basle.

211 Jacques Heim models wearing Sonia Delaunay's "simultaneous" costumes, one of them at the wheel of the journalist Kaplan's automobile, its paintwork based on a Sonia Delaunay material. Photograph taken in front of the Tourism Pavilion of the 1925 Exhibition of Decorative Arts. Archives Sonia Delaunay, Paris.

212   René Lalique: *Victory*. Radiator cap. C. 1930. Colorless molded glass, W. 25 cm. Private collection.

213   Prototype of a "Cubist" Panhard-Levassor automobile. 1923.

214   Georges Lepape: *Matching Dress and Coachwork*. Watercolor and gouache for the cover of *Vogue*, November 1, 1924. Private collection, Basel.

The Cubist Woman

In 1928, Jeanine Jennky beat Louis Chiron in a supercharged Bugatti in the Boulogne 4-hour race; Helle Nice broke a number of records with an average speed of two-hundred kilometres an hour on the racecourse in Montlhéry; Miss Friedrich and Miss Shell took part in the Paris-Nice trial.

The Twenties ushered in the Age of the Beauty and the Automobile: the female revolution had begun. Victor Margueritte took note of this phenomenon, commenting in the pages of *La Garçonne*: "Sporting a red leather beret, bare-necked in an open coat, she drove with an alert decisiveness, so delightfully boyish that Regis, bad tempered as he was, could not help but admire her.... Yes, all the same, this was a new example of feminine grace! A being still altogether surprising, although her ranks are rapidly multiplying—a being who from now on would have to be counted as an equal."

In the previous decade, society women had already adopted the automobile as an exclusive addition to the realm of feminine accessories—a curious choice when one recalls the kind of dustcoat falling to the feet, topped with an immense muffler, and transparent mica viewing panel. Coachbuilders pandered to the slightest whims of these beauties, allowing them to choose the color of the seats, to stipulate cushions for the back and for the feet, parasol holders, hearing devices, glove compartments, mirrors, elaborate trunks, and the like. Colette noted in *Gigi*: "The style for automobiles that year was high and rather wide, because of the enormous hats imposed by Caroline Otero, Pascaline de la Drôme, Liane de Pougy.... The autos also slid gently around the corners."

World War I had given an impetus to the phenomenon of female liberation. Had women not replaced men at work in hospitals, shops, public services? The female wardrobe was modified to suit this new role calling for agility and freedom of movement. Corsets were banished, dresses became shorter, hats smaller. With the return of peace, the craze for freedom took control. The change was spectacular. The "Cubist woman" came into being, defined by René Bizet and described by Colette in *Vogue*: "short, flat, geometric, square." A final snip of the scissors at the neckline completed the metamorphosis. Women announced their freedom by adopting an androgynous look. To take the wheel—hitherto an essentially masculine prerogative—was the most startling expression of this emancipation. In 1926, the lively Duchess of Uzès gave her blessing to these developments by presiding over the foundation of the Women's Automobile Club.

The 1920s automobile, as it appeared in *La Garçonne* and in *L'Homme à l'Hispano*, was no longer the vehicle it once had been. It emerged from the war years covered in glory. The taxi episode at the Marne, the transport of munitions and the wounded, endowed autos with a warriorlike aura. From a technical point of view, as is usually the case in times of war, the automobile

The Mechanics of Beauty

benefitted from the manufacturers' efforts to meet the demands of the military authorities. Mechanically it was considerably improved.

"A work of art should reflect its own epoch," wrote Fernand Léger. "If our pictorial expression has changed, it is because modern life demands such change.... Beauty is no longer to be catalogued or graded, it is everywhere.... Modern beauty almost always comes together with day-to-day needs.... The automobile of today, subject to the requirements of speed, has been lowered, lengthened, refined, and has achieved a balance of curved and horizontal lines that stems from a sense of geometric order."

The decorative arts did not fail to take up the new subject. Hervé Poulain, an auctioneer with a keen understanding of the connection between art and these iron horses, noted the marriage between the decorative arts and the automobile. Both partners were generously endowed and left their mark on each other. On the one hand, the auto had its rationality and its functional character. On the other, the decorative arts determined the colors of the coachwork, the accessories, the interior fittings—in short, the finery of which woman herself is the finest flower.

The union was witnessed by artists. Women, fashion and the automobile combined to form the favored thematic trilogy of illustrators and commercial artists, incense bearers of a privileged society and past masters at evoking the ephemeral. Thus woman and the automobile were linked together, as Hervé Poulain argues in his book *L'Art et l'Automobile* ("Art and the Automobile"); complementary archetypes of worth, luxury and beauty. The whole Art Deco epoch is implied in this fleeting vision of a pretty woman with khol-lined eyes, cherry lips and close-cropped hair with a cloche hat, wearing a short dress by Madeleine Vionet or Coco Chanel trousers, and driving a Bugatti through Montparnasse, en route to Deauville or Saint Moritz. Glittering star of the age, the Amazon was asserting her supremacy.

Sonia Delaunay—faithful to the general concept of not separating art from the environment—achieved the perfect synthesis: for the 1925 Exhibition, she painted an auto body in colors similar to her dresses and her materials. The cover of the second number of *Vogue*, entrusted to Lepape, showed a model standing before an automobile, the coachwork of which harmonized with the geometric patterns of her dress.

These signs of emancipation, albeit concerning only a thin stratum of society, were nonetheless highly ambiguous. The problem of "woman as object," which was their natural result, is raised by Pierre Gascar: "Between the two wars, automobile elegance competitions were invented. The participants descended from their vehicles before the jury, froze in a graceful pose, one hand placed on the front of the car. Woman and object as precise equals—the one bearing the label of the great couturier responsible for her dress, the other

the label of its manufacturer and coachbuilder. The two elements of the picture are transposed: the woman has herself become an object, in a society based on ownership, and the car appears as a projection of the virility of the man who owns it. It can escape no one that by placing her hand on a hood housing forty horses

215   Liubov Popova: Cover of a fashion magazine. 1924.

LA 40 CV RENAULT

waiting to be sparked into life, the woman, graceful in her 'Twenties' dress, displays her submission to a force that is perhaps most faithfully represented by the power and even the streamlined form of the machine itself."

Was there, as Cocteau is supposed to have thought, a catch behind this symbolic freedom, referred to poetically at the time as the "fabulous unicorn"? The unique and superb self-portrait at the wheel by Tamara de Lempicka, at the beginning of this book, gives expression to high aspirations and proclaims the dawn of a new era. The artist paints—and sculpts—the face of a cold, disturbing beauty, heavily made-up, gloved and helmeted. The machine has the ambiguous character of an all-devouring sorceress—filled with loathing, yet enticing. It is simultaneously armor and flesh, mythological and contemporary. This woman is free to live. She can also die by the automobile: for example, strangled by her scarf, caught treacherously beneath a wheel. Jean Cocteau spoke in his typically flippant manner of this incident: "Yesterday Isadora Duncan died.

This drama is connected in more ways than one with an order of things we consider worrying. It requires too close a complicity between a profligate little racing car and a fringed shawl not to arouse our suspicions. The shawl harbored a deep hatred for the victim. I have often seen it caught in the doors of elevators, of bars, tangled in branches. The aim of the shawl as I see it is quite clear: to strangle Isadora and thus ensure for her the death of Jocasta predicted by Duse. But what could the car's motive have been? Well, we have just learned of the acquisition of this particular automobile by an American collector. P.S. Now they tell us that someone has bought the shawl as well. Perhaps the two criminal objects have found a way to be reunited?"

Italian Futurists were already serenading the automobile. Thus Boccioni declared: "A valve opening and shutting creates a rhythm as beautiful as, but infinitely more original than, that of an eyelid." In the twenties, Derain was even more categorical: "My Bugatti is more beautiful than any work of art...."

216 Marcelle Pichon: *La 40 CV Renault*. C. 1921. Watercolor for the *Gazette du Bon Ton*. Mr. and Mrs. Hervé Poulain Collection.

The 40 CV Renault assured the make's prestige from 1921 to 1930. Presidents of the Republic rented them at 1,500 francs a month and they were chosen by beauties for the *Concours d'élégance*.
The car was more than five meters long and its immense snout housed an extraordinary motor with a cubic capacity exceeding nine liters. The dinosaur rolled onto the track at Montlhéry on May 11, 1925, and drove for 24 hours at an average of 173 km/h., a world record!

Fashion for Everywoman

217 Presentation at Deauville of a collection of Chanel furs, on Russian models. Sketch from *Vogue*. 1923.

218 Georges Lepape: A woman of fashion in a *Vogue* studio, in front of Manhattan skyscrapers. *Vogue* cover. 1928.

219 Jean Dupas: *Woman in Furs*. 1925. Oil on paper, 60 × 50 cm. Galerie Félix Marcilhac, Paris.

The End of a Reign

220–221 Paul Poiret: Evening dress and cocktail dress on period Siégel mannequins. 1925. Exhibition of Decorative Arts, Paris.

In 1920, the *Gazette du Bon ton* assured us that "the dress reflects the spirit of its era" and that it was "an authentic document of the times." The first issue of the French edition of *Vogue* also appeared in 1920. This famous periodical devoted itself essentially to fashion, and its repercussions on practical, artistic and social realms. One could read, for example, that "the Torpedo will never be a woman's car, as it is injurious to the complexion of the smart woman," or "up with the warm, closed automobile, where one can wear open necklines," and everything was known about "Mrs. Charles Max, a woman of legendary good taste, who adopted a delightful sort of hat for motoring, inspired by the cap of Mephistopheles. Made of grey taffeta, it completely covers the head, the rear part has two strings which cross under the chin, in order to protect the wearer from clouds of dust. In front there is a kind of bib, to be raised or lowered as you wish."
With the end of the war, Paris became once again the Mecca for artistic activity, but the atmosphere remained that of a people in convalescence. Prices had risen alarmingly, sugar and wine were scarce, butter still sold on the black market, milk was forbidden in pastries: the scarcity of meat even led to some disturbances in the Halles district, and electricity shortages obliged the Government to close the Metro after eleven p.m.
In times of crisis, people turn to large-scale entertainment and, of course, to dancing.... Everybody set to dancing. The dance halls were permanently full. The tango and the fox trot took the city by storm, to be followed by the black bottom, the shimmy and the Charleston, while dance bands recently arrived from the States hammered out their violently syncopated rhythms. During the day, Julian Robinson remarked in 1921, dresses were simpler than before the war, but in the evening fashion recaptured an extraordinary splendor. Dresses were luxurious works of art, each conceived and executed with infinite care for one society woman and for her alone. Each was put together piece by piece, with linings, paddings, whalebone, fastenings by the hundred. Sumptuous fabrics alone were not enough: gold lace, elaborate embroideries, beads, sequins and colored stones had to be tacked on. It was all part of Paul Poiret's ultimate triumph, before he was finally deposed by the novel ideas of a certain little dressmaker—Coco Chanel. Before Chanel succeeded in bringing women into line, making them "all the same" as she wished, one witnessed the swan song of fantastically rich beauties the world over, particularly Latin American women and the rare demi-mondaine females who still clung to the pre-war taste for showy extravagance and whose jewels—considered, as we have seen, the highest mark of success—signaled their ruinous tidings throughout this period of doomed luxury....
Something new was happening. By 1922, journalists in fashion magazines were talking openly about the new craze for jazz, for costume jewelry, for cigarette smoking,

PAUL POIRET
MANNEQUIN SIEGEL

for dance. Already dictators of fashion, they insisted that the modern woman must be slender. Slimness was the new canon of beauty. To be plump was altogether out of fashion. Journalists in London or New York with their eyes focused on Paris claimed to be scandalized by the "daring new decolleté," at "ever shorter and shorter skirts", and above all at the "scanty bathing costumes worn on fashionable Brittany beaches." Not that this prevented these worthy Anglo-Saxon colleagues from filling their papers with photographs of "these revealing swimsuits worn by daring girls," no doubt with a view to condemning such indecencies more effectively!

But, all things considered, what stamped the Twenties most clearly and became its symbol was the small "cloche," with its rounded crown and turned-down brim, which, as the new luxury fashion magazine *Styl* noted, was "all the rage." This German Art Deco magazine also declared that "just as surely as the women of yesterday were made to travel in automobiles, today's women are made for air travel." The new fashions for traveling by air were also described, for example "a costume of thick suede, fur-lined and trimmed with mink" and a "carefully fitted hat," worn with "soft, calf-high boots" and a "specially designed overcoat, shut at the side and split at the front, which buttons up to form a pair of trousers during the flight, but can be adjusted without taking up space on landing."

Fashion writers had no difficulty destroying today what they had admired yesterday. The taste for sport became more and more pronounced as the decade advanced. Everyone claimed to be the inventor of the "sporty look," a trend whose impact is still as strong as ever.

This taste for sport, for speed, for the emancipation of women, the cult of novelty, the continuous urge to have a good time, and the new freedom of manners, defied—successfully—the traditional code of conduct of Saint-Germain, with its outworn pomp and display. Patou dressed Suzanne Lenglen, star of women's tennis, then her rival Helen Wills and the woman pilot Ruth Elden. Society women such as the Duchess of Penaranda thought of nothing but suntans, short hair and a sporty look. They adopted blazers, sweaters, cardigans or twinsets as their favorite dress, worn with a headband and a pleated skirt.

Europeans were shocked that American models with boyish figures were now acclaimed. They became the triumphant rivals of the former Latin "Venuses." These elegant Americans, from Pola Negri to Gloria Swanson, from the tiny Mary Pickford to the sublime Louise Brooks, were delighted that elegant clothes should be produced to suit their particular physical characteristics and they came to Paris to spend millions.

Coco Chanel, herself at the outer limits of orthodoxy, became a resolute exponent of this new youthful chic, which she publicized by wearing her own models in the extremely elegant circles in which she developed her talents. A suntan went very well with these sophisticated

The Fashion Magazine

222   Martial and Armand, Jenny and Jean Patou models featured in the review *Art, Goût, Beauté*. 1930.

EN FAVEUR. — Vêtement de ratine avec fourrure de karakul. Le col donne un mouvement d'écharpe croisée en gilet. Découpes incrustées. Le bas du devant, côté fermeture, est coupé en biseau.

Création MARTIAL & ARMAND.

COTE D'AZUR. — Manteau pour le sport en tweed moucheté avec bandes de cuir. Col Danton souple. Grandes poches retenues dans un encadrement incrusté.

Création JENNY.

TOUT VA BIEN. — Manteau de tout aller élégant en lainage fantaisie garni de loutre. Les manches sont étroites du haut et de forme gigot du coude aux poignets avec travail de nervures.

Création MARTIAL & ARMAND.

FIORETTI. — Manteau d'après midi en tissu vigogne noir paré d'astrakan du même ton. La fourrure est posée en découpes au bord du manteau. Elle recouvre la moitié des manches et le col droit.

Création JEAN PATOU.

223 Georges Barbier: Evening dress by Worth in the August, 1921 number of the *Gazette du Bon Ton*.

By democratizing fashion, by bringing it "down into the street," Chanel also set in motion the reign of the copy and the era of the home dressmaker. People took their ideas from the fashion magazines, and sewed their own Lanvins, Patous or Chanels, or had them made up by their "absolute darlings." Chanel herself declared: "Fashion does not only exist in the dresses; fashion is in the air, brought by the wind, we feel it, breathe it, it is in the sky and on the streets, it draws on ideas, manners, events."

From now on the creations of *haute couture* were destined to be shamelessly copied. It was inevitable and Chanel said it was "better just to

sports clothes, and with the masculine blazer, which Coco Chanel claimed to have introduced almost by accident, by wearing one in Paris society that she had borrowed from the captain of a yacht on the Mediterranean. But above all her name became synonymous with the short, close-fitting two-piece outfits she introduced, the celebrated "Chanel suits," copies of which one still meets in city streets from New York to Tokyo.

The success of Art Deco is an undisputed fact. So decisive a word of command had never before been so well obeyed. As had been the case of the Pavillon de L'Elégance at the 1925 Exhibition, fashion necessarily fell into line with the new furniture, free of sculpture and unadorned. Naturally, the "old brigade" was in full

opposition to the new tendencies: "What Chanel has invented," said Paul Poiret, "is high-class miserabilism." Or again, "In days past, women were architectural and beautiful, like the prows of ships. Now they look like little half-starved telegraph operators."

Sem, the caricaturist, ironically observed: "As for the hats, they are nothing more than shapeless filters made from soft felt, into which women push their heads, tugging them down with both hands.... Everything disappears, swallowed up in this elastic pouch: hair, forehead, ears, cheeks, down as far as the nose. They would even use a shoe-horn, if the idea had been put to them."

Edmonde Charles-Roux—once director of the French edition of *Vogue*—remembers how, in 1926, the

American edition of *Vogue* predicted that a certain black dress by Chanel, a close-fitting, plain crepe de Chine sheath, with long sleeves, would become a sort of uniform that women everywhere would want to wear. The prediction that women in large numbers could accept the idea of wearing the same dress seemed highly unlikely. Then, to bring readers to agree that perhaps the very "impersonal" simplicity of the dress would be its key to success, the magazine hazarded a comparison: would one hesitate to buy an automobile because it was the same as others of the same make? On the contrary, this similarity guarantees the quality of the car. Witness the arrival of the Ford, signed Chanel.
Despite the virulent criticism that heralded its appearance, Chanel's "Ford" enjoyed its predicted success.

Nothing could stop it. Male reporters deplored its effects on the female form—"no more bosoms, no more bellies or backsides. As for the skirt, it has been slashed to the knee." They jested in vain that the feminine fashion of this moment of the twentieth century would become known as "cut-away." It was no longer on men alone that women depended for their choice of fashions. They now placed their trust in the simplified Chanel styles. Thus even fashion had entered the age of standardization: alas, no doubt an irreversible process of evolution.
In the autumn of 1927, for the first time in the history of the Western world, the sight of the female knee became something admissible and respectable in the eyes of polite society. But one problem arose: what was to be done about garters, worn by most women to keep their

ignore it." Later she was to say that even the great couturiers copied her, but that only Yves Saint Laurent knew how to do it well.
Photographed here, several imitation Chanel models, from the back and the front, at the races in 1922.

dreamy, murmured: "He was always so gentle, affectionate... the most caring lover imaginable. At night, next to me, he slept like a child."

228   Jean Dupas. *Woman with a Flowered Hat.* 1924. Oil on canvas, 50 × 40 cm. Galerie Félix Marcilhac, Paris.

227   Kees van Dongen: *The Dolly Sisters.* C. 1925. Oil on canvas, 91.5 × 73 cm. Private collection.

226   Landru and Fernande Segret:

On January 23, 1923, a worn out cast iron cooker, heavily rusted, was put to auction. In the flea market it would have fetched pennies. But a price of 500 francs, or even 4,200 francs? Going, going, gone! "Did you see?" whispered an excited stout woman, "there was still some blood on it!" It was the end of the Landru affair. Ten women had been put to death in this cooker, bringing Landru 35,642 francs, or an average of 3,564 francs per victim. Fernande Segret, one of the rare escapees, still loved him and stated at the trial: "He was a poet. Alfred de Musset was his favorite author.... He was mad about opera...." But the French knew of worse culprits at the time: what assassin could compete with the Kaiser, what number of corpses with the ten million war dead? "Me? Have I made someone disappear?" Landru said to the judge. "If you believe everything they say in the press!" Nine hundred and ninety six grams of human bones, three hundred remnants of skulls, six petrosals, five metatarsals, the remains of knee caps, feet, and forty-eight phalanges all spoke against him. Colette noted down her impressions. Quipped Landru: "If the ladies have something to reproach me with, they have only to lodge a complaint!" To the judge: "I only wish I had several heads to give you." France laughed at this melodrama. Fernande Segret, her eyes

174

Summer Vacationing

229 Summer holidays for Monsieur and Madame Néret, the author's parents, as a young married couple. He is an administrative inspector, she the daughter of Louis Leperche, who finished top of the class at the Ecole Centrale and designed the first automobile financed by his friend Delage. Monsieur has his clothes made for him at his tailor, Desnoux, Faubourg Saint-Honoré. Madame buys her outfits from the Grands Magasins du Louvre, place du Palais Royal, and her hats come from a small milliners. At the time, it was very smart to be dressed at the Magasins du Louvre, where one was greeted, as in a modern-day *boutique*, and offered an orangeade or a grenadine.
Roger Néret served in the army for four years of war, then during the occupation of Germany. He came home with a taste for photography and some war booty: a film pack Voigtlander. The bicycles are English, with wooden rims and three-speed gears. At home, the furniture is signed Ruhlmann. My parents were "with it." This picture was taken on a bridge over the Indre River, near Azay-le-Rideau in the Loire Valley. A tripod with a delayed action device was used.

230 *La Garçonne*. 1925. Anonymous photograph. The year before, a song by Dréan at the Alhambra had immortalized the short hairstyle adopted by emancipated women: "She had her hair cropped short, like a little girl, so sweet; she had her hair cropped short, saying that suits me better now; women are doing what men do, because it's the fashion, and so easy; they're all cropping off their hair."

stockings from wrinkling? To deal with this new style, garters rapidly appeared in all forms, sizes and colors, worn above or below the knee, but always attracting attention to the legs of the wearer. Montaigne said: "Certain things are covered, so much the better to display them." Now, things were no longer covered. Otherwise it would have been quite impossible to dance the Charleston—the dance that reintroduced the potential eroticism of a high kicking leg. "The same woman who at eighteen was dressed in a sort of armor, will be unprotected from the slightest draft around the age of thirty," wrote Jacques Laurent, not without a certain relish. The more daring even wore shorts, with flesh-colored stockings rolled to the knee.

Underwear, like the other articles of feminine "gear," could be put on or taken off in a few seconds. At dances, male partners had considerable difficulty in hiding their feelings at the fleeting visions of bare thighs above silken stockings. The time of hesitation was over. Women had discovered their bodies.

Among the many changes that were taking place, none was so revolutionary as the new style of underwear. The Belle Epoque woman had been clad in voluminous underwear of cloudy cambric. The young beauties of the twenties were content with panty-chemises and slip-on petticoats as simple as possible in plain silk, tussor, crêpe de Chine, georgette or rayon. "Peau d'ange" satin was the height of luxury. Undergarments were no longer merely functional; they had become, under new forms, what they remain today: "obscure objects of desire."

On beaches, bathers sported the most clinging of bathing costumes. Gone forever the skirt and the thick, heavy jersey, which used to soak up water like a sponge. It was replaced by a fine woolen jersey that shamelessly accentuated the female shape.

But it was not as easy as all that. In order to look chic in the swimsuit which in 1928 was all the rage at Deauville—the fashionable spot where smart Parisians crowded together with not-so-smart Parisians—you had to be flat-chested and built like a boy. Otherwise you looked like a survivor from the Belle Epoque. Fashion was less and less suited to plump women, while bodily comfort assumed progressively greater importance.

This rather special brand of eroticism to be encountered at Deauville was not lost on the magazine *Crapouillot*, which sardonically proposed the following description: "Women poured into silk swimsuits are on display there, sitting around tables. Their made-up faces contrast strangely with the rest of their bodies, which keep their natural color."

Lanoux observes in his *Paris 1925* that Deauville, whether one went "the 40-centime way" (the fare for the trip), or by the "pleasure train," was, finally, a suburb of the Bois de Boulogne and he added that "every young woman who owns a little dog also has a little automobile." He forgot to include "her little Kodak," for photography had also become a mania, with as many

Underwear:

from the Iron Collar to Unbridled Nudity

231 At the beginning of the Twenties, underwear was still a mixture of the plate armor of the Belle Epoque and the looseness brought about by sports and emancipation. Witness this postcard of a period "pin-up," at once undressed and triumphantly decked out—every square inch of bare skin or underwear intended to arouse.

232 C. Hérouard: Illustration for *La Vie Parisienne* ("Parisian Life"). 1929. Art Deco pin-up or Cubism as rounded as it got. Period furnishings, Iribe-type roses, fashionable furnishing fabrics.

A Shock
to the Senses

devotees as one would expect in an essentially narcistic age. For women, the photo was like a mirror: yet another means of assessing their charms.

The year 1929 sounded the knell of this folly. In the autumn Patou lengthened skirts. Women twisted themselves in their chairs to pull down the hems of their dresses. Hollywood found itself from one day to the next with a stock of out-of-date films, in which famous stars paraded about bare-kneed, thus providing an unwitting comic element.

But Chanel was to go further that year. As the ultimate mirror of the new freedom of manners and the sporting opportunities offered to well-off women, the wearing of trousers was the most spectacular of all Chanel's innovations. She alone is responsible for making acceptable this version of male attire, to recall the words of Edmonde Charles-Roux. It was she who adapted this style to all occasions, altered it according to the requirements of fashion, varying its interpretations, making it in turn casual and sporting, or elegant and sophisticated.

Clearly, in 1929, the wearing of trousers was an emancipating step that could be taken only by women of sufficient means. But the barrier had been crossed and, with the advent of the age of leisure and standardization of dress, the Chanel fashion would descend into the street, where thousands of women would opt for trousers. The era of jeans-for-all-seasons and unisex styles was now only a step away. Chanel forestalled all those who, by affecting a taste for workclothes (sailors' smocks, dockers' T-shirts, plasterers' white tunics), consider themselves to be trendsetters. She was the first to turn anti-fashion into fashion. This, to the traditionalist, was truly outrageous.

In September 1929, while the United States experienced the effects of Black Friday, when all the banks closed their doors and the Great Crash began, in Paris the crisis was less severe and the franc was stable. An opulent decade opened for high society—an era of magnificent parties where, as Edmonde Charles-Roux notes, the women appeared robed in white satin....

As we know, the Belle Epoque did not exactly coincide with the beginning of the century, but began, rather, in 1899, the year in which Dreyfus was pardoned. Nor did it end in 1910, but in 1914, with the declaration of war. Similarly, the Roaring Twenties do not correspond exactly with the period from 1920 to 1930. According to Lanoux, "the 1925 period began with the 1919 demobilization and ended with the 1929 crash."

However, a bizarre characteristic of the new decade soon became evident. When times are dark, fashion tends to go light. The dark lady of the Roaring Twenties took her bow and left the stage to the white lady of the Thirties. The wheel had well and truly turned full circle, and slenderness was giving way to more generous shapes: black is slimming, while white enlarges—a beauty tip that no fashion magazine fails to mention regularly!

233 The "Diana bathing" style of postcard of the 1920s. Women no longer ran the risk of drowning, dragged under by the weight of bathing costumes that covered them to their ankles. A fine jersey was far more revealing, and they no longer hesitated to display their breasts proudly when the occasion presented itself.

234 After 1925, not only ankles were on display, but also knees. It was important that no underwear should be peeping out from under ascending hemlines. Even bras were no longer obligatory. "The woman of 1928," writes Jacques Laurent, high priest of feminine undergarments, "was subjected to a shock to her sensibility less strong than it would be for a Moslem woman, but nevertheless sufficient for her behavior to be affected. The impression of nakedness beneath her dress was new for her.... The touch of thighs, brushing against each other, had characterized female ambulatory motion throughout the entire history of the Western world, but, after eighty years of drawers, it now came as a disturbing discovery. The disappearance of the corset introduced an altogether dizzying degree of freedom." *(Histoire imprévue des dessous féminin)* ("Impromptu History of Feminine Undergarments").

Stage Design

235   Oskar Schlemmer: *The Triadic Ballet*. 1926.

Interest in the Theater and Stage Design

236   Varvara Stepanova: Constructivist costume for *The Death of Tarelkin*, presented at the Gitis Theater, directed by V. Meyerhold. 1922.

237   Oskar Schlemmer: Schlemmer dressed as a Turk in *The Triadic Ballet*. Dessau, Bauhaus. 1926.

238   Oskar Schlemmer: "Wire" figure from *The Triadic Ballet*. Dessau, Bauhaus. 1926.

239 Fernand Léger: Costume for Rolf de Maré's Ballets Suédois. 1920–1925.

Europe was in a festive mood: everyone took to dancing in order to forget five years of horror and carnage, and perhaps even more to avoid confronting the future. In Paris, the Ballets Russes were cultivated like an exotic and delicate flower that required the constant care of the best possible artists.

Diaghilev's genius had been to attract the top decorative artists and the most talented musicians. In 1920, the phenomenon was twofold. Firstly, the established Russian artists such as Bakst, Benoit, Goncharova, Larionov (who were refugees from Bolshevism) were joined by painters living in France, among them Picasso, Braque, Matisse, Derain, Marie Laurencin, Juan Gris, Max Ernst, Miró, Utrillo, Gabo and Pevsner (also refugees), who carried out the stage design and the costumes for forty shows. Another contributor was Jean Cocteau, in the case of *Parade* and *Le Train bleu*. An occasional touch was also added by Coco Chanel. Soon afterwards, Stravinsky and Prokofiev were surrounded by Satie, Auric, Milhaud, Poulenc and Manuel de Falla.

Presented for the first time at the Théâtre des Champs-Elysées, *Le Train bleu* was part of the "art season of The Eighth Olympic Games" in which the Ballets Russes played a leading role. The Baron de Coubertin, president of the Olympic Committee, and the members of the committee, all of whom were present and duly listed, filled the theater.

Armand Lanoux remarked: "Fundamentally, the only revolution is sport. 1900 saw the bicycle, horses, the first motor races. 1925 brought with it athletic events, boxing and stadiums...."

In order to give choreographic strength to a scene where bathers, tennis players, golf champions and other beautiful people in search of adventure were brought together, Diaghilev chose Bronislava Nijinska, who was as stubborn as her illustrious brother. She could not speak a word of French, relates Edmonde Charles-Roux in *Le Temps Chanel* ("Chanel and Her World") and what was more, had never heard of this *Train bleu* that everyone was talking about. Separated from the Ballets Russes throughout the war, detained in Russia and marked by the Revolution, she had a taste neither for luxury nor for humor. Cocteau suggested to her as possible sources of inspiration photos of Suzanne Lenglen at tennis, of the Prince of Wales at golf.... She danced as a tennis player, tennis racket in hand. Diaghilev called her the greatest choreographer of her time: "Whatever one may think, this extravagant woman is a true Nijinsky, and that is the end of the matter."

Within the new concept of the "total show," englobing everything from costumes to sets, the artiste became more and more an element of the whole production. A notion as new as the development of the set itself, which was little by little becoming a vast, omnipresent "machine," a kind of leading player, swallowing up the actors and reducing them to mere cogs in the huge machine-spectacle.

240   Liubov Popova: Stage set for the mass theater *Combat and Victory*. 1921.

241   Aleksandr Rodchenko proudly wearing the worker's suit designed by his wife Stepanova, which resembles, pipe included, the theater costume by Popova, below. 1920.

242   Popova: Theater costume. 1920.

Constructivism on the Stage

Erwin Piscator founded the Proletarian
Theater in Berlin. It was no longer a
theater of dreams, of escapism, of
diversion—nor was it either Expressionist or naturalist. It was political theater
at the service of the renewal of society.
In 1920, he put on *Russlands Tag*
("Russia's Day"), in which the actors
were non-professionals and the protagonists were the masses.
The Théâtre National Populaire moved
into the premises of the former
Trocadéro, under the direction of
Gémier. The aim was to offer shows for
everyone, with inexpensive tickets.
Meyerhold, a Russian director, the
pupil of Stanislavskii, inaugurated the
first Theater of Propaganda, the
Theater of the Soviet Republic, establishing his "biomechanical" concept.
The actors followed finely calculated,
almost mathematical movements. The
stage and the set were characterized
by a "Constructivist dynamic."

The Russians, whether in Paris or Moscow, were the real
innovators. A new covenant emerged—the adaptation of
the artist's easel and concentrated vision to the
dimensions of the stage. Taking note of the three basic
elements in ballet—dance, music and stage design
—Diaghilev, aware of his role as master producer, said:
"When I am producing a ballet, I never for an instant lose
sight of these three factors." Success depended on their
balance. Through dance, painting could at last veritably
conquer the third dimension: volume, dynamism and
movement. At the same time, thanks to the painter, color
invaded and liberated a stage hitherto limited to neutral
tints and over-ornate decoration.
Thus, in 1920 Matisse brought to the ballet *Le Chant du
Rossignol* ("The Song of the Nightingale") a refined
harmony based on white and turquoise, contrasting
sharply with the red cloak lined with black worn by the
figure of Death. At the same time, Derain introduced
Black art into *Jack in the Box*, a lighthearted piece by
Satie and Milhaud. Braque, in *Les Fâcheux* ("The
Bores"), developed his very personal range of muted
browns and beiges, occasionally set off by a very deep

green. While Survage imposed the austerity of the
Cubists in *Mavrz*, in *Romeo and Juliet* Max Ernst took the
opportunity of asserting in no uncertain terms his
Surrealist anxieties.
Like Diaghilev, the Ballets Suédois of Rolf de Maré also
called on the Groupe des Six, on Claudel, Cocteau and
Cendrars. Much of their success can be attributed to the
high quality of the painters who contributed to their
productions. One example was Fernand Léger, who drew
his inspiration from Africa in order to create, with
Cendrars, in a flickering chiaroscuro, Darius Milhaud's *Le
Création du Monde* ("The Creation of the World"). There
were some protests. The Russian critic André Levinson
remarked disapprovingly: "Never will we create a true
work of dance by translating through jumping
movements the conventions proper to the plastic arts."
In *Relâche*, a sort of instantaneous ballet in black and
white, Francis Picabia was looking for an artistic form,
both spontaneous and anti-intellectual, in opposition to
the leading thinkers and heads of the various schools. All
possible directions were being explored simultaneously.
In Russia as in France the avant-garde sought to make

244 Pablo Picasso: Costume for the Russian ballet *Pulcinella*. 1920.

The Ballets Suédois, which appeared in 1920, created an event in Paris along with the Ballets Russes of Diaghilev. The ballet's instigator and director, Rolf de Maré, surrounded himself with the most important artists in Paris: Cocteau, Léger, Picabia, Bonnard, de Chirico, to work on the themes and the sets; and musicians like Milhaud, Satie, Poulenc and Honegger to create the scores. That year, there were no less than seven premiers: *Jeux* ("Games"), *Iberia, La Nuit de la Saint-Jean* ("Midsummer Night"), *Maison de Fous* ("Madhouse"), *Le Tombeau de Couperin* ("Couperin's Tomb"), and *El Greco et les Vierges folles* ("El Greco and the Foolish Virgins").

A Festive Atmosphere

use of stage space. Even Constructivism, condemned by Jacques Copeau for its excesses, was in on the show, with Alexandre Exter, Georges Annenkov and Liubov Popova, among others.

Pevsner and Gabo made much use of new materials—including translucent plastic and oilcloth—emphasizing the movements of Nikitina and Lifar in *La Chatte* ("The Cat") by Henri Sauguet and George Balanchine. Enthralled both by mass theater and by Marinetti's Futurism, Iakulov introduced mechanical sets for Meyerhold. For *Le Pas d'acier* ("The Steel Step") by Prokofiev and Massine, he designed ladders, platforms and cogwheels which provided a background for the movements of Danilova, Chernicheva, Lifar and others, thus anticipating an aesthetic style that Calder and Tinguely would handle in their own fashion in the following decades. Pavel Chelichew designed the aerial scenery for *Ode* by Nicolas Nabokov, by hanging shapes in the air using metal wires, with the soloist suspended in one of the loops. He also used four projectors in various positions, including one in the dome that cast images of geometric motifs onto the curtains—a technique used frequently since then. Finally, Giorgio de Chirico, the metaphysician, brought his own style to bear on stage setting by transforming the dancers into fragments of architecture, mixing together the broken capitals of columns with the frozen prancing of a fantastic horse.

The Folies-Bergères sought the aid of Erté, and Raoul Dufy was responsible for the sets of *Bœuf-sur-le-Toit* ("Ox on the Roof"), an avant-garde show by Cocteau which was presented at the Champs-Elysées Comédie. The cinema also began to appreciate the use of the plastic arts. Louis Delluc commissioned Germaine Dulac to produce the costumes for *La Fête espagnol* ("Spanish Festival"). Marcel L'Herbier assembled a painter, architect and designer team for each film.

Germany also fell under Russian influence. While France absorbed principally the aesthetic side of Moscow's teachings, the scenic experiments of stage director Erwin Piscator, in Berlin, were closely bound up with the prevailing climate of insecurity, political upheaval, and social and economic reverses. As Expressionism came to a close, Piscator conceived the idea of presenting a "total view" on stage, that was the whole of history, explaining events by an "analysis of their beat." His overall aim was educational: "to conquer this world of hatred, hunger and destruction, and to build a new world based on community and sensible order." The path he chose was not aesthetic, but instructive. Jeanne Lorang, in a chapter of the catalogue for the Centre Pompidou's Paris–Berlin Exhibition dealing with theatrical and scenic developments in Germany in the Twenties, lists a number of examples. Thus, in *"Russia's Hour*, at the Proletarisches Theater in Berlin in 1920, the backdrop was a map of Europe, with its frontiers, painted by John Heartfield on a large panel." She also points out that "Piscator used films and slides in his productions. In 1924, for *Flags*, by Alfons Paquet, the title of the play, together with a short historical introduction, were shown on a screen halfway up the proscenium. Portraits of the characters appeared and a narrator introduced the 'actors' ready to 'reconstitute' what had already been described. Cuttings from newspapers, slogans, statistics displayed on screens set up on both sides of the front of the stage then formed an accompaniment to the stage itself." Piscator played in local halls, factories, the courtyards of apartment blocks, and sports grounds, modifying the texts according to the setting. *Oops! We're Alive!* by Ernst Toller, with its scaffolding of metal tubes 11 meters wide and 8 meters high, called Constructivism to mind. In *Rasputin*, the Czar, surrounded by the officers of his general staff, was seen admiring photos of battles projected onto the dome. On these horrific images an authentic extract from one of the Czar's letters was displayed at regular intervals: "My life here at the head of my troops is healthy and invigorating"; the whole effect was disquieting, to say the least! In Piscator's stage adaptation of Jaroslav Hašek's famous *The Good Soldier Schweik* (1928), caricatures by George Grosz were projected on the backdrop. The cast of this subversive comedy consisted of "grotesque marionettes," brought onto the stage by conveyor belts. We are also told by Jeanne Lorang that Brecht considered Piscator to be the leading dramatist of the age, with the exception, of course, of Brecht himself, even though Piscator had never written a single play.

With Schlemmer, it was straightforward Bauhaus brought to the stage. The characters were based on such simple shapes as spheres, cones, cylinders, circles, spirals, and so forth, corresponding to standard shapes of the human body or to the movement of the body fixed in a form. Dance consisted of the same elements, with the addition of color. The "abstract" nature of the costumes lay in the beauty and novelty of the materials employed. The style was as far removed from the historical—the very opposite of the working man's theater of Piscator—as from the tinsel of a Parisian revue.

Of course, none of this could survive the Nazi regime and the artists would be reduced to silence by internment in the concentration camps.

Meanwhile, in Paris, nobody wanted to listen to Le Corbusier, that spoilsport, who was troubling the easy conscience of the Roaring Twenties—which were, in a way, doing their best to continue the Belle Epoque—with his talk of impending reductions in living standards and his projects for environments suitable to an austere new life-style. Everybody was terrified at the thought of it. Indeed, what the world set out to do was to enjoy itself, to preserve its comforts and luxuries, to bring Ruhlmann's theatrical style into their own homes. (Significantly, at the 1925 Exhibition of Decorative Arts, it was Jacques-Emile Ruhlmann's pavilion, rather than Le Corbusier's or the Russians', that people flocked to see.) Ruhlmann was reassuring; he fell into the tradition of eighteenth-century cabinetmaking, enhanced by the skilled finish of the nineteenth century, with the addition of a few inventions, such as tapered, slightly curved legs (one of his secrets), or the use of such marvelous materials as ivory, tortoise shell and mother of pearl, virtually unknown to French cabinetmakers before him. All this was far from cheap, but that was of no consequence, since Ruhlmann worked only for the very private club of the elite.

246   Demonstrators carrying the model of Tatlin's Tower, May 1, 1926. Leningrad.

Agitprop

Despite the Revolution, a festive atmosphere prevailed in Russia too. The fall of the Winter Palace was enacted by a Red Army battalion and some thousands of proletarians. On stage, fifty actors, dressed like Kerenskii, mouthed the same speeches and imitated his gestures. Relentlessly, the Red Army and the proletariat advanced, driving

Russia been so close to collapse and never before had the country rejoiced in such a wave of carnivals, marches, boats on the Volga, propaganda trains or buses in the countryside, covered with posters and slogans, "Rosta Windows" written by the poet Maiakovskii, of whom it was said—as, indeed, we might say of many contemporary artists, painters, sculptors, musicians and architects—that "he entered into the Revolution as if it were his own house, at once throwing open the windows."

Everyone expected that the Revolution, which they had longed for and brought about, would totally transform society. Tatlin's famous tower, which became a leitmotif, symbolizing both the Revolution and a certain festive mood, was designed to be twice as high as the capitalist Eiffel Tower (though for the time being, it was only at the maquette stage) and was carried about from festival to festival like a holy sacrament. It was a lighthearted creation. It contained, in the interior of its spiral, three suspended spheres, designed to revolve on their own axes, the first completing one revolution in a year, the second in a month and the third in a day. The largest sphere was to serve as offices, as a place for meetings or congresses. The tower would also make music, disseminate information and even project images onto the clouds so that everyone would be able to see them. But the commanding officer of the Red Army battalion which had enacted the fall of the Winter Palace was to suffer a reprimand for having participated in such a masquerade. Indeed, the party was nearly over. Lenin, confronting an illiterate nation, would have no use for the avant-garde, even if it was doing its best to make itself useful, what with Malevich and his Suprematist ideas for teacups and teapots, and Tatlin with his stove designed to give out more heat while consuming less energy—scarcely relevant at a time when wooden houses were being demolished to provide fuel. Luckless creative artists and utopians would soon be scattered and ground down by the implacable engine of Bolshevism. Those who did not leave ended up miserably, like Malevich, or, if they managed to keep afloat under Lenin, were subsequently cruelly subjected to the stereotypes imposed by Stalin, whose paranoiac sensibility could tolerate only the Caucasian bourgeois style of 1910.

During Agitprop's prime, this art of "revolutionary propaganda," the festival, became a specific art form that would soon be found throughout the world, even as far as Maoist China. The facades of buildings were, for example, adorned with large panels resembling modern paintings, but with the dimensions appropriate to an urban setting. Tramways were decorated in the same way as the New York subway today. If people were not given bread, at least they were provided with grand spectacles representing, for example, the funeral of the Old World, depicting ridiculous pot-bellied capitalists with their fat cigars, religious rites and superstitions, popes, rich peasants, the idle, and the drunk.

"Propaganda trains"—a phenomenon of fundamental importance—stopped briefly in each town, bringing with them the possibility of contact with several forms of art at one time (frescos, posters, tracts, cinema, theater, and the like), thus reaching the public in the most direct and effective way. The people were not surprised at all this. They even compared these colorful propaganda trains and floats to the wedding chests at peasant marriages and to the Easter eggs they knew well.

247   The Agitprop boat *Red Star*. 1920.

before them the anti-revolutionary forces, amidst the clamor of bells, whistles, sirens and cries. Powerful searchlamps, requisitioned from a contractor, distorted the scene to the point of caricature.
In *Bread and Circuses*, we find ourselves in Petrograd in 1920, at the end of the civil war. Never had

248 Auguste Helligenstein. *Dancer with a Garland*. 1927. Blue enameled glass, H. 18 cm. Galerie Félix Marcilhac, Paris.

249 Demetre Chiparus: *Russian Dancers with Cymbals*. 1930. Gilded bronze, marble and ivory, H. 50 cm. Galerie Félix Marcilhac, Paris.

Suzanne Lenglen, the French tennis champion and invincible queen of Wimbledon at singles and doubles, provoked the laughter of the British public with her extravagant leaps. As we have seen, she inspired the character of the woman tennis player in Jean Cocteau's *Le Train bleu* of 1924. Her way of dressing became part of her legend. No champion before her had worn two cardigans, one on top of the other, or used rolls of cloth to make a headband, a novelty that Chanel employed for Nijinska's headgear. In 1924, the Davis Cup, as old as the century, guaranteed tennis an international audience, but its popularity in France was above all due to the personality of Suzanne Lenglen and her exploits. She symbolized graphic art in motion.

A richly bronze Josephine Baker, her armpits shaven, shimmied through *The Black Revue* which, as opposed to the elite Ballets Russes, was a great success with the general public. Her body seemingly disjointed, Josephine posed nude for Dunand's panels in lacquer and egg shells. Man Ray photographed her and Horst painted her. Her nakedness undulating in a wind of pleasure, her agility, her beautiful black idol-like body, her perfect breasts, delicate arms, long legs, and the exotic charm of her silhouette were all crystallized in an arabesque—another graphic symbol of the era.

The search was on for the authentic and the natural,

qualities which were to be captured in every way possible.

Paul Morand, the king of the Twenties, dressed in his diving suit—he was the most sporting of contemporary writers—points out in *Magie noire* ("Black Magic") the irresistible and disturbing attraction exercised on this "civilized" society by the Black world: "In bars after the armistice, jazz has accents which are so sublime, so heart-rending that we all understand that a new form must be given to our way of feeling. Sooner or later, I believe, we shall be impelled to answer this call from the shadows, obliged to find out what there is behind the wild melancholy emanating from saxophones." His dictum, "The real snobs are in sweaters" provides the best definition of the inverted snobbery of the Twenties. Suzanne Lenglen, Josephine Baker, Paul Morand, Isadora Duncan and Caryathis were archetypes of exuberance, the kings and queens of thrilling motion,

Art is Alive and Well

250 Paul Colin: Study for the *Tabarin*
poster. Oil and charcoal on canvas,
120 × 120 cm. Paul Colin Collection.
This renowned graphic artist always
began each project with an oil or
watercolor study. At the end of his life,
he regretted being so famous as a
poster artist and so little known as a
painter.

251 Thor Bögellund: Danish poster
for the famous Copenhagen public
gardens. 1920. Color lithograph,
86.2 × 59.7 cm. Victoria and Albert
Museum, London.

born out of the vogue for sport and the Black style with
which they identified.

Caryathis's name will always be associated with *La Belle
Excentrique* ("The Beautiful Eccentric"), a ballet she
danced bare-bellied, a velvet heart adorning her crotch.
Erik Satie wrote the scenario and composed the music.
He also took her round the costumers: "My music
demands outrageousness, and 'a woman more like a
zebra than a doe.'" This "new" woman, so described,
could be found everywhere, her hair cut short to facilitate
practising all kinds of sports. The languid, soft, luxuriant
woman of the beginning of the century, by discarding her
corset, as we have seen, had become, in 1925, highly
strung and slender—a post-Cubist type. She was
constantly on the move and, in this, she was not alone.
All the celebrities of the age were on the move as well.
They were on horseback, dancing, driving open-topped,
and anticipating "jet-set society" by traveling from capital
to capital by plane.

They were turned on by motion, and dedicated to action;
they became the slaves of speed. Nothing could stop a
Paul Morand. From New York to Timbuktu, he traveled
ceaselessly. Everybody was enticed by change—change
which was often nothing more than a semblance of
movement. What in 1900 was the spineless style—the
reign of the vegetal, creepers, branches and flowers

arranged artistically—was now twisted by a gust of high
wind. Veils, ribbons and clothes were set dancing in the
breeze. For the war was over, why not say it out loud? To
forget the horrible past one had to enjoy oneself, ignore
the anxiety of the present and not look towards a future
which, to say the least, was uncertain.

Morand cultivated a cold humor: "After *Magie noire* even
my photos began, shades of Dorian Gray(!), to assume a
Negro character." For Black fashion—another aspect of
motion—burst upon the scene in 1925, giving a
completely new character to every field of everyday life.
Decorators and ceramic artists, jewelers and cabinet-
makers, goldsmiths and bookbinders, silk makers, poster
artists, and glass workers all "went Black," right up to the

great fashion shops, where, for example, the latest mannequins created for Siégel by Vigneau were lacquered black. The latter did, however, give rise to a certain amount of indignant protest.

Since 1905, knowledge of Black art had been the province of a very limited number of enthusiasts. Suddenly, two successes attracted the interest of the press. First of all, the advent of jazz. The socialites began to frequent "Black balls" and dance the black bottom. Fierce competition arose among nightclubs where one could dance with Blacks. People flocked to the Bal nègre or the Boule noire. All this led on to the *Black Revue* which, by its explosive force, renewed the impact of the Ballets Russes, revealing to the Parisians of 1926 an art of bewitching authenticity.

"Fashion is dying, fashion is dead," lamented Paul Poiret, who ended up unemployed, borrowing 20 francs from a friend, and reciting *The Grasshopper and the Ant* in a Cannes cabaret for a mere pittance; he stitched an overcoat for himself out of an old bathrobe.

Chanel, with her tailored dresses in jersey or black wool, simple and understated, suited as much to grand-mothers as to their granddaughters, had killed him off. Where Paul Poiret had draped ten meters of cloth in an oriental-style tunic and trousers, in the 1920s no more than one meter would be needed to cover the boyish chests, expose the bare backs and hide the tops of the knees. Constant motion pushed belts lower and lower down these tubes, until they reached the non-existent thighs, where, miraculously, they stopped. At one show, a couturier amused himself by mixing a couple of youths with his nymphs and no one spotted the ruse.

This miraculous change, this deference to sport and to Black fashion, was decided by Chanel one evening in a box at the theater, her companion a well-known English peer. Leaning over the purple edge of her box, she looked at the crowd of women kitted out in Paul Poiret style and murmured: "This can't last, I'm going to slap them all into black...."

Schiaparelli used nothing but fabric for dusters and sacking for daytime wear, and a blue-haired milliner, Mme Agnes, launched onto the market a turban made of jersey that could be slipped into a pocket.

One recouped on the accessories: spangled handbags, 75-centimeter-long cigarette holders, powder puffs encrusted with eggshell and ostrich feather fans.

The new rich no longer wanted to display their ostentatious strings of pearls or diamonds—that was all old hat. The only necklaces worn were those of Black chieftains, with rows of wooden bracelets, pebbles colored or painted with barbarian designs, whose weight almost bent the new woman double, but which she insisted on wearing, even with her bathing suit.

Paul Poiret's Oasis, where one still danced the tango, fell out of favor. People preferred the Bœuf-sur-le-toit which had just been launched by Moysès and named after Cocteau's latest work. It was a small place in the rue Boissy d'Anglas, decorated with Dadaist paintings on the walls, and featuring Picabia's *L'Œil cacodylate* enthroned over the bar. "The prettiest women of Paris are to be seen there," Jean Oberlé recounts in his memoirs "accompanied by men in evening dress or tuxedos, rubbing shoulders with someone like Picasso in a sweater or Derain smoking his pipe." The lovely Caryathis, between ballets, was to be found dancing on the tiny stage, just as what were later called "go-go girls" would do in the 1970s.

One would have thought that nobody in Paris had anything to do. Dancing had taken over the city. No hotel, however modest, was without its *thé dansant*, and its evening dance hall. At private gatherings, everyone took a turn at the piano, and passers-by, drawn by the noise, came up to mix with the guests.

Fortunes were made and lost daily, amidst general indifference, and the only really stable currency was the Black or South American dancer.

Flossie Mills was the star of the *Black Revue*—a kind of exotic South-Sea island bird, with a skin of coral pink, and long legs dancing out a rhythm that no orchestra but her own could hope to follow. For the first time, Europeans discovered a music hall law they had never before dreamed of—the Americans called it "timing." Guilbert Guilleminault in his *Roman vrai de la IIIe République* ("True Novel of the Third Republic") relates how in the speak-easy of the first tableau, scenes

followed each other at such a pace that it was impossible to determine, other than by the color of the clothes, who were the owners of all the dark arms, all the legs moving in all directions, gyrating, jumping, interlacing, twisting, pushing, an onslaught of heavy, fat-jowled Black women, their hair jet black, bottoms and breasts bumping in time to the breathless, hiccupping rhythm of the jazz. Sweat made their dark, silken skin gleam; they only touched the floor to launch off again towards the roof. The whirlwind did not stop—another scene followed instantly. One spectator, eyes popping out from her head, jumps from her seat: "Enough, that's enough! Stop the show. We didn't come here to see such ugliness!" No one heard her. The public was stunned, overwhelmed, astounded.

People rushed to Paris from every corner of the globe. Aging American women, artificially slimmed down, recaptured some of the freshness of their youth in the arms of dark gigolos who absorbed their pearl necklaces at the same time as the latest perfume, *Vierge folle*. Exiled Russian princesses set the tone, selling off their jewels. Complete strangers invaded one's apartment, bottles under their arms, an orchestra at their heels—this was the era of surprise parties. Half an hour later the orgy was in full swing, in the light of black candles, women reclining on cushions, bare-backed, with long cigarette holders between their teeth.

France already numbered 180 feminist societies, with 160,000 members, directed by women who were quite certain they had been men in a previous existence. At the same time, Mrs. Pankhurst, queen of English sufragettes, passed long periods of her life in prison. Newspapers carried absurd articles: "A man has locked up his wife because she had her hair cut like Joan of Arc's".... "A father kills his daughter for the same reasons...." Never had there been such a field day for caricaturists—Albert Guillaume sketched a woman at the theater, her back completely naked, with the caption: "The ideal bathing dress." Poulbot depicted a young woman, rather unsteady and in a gay mood, entering the family home: "But Mademoiselle is drunk!" exclaims the dignified but worried butler. "Just you wait," the girl replies. "You'll laugh your head off when you see Mother!"

Women wanted to "live their own lives" and called for the "free love" that they believed Bolshevik amazones were practising so enthusiastically in a Russia engulfed in anarchy; at any rate, they called for full political equality. The heroine of *La Garçonne*, disappointed in men, decides to have a child outside marriage, so that she can bring it up according to her own ideas, despising the male sex. Madeleine Auzat, wife of the author Victor Margueritte, wrote a book herself, *Femme toute nue* ("Naked Woman"), in which she gave explicit accounts of the love affairs of a Senegalese and several Parisian women. Victor Margueritte sold a million copies of the book and was expelled from the Légion d'Honneur! "He should have kept his buttonhole clean," Bailby, director of *L'Intransigeant,* remarked ironically.

In 1921 Isadora Duncan was invited by the Soviets to make her home in the USSR. She was offered a school with a thousand pupils financed by the State and an orchestra to train them—a wonderful contract. This "true Tanagra," "this creature escaped from an antique bas relief," who danced barefoot and mimed flight on stage, her beautiful flashing legs treading the boards in broad strides, tantalizing in a drape that accentuated her taut breasts, falling at last like a piece of diaphonous material,

252 The English dancer Margaret Morris performing in *Tribute to Spring*, "in graceful harmony with the tender green leaves." 1923.

253 Students from Margaret Morris's summer dance course. 1923.

The students danced in tunics inspired by ancient Greece and also practiced swimming and sailing. Morris confided to *Vogue* that in her opinion the best artistic expression was the result of health and vitality.

Dance Your Troubles Away

A Festival of Beauty

and freezing, with a final shiver of cloth shaken into stillness, was to realize her dream: to teach her own art of graphics in motion.

Miss Chaikovskii, daughter of the composer, begged in vain: "Don't go, Isadora, for heaven's sake. Appalling things are happening there. A friend, absolutely trustworthy, has recently written a letter to my father. Everybody is starving. They are chopping up children for food and their remains are to be seen hanging in butchers' shops." It was in fact the very period when Russia was represented in Western eyes as an enormous bearded *muzhik,* his arms folded, booted, with a knife between his teeth. Isadora looked in vain for the Bolsheviks in Moscow, but was unable to teach for lack of roubles.

Never before had countries been so closely in touch with each other. The most trifling incidents took on dimensions of international importance. "Would it be a great disappointment to France if Silesia were given to Germany?—Not at all—But if Carpentier were beaten by Dempsey...." In the Paris of 1921, the only event of any significance was the "fight of the century" and this caricature in *Cri de Paris* was scarcely an exaggeration. Mistinguett, the music-hall star, proclaimed: "This Dempsey, he has a jaw like everyone, hasn't he? Well, George will floor him like all the others." The fight even led to an exchange of views between the President of the Republic, Mr. Millerand, and His Majesty King

254　Max Le Verrier: *Bacchanal.* 1926. Bronze, subsequently chromed. Private collection, Cologne.

255　Reebecke: Photographic study published in *Paris Studio*, No. 6. 1926.

198

Alfonso XIII. The king of Spain sent his best wishes. The Japanese Crown Prince Hirohito, at the Longchamp Grand Prix, while admiring the elegant floral mat silk prints and the Liberty prints, admitted to a journalist how much he regretted being unable to go to New York to see the fight.

The Government had the bright idea of arranging for airplanes to streak across the Parisian sky as soon as the result was known, firing red rockets for a Carpentier victory, white for Dempsey, and green if the fight were a draw. For this outstanding event, the Americans, never lacking enthusiasm, built a stadium at Jersey City. It was the largest open air arena ever to have been built. An immense wooden basin, octagonal in shape, it could hold 120,000 spectators. All the celebrities had booked seats: Henry Ford, Rockefeller, Alice Roosevelt, daughter of the former president, Charlie Chaplin, Douglas Fairbanks, Mary Pickford, Rudy Valle and others. Even the famous Black boxer, Jack Johnson, for years the holder of the world title, was released from prison, where he was serving a sentence for debt, to be present at the fight.

A hairdresser made a fortune selling locks of hair cut from the head of "Gorgeous George"... then a deathly silence gripped Paris. A million Parisians gathered in the

256   The dancer Claire Baurov. 1928.

257   Max Le Verrier: *Madness*. 1926.
Bronze with patina and marble. Private collection, Cologne.

The Transatlantic Craze

258 Edward Steichen: *Wind Fire: Thérèse Duncan on the Acropolis.* 1921. Photograph.

259 André Kertész: *Satiric Dancer*.
1926. Photograph.

streets of the city could not believe their ears; they were astounded, stupefied: "Carpentier knocked out in the fourth round." Everyone was speechless. They avoided each others' eyes. The crowd was crushed, struck dumb. A pretty woman was weeping, her car drawn up in the Place de l'Opéra, shaking her fist at the photograph of Dempsey decorating the facade of the *Echo de Paris*. Carpentier had fractured his thumb in the second round. "I thought I was dreaming," he said, "on my return to Paris... they stretched out their hands towards me, they wanted to carry me in triumph. Good grief, for a moment I was lost. Perhaps I was mistaken and had defeated Dempsey without realizing it?" France, ever maternal, loves a loser. It was a splendid opportunity also to pay homage to the inventor of the wireless telegraph. In his editorial in *L'Intransigeant*, entitled "Consolations," Léon Bailby wrote: "Yesterday was a great day for us all. We were able to celebrate one of the unquestioned glories of our country, the achievement of that great but modest scientist, Branly.... When the result took a little less than twelve seconds to be transmitted from New Jersey to Paris, the remarkable nature of Branly's invention, perfected by Marconi, was brought home to us, doubtless for the first time." *Le Peuple* adopted a lighthearted tone: "Since present-day journalism forces us to publish photographs of two well-known pugilists, allow us to make amends for this concession to popular taste by placing them against photos of two learned figures: Mr. Branly and Mrs. Curie."

Finally, in *Le Temps*, Paul Souday adopted a sufficiently solemn tone to impart conclusions of thoroughly good sense: "Fortunately the greatness of a country depends on things far more significant and far-reaching than winning a boxing match. This particular sport has rather less importance than gifts of a scientific, artistic, literary or military character." National honor had been saved!

So, against this general background of sport, speed, jazz and dance, there was a tendency towards stereotyping; model attitudes were fabricated. The female body, endlessly represented by artists, craftsmen, graphic designers and advertisers, changed irrevocably, became slighter, more refined. Millions of women cherished the hope of conforming to this new style and of becoming a sort of abstract woman, nothing but eyes and mouth, freed body undulating to the rhythms of the Bal nègre, effortlessly sporting, always dressed in the new hazy clothes—costumes for the "follies of trans-Atlantic life," as Caryathis called them. This shattering entry of movement into art was faithfully recorded by graphic art, by photography, by the naturist cinema, by mantelpiece sculptures, reflected as though in a mirror, amplified and passed down to us, a moving message, immobilized by time. From now on this art in motion offered artists of all sorts a new field for investigation, which each, naturally, used in his own way.

Graphic Arts

260 Cassandre: *Le plus fort l'Intran (L'Intransigeant)* ("The Intransigent"). 1925. Poster; color lithograph, 169 × 117 cm. Mr. and Mrs. Donald Karshan Collection, Paris.

261   Charles Loupot: *Valentine peinture émail* ("Valentine Enamel Painting"). 1928. Poster; color lithograph,
158 × 118 cm. Musée de l'Affiche et
de la Publicité, Paris.

In the Twenties people no longer stopped, as they did before the war, to admire a Muche or a Toulouse-Lautrec on a wall. They passed quickly by. So much the better, or the worse, if their attention was held momentarily by a poster, or by a piece of graphic art. "The lazy eye must be continually surprised by simple and perfect graphics," said Loupot, whose poster of an automobile at high speed was, in his own words, "the graphic expression of an idea." The influence of abstraction made itself felt in a tendency to synthesize in order to get the advertising message across, and to add poetry by means of color. Did not Brancusi employ the same principle when he represented a bird in flight as a sculpture in the form of a rocket—a form which, incidentally, was rediscovered five decades later by the computers calculating the lines of another bird, the airplane *Concorde*: what better example of the prophetic gift of an artist of genius? As distinct from the turn-of-the-century posters in which the characters occupied more space than the object being sold, the characters, if they proved really indispensable, now became stylized, rendered in a sort of Cubist manner. In Loupot's work, women's faces were barely sketched in, while Lebedev's revolutionary soldiers were stylized to the point of anonymity, thus constituting a more powerful representation of revolutionary triumph. Loupot gradually went further and further in his simplification and use of geometric forms, with the popular *Bonhomme en bois* in the Galeries Barbès or the "Valentine" character.

"Cassandre soars above his generation as did Toulouse-Lautrec," maintains Alain Weill, founder of the Musée de l'Affiche et de la Publicité (Museum of the Poster and Advertising). "He had something to say and that something was visible." Close to the Bauhaus and to

Walter Gropius, convinced that an artist should not live in an ivory tower, but must reflect his own times, the author of the unforgettable *L'Intransigeant* and of *L'Etoile du Nord*, as well as the inventor of *Dubo, Dubon, Dubonnet,* stated as early as 1926: "The poster is not, and ought not to be, as a painting is, a work instantly set apart by its 'manner,' a unique example designed to satisfy the shadowy love of a single, more or less informed enthusiast; it must be a mass-produced object reproduced thousands of times, like a pen or an automobile, and like them, it should render certain services of a material type, achieve a commercial purpose."

He drew his points of reference from Cubism, "a reaction against individualism" leading to "a representation of the absolute nature of the object." He was Cubist in the

263   Cassandre: *L'Etoile du Nord* ("North Star"). 1927. Poster; color lithograph, 105 × 76 cm. Kunstgewerbemuseum, Zurich.

262   Joost Schmidt: Poster for the Bauhaus Exhibition, Weimar. 1923. 83 × 65 cm. Bauhaus-Archiv, West Berlin.

264 Charles Loupot: *Bugatti, le pur-sang de l'automobile* ("Bugatti, the Thoroughbred"). 1924. Poster; watercolor and gouache, 31.5 × 22 cm. Hervé Poulain Collection.

The Surprise Factor

sense that his method was essentially "geometric and
monumental: architecture, the art I prefer to all others,
has given me an intense dislike of distorting detail, and
has made me love the wide spaces whose impersonal
bareness lends itself to great advertising frescos."
He was more concerned with form than color, with the
arrangement of elements than their details. He went on
to stipulate that, in this arrangement, letters played an
increasingly important role (he also designed typographic characters, too avant-garde for the period; in
1968s, when his "Cassandre" was refused, he committed
suicide). The letter was "the leading star of the mural
stage, since it, and it alone, is responsible for
communicating to the public the magic selling formula."
The poster artist should, according to Cassandre, begin
by positioning his composition around the text: "For the
poster is not a picture. It is above all a verbal message. It
is the word which is in charge, which conditions and

gives life to the whole advertising scene." With his
J'achète tout aux Galeries Lafayette (1928) ("I Buy
Everything at the Galeries Lafayette"), he even succeeded
in inventing the non-illustrated poster.
Prophet of the poster in his own time, reflecting all that
was happening from Berlin to Moscow, Cassandre
turned therefore "towards a pure product of the square
and the compass, towards primitive lettering, lapidary
lettering, the work of the Phoenicians and the Romans,
the true, the only lasting monument." Starting from the
written word, he found the image. "The verbal element"
became the "spatial element." His approach had little in
common with Leonetto Cappiello's, who was still
exploring spots and arabesques. To line Cassandre
added style. In 1927, the railroad was the inspiration of
two masterpieces: *Nord Express* and *Etoile du Nord*. The
combination of space and speed is as operative in his
method as in his subject matter: the unfinished

268 El Lissitzky: Project for the Lenin Tribune, Unovis. 1920.

To answer Lenin's call for "propaganda for monumental art," El Lissitzky conceived projects, posters, typographic characters and page settings in which the dynamic effect was frequently obtained by the use of diagonals and asymmetry. His work has had a considerable influence on modern advertising. The "drawing of the Lenin Tribune" sums up his symbolic and graphic aims. A photomontage shows the revolutionary leader preaching from the top of a steel structure. El Lissitzky, who had adhered to Malevich's theories and who was, moreover, an enthusiastic supporter of the October Revolution, was to become the propagandist of Constructivism abroad, particularly in Germany, where he spread the word to the members of the Bauhaus.
From 1919 to 1922, Maiakovskii, with a group of painters and poets, made posters inciting agitation for the front and rearguard, on up-to-date political, military and economic theories. These hand-made posters became known as "Rosta Windows," from the name of the Russian Telegraph Agency (Rosta) and because they were exposed in the windows of empty shops. Maiakovskii always produced the texts and often the design for these works, and they represented "the summary report of the three hardest years of the revolutionary struggle, expressed in splashes of color and the noise of words of command." (Maiakovskii, *I Demand to be Heard*, 1930.)

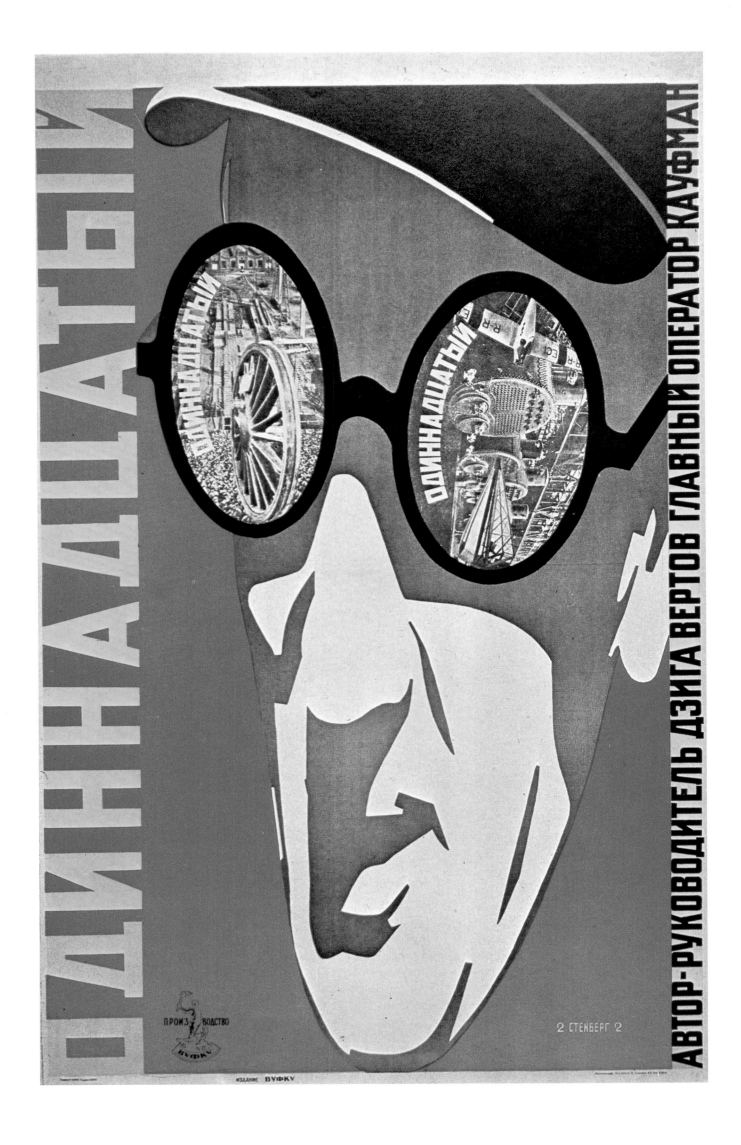

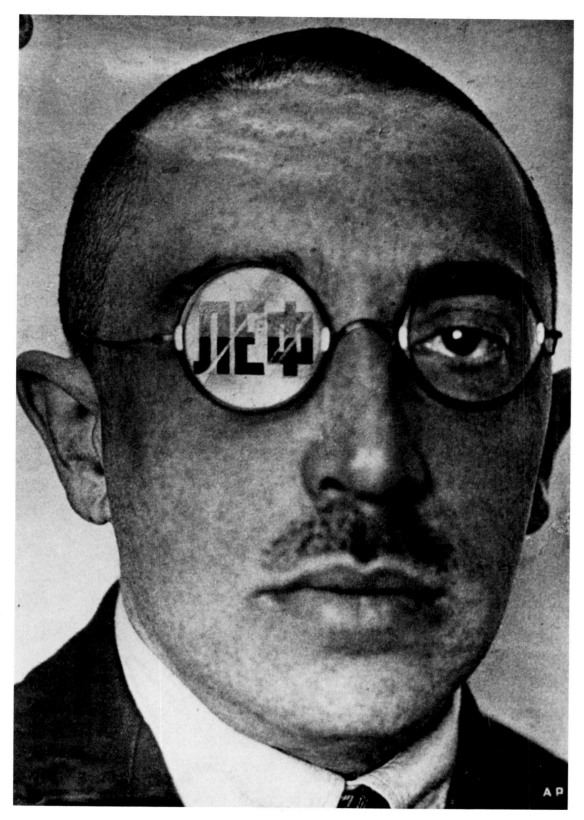

269 Vladimir and Georgii Stenberg: *The Year 11*. 1928. Cinema poster; Color lithograph, 107 × 71 cm. Lenin Library, Moscow.

270 Aleksandr Rodchenko: Photomontage of Osip Brik. 1924.

know Deauville or Le Touquet, to own an automobile and a wireless. Standardization, mass-production and design had all brought the prices down. It was a matter of making the public aware of all the marvelous inventions which had become available. The impetus had been given and we now know where it was leading.

Agitprop, the art of revolutionary propaganda in Russia was, on the other hand, linked closely to social life in all its manifold aspects. Its role was to help "construct life"—to participate in the education of the people. It was radically opposed to the concept of the consumer society; its function was neither to delude nor amaze. As previously mentioned, it circulated through all the provinces—Soviet Asia, the Caucasus, the Polish front—thanks to the propaganda trains and boats. Brightly colored posters were to be found amid the mural paintings, the tracts, the cinema and theater. Despite the shortage of paper and the collapse of the printing industry, the best-known artists began producing a special sort of revolutionary poster, the famous Rosta Windows, which owe their creation to Maiakovskii and were in fact produced under his direction. They were hand-stenciled, an economical substitute for printing, which had largely disappeared. The pictorial style was stylized and spare, but also expressive, even aggressive. The same type of poster appeared during the Spanish civil war, the Cultural Revolution in China and in May, 1968 in Paris, where one proclaimed: "It is forbidden to forbid."

Another kind of revolt was finding expression in Germany: the opposition of artists to the Weimar Republic, which Raoul Hausmann condemned as "nothing but falsehood, an attempt to disguise Teutonic barbarism," while Grosz shouted: "Make trouble! Explode! Rise up!" The new aesthetics were based on ugliness and shock images; drawing was used to expose moral and physical debility—though this technique was considered too slow by the Dadaists, who held that photomontage was the only adequate means to rival the speed with which the bourgeois press disseminated its lies.

Beneath such different skies, the poster and graphic arts were united to promote, on the one hand, consumerism, and on the other, community life. But in both cases, these new art forms drew level with their elders. They can even be considered as the best ambassadors of the art world. Cubism, Futurism, Fauvism and the opulence of the Ballets Russes were all absorbed by graphics and provided a great variety of forms and colors. In turn, poster artists made the avant-garde more acceptable to the public, paving the way to a fuller understanding of it. The eye gets used to everything, regardless of quality. Once accustomed to something, it becomes avid for new sensations. From Moscow to Berlin, in Paris, London or New York, the streets became a sort of art gallery. Any means were acceptable—photography, collage, distortion, caricature, Cubist analysis, provocative Dadaism or Expressionist drawing, as long as they got results.

Little by little creative work in other fields, such as painting, sculpture or architecture, began to seem less shocking to the "educated" eyes of the public. This was the service rendered by graphic arts, for all the occasional abuses. For the moment, the graphic arts that made their appearance on walls, in periodicals or in books were simply mirrors, reflecting the events that were taking place in each country, as well as changes in national habits and developments in technology.

perspective lines never fail to stir the imagination with their own dynamic character.

If graphic techniques were much the same, the aims sought in the capitalist states and in revolutionary Russia were totally different. In the West, it was efficiency, sobriety and profitability that were called for, following, to that extent, the principle voiced by Cappiello: to create forms that embodied the product, and that, even in the most varied settings, could quickly evoke the trademark, the idea or message, simply by their appearance. It was an art of the consumer society.

Posters grew larger, in order to increase their impact. They occupied the most privileged spots. In postwar Europe, one had to visit the Black Forest, to see Italy, to

Photography

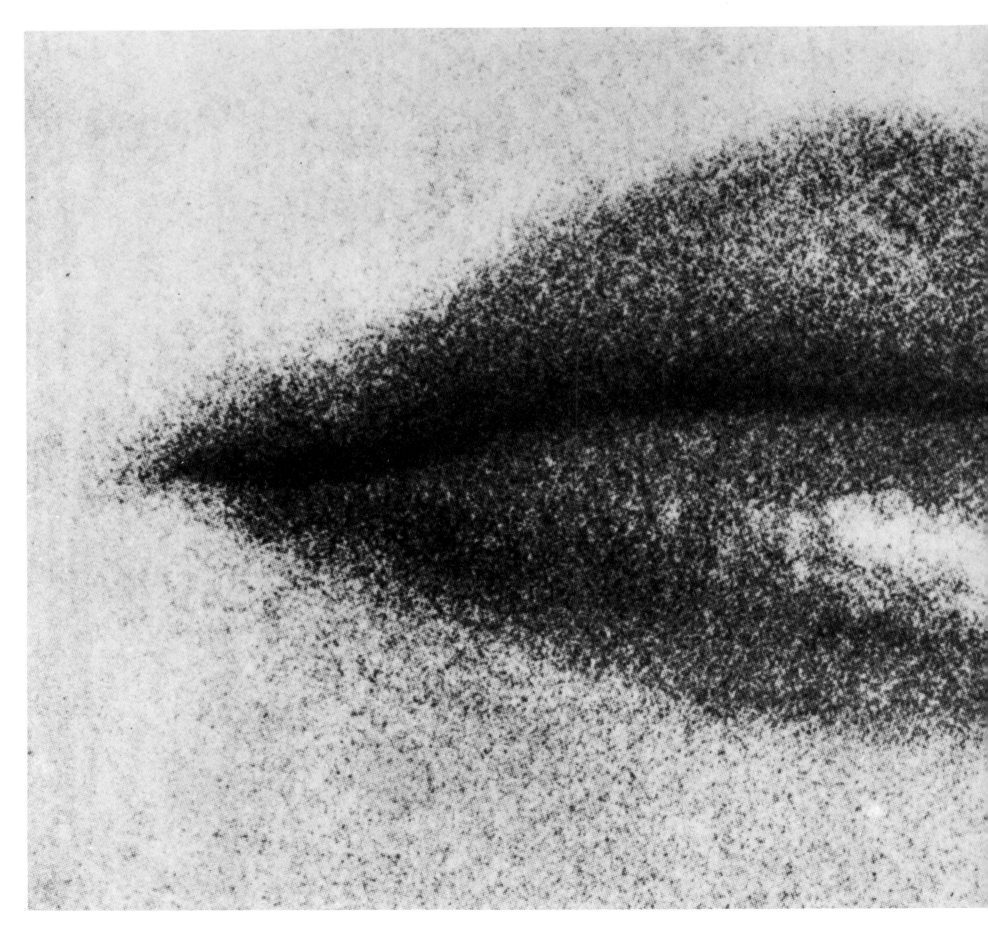

271 Man Ray: *Lips* (detail). C. 1925.
Photograph.

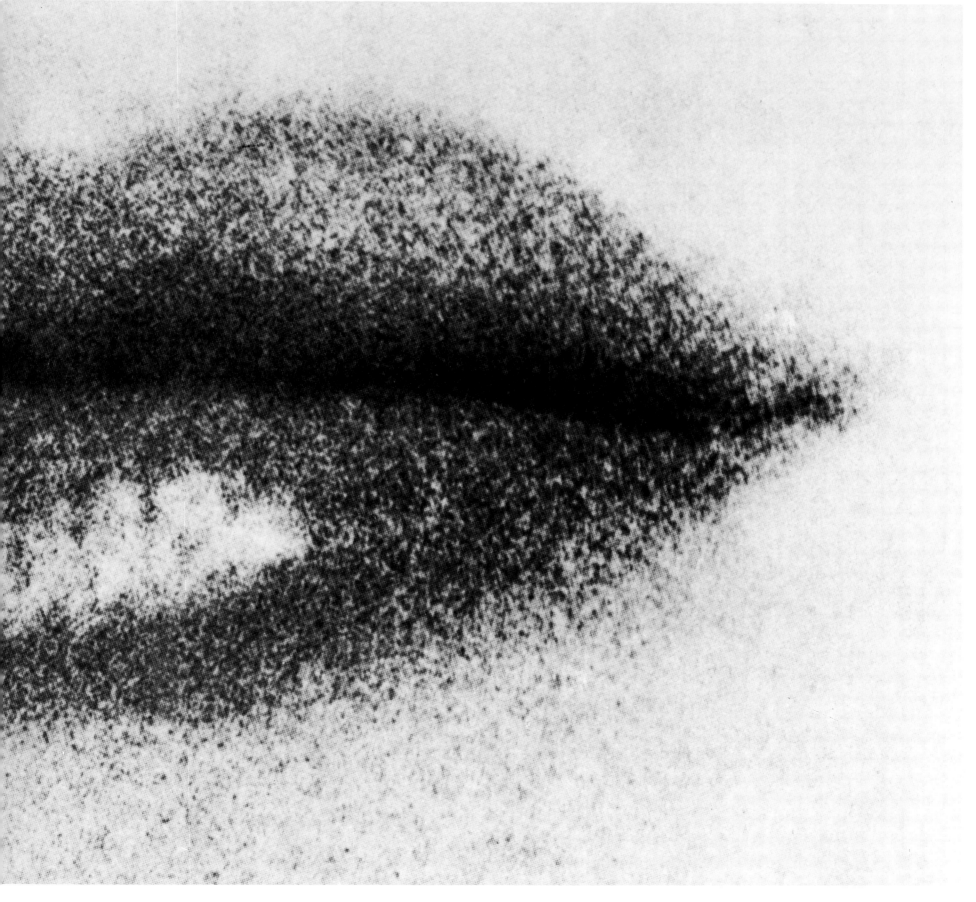

The present craze for creative photography gives us a chance to observe a rare historical phenomenon with our own eyes: the transition from a technique to an art. While the first awareness of sculpture as an authentic art form is lost in prehistory, that of painting, at least painting in its modern connotation—the canvas on the easel—was established about five centuries ago. As for engraving, the battle for its recognition has only just been won. It is perhaps worth considering painting with canvas and easel as an important step towards photography: from then on, the work of art possessed its own space, cut off from the world and portable. Engraving brought a further element with it: the notion that it was possible to reproduce an image in infinite quantities without impairing its artistic quality.

That painting at the easel, engraving and photography had to wait until long after their births as techniques to gain recognition as genuine art forms did not of course

The New Cézannes

mean that those fields had to wait for such recognition before producing masterpieces. The primitive painters, and many engravers since the first printed books, were admirable artists; so were the photographers Nadar, Atget and many others. But the acceptance of a human activity by the world of culture is less an event in the history of creative art than an indication of the changing manners of society itself. What may prove decisive today, notes Jean-Claude Lemagny, custodian of the Photographic Department of the Bibliothèque nationale (National Library), is the entry into the museum, and the museum of the imagination, of all photography, including bad photography.

Hence our scrupulous preoccupation with representing the photography of the Twenties in this volume with just a few outstanding examples. How can one begin, or go on, without the criterion of quality? Surely it is only through the very great works that all the others become noteworthy.

In the Twenties, creative photography emerged from an era in which indistinct outlines were regarded as a hallmark of artistic achievement—a failing or hypocrisy still present in our times among photographers who are either attempting to be "artistic," or are simply irremediably incompetent. To the hard, summary, prosaic nature of the ordinary photo, blurred outlines presented a contrasting "poetry of imprecision." Straight off, Alfred Stieglitz asserted that the photograph ought not to be ashamed of looking like a photograph. Since clarity,

exactitude and instantaneousness are the essential characteristics of photography, why not acknowledge this? But the accurately regulated lens sees things more clearly than we do, or rather, we experience them less clearly than the lens shows them. This demonstrates the difference between clarity and exactitude. We live by several senses, including the sense of touch: we know that the smoothest fruit is covered with an invisible mist, the faintest of blooms.

A great photographer is not content simply to press the little button on his Kodak. In order to take his celebrated photograph of a *Pear on a Plate*, Steichen—the new Cézanne—placed his subject under an awning of thick coverings and allowed only a ray of light to pass through a small opening. The whiteness of the coverings that formed the interior of the awning diffused the light faintly. Steichen focused exactly on the fruit's surface and left the lens open for thirty-six hours. It was, he explained, a matter of "rendering volume and weight." The fruit breathed. During the space of a day and a night, it expanded and contracted. "Instead of producing one meticulously sharp picture, the infinitesimal movement produced a succession of slightly different sharp images, which fused optically as one. Here for the first time in a photograph, I was able to sense volume as well as form." By abandoning instant photography, Steichen also succeeded in reconciling complete clarity of outline with the greatest possible accuracy. In fact, instantaneousness is the most relative of the three characteristics of

274   Edward Steichen: *Time-Space Continuum*. C. 1920. Photograph.

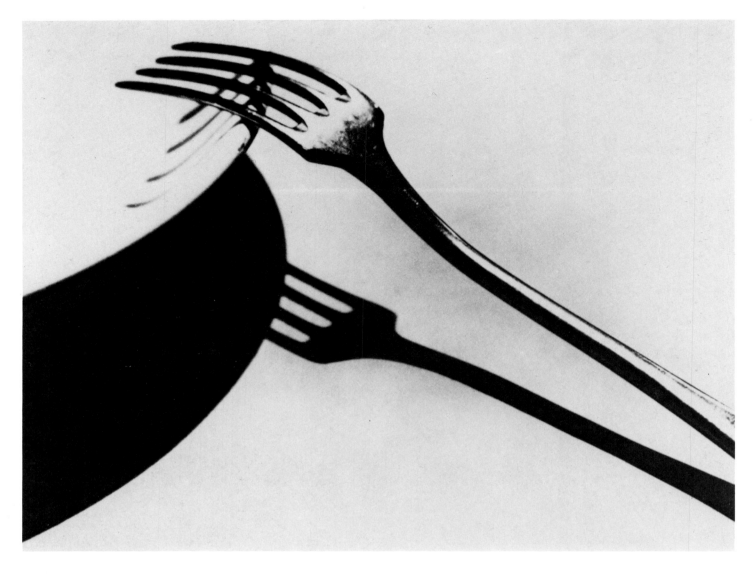

275 André Kertész: *Fork*. 1928. Photograph.

276 André Kertész: *Paris*. 1925. Photograph.

277 Aleksandr Rodchenko: *Cog Wheels*. 1930. Photograph.

Total Synthesis

photography, for every picture consists of the more or less rapid absorption of light by a sensitive surface. In letting such a long time elapse, Steichen enabled photography to move in harmony with the breathing of nature itself. He thus separated sharpness of image from exactitude—the two elements yoked together in a hard, cold photograph. Yet at the same time he reconciled them, for the lens provides sharpness and the film adds exactitude. The sensitive plate was saturated and filled as though by an excess of matter, which then remained fixed in the clear outline of the object. Thus, through the richness of the surface, volume was created. What Cézanne achieved by bringing together the true nature of reality and that of art, was done here for photography by Steichen.

On the other hand, in his no less famous *Wheelbarrow with Flower Pots*, Steichen achieved a perfectly realistic image. What surprised him was the discovery that this image called completely unexpected subjects to the minds of his friends. He "began to reason that, if it was possible to photograph objects in a way that makes them suggest something entirely different, perhaps it would be possible to give abstract meanings to very literal photographs." Edward Steichen—an emigrant in childhood from Luxembourg to the United States, apprentice lithographer, painter then photographer, learned authority on the limitations and essential nature of photography—broached the subject of photographic equivalents, which another American, Alfred Stieglitz, studied in depth from 1923 onwards, with his *Clouds* series.

Enthralled by Einstein's theories on the relativity of time and space, Steichen wanted to go further and give expression to the theory by linking together objects which, for him, acted as symbols. But in *Time-Space Continuum* (1920), he came to see that the very friends whose imagination had proved so prolific when faced with the *Wheelbarrow* proved incapable of interpreting the meanings with which he had sought to invest this new image: "I began to realize," he said, "that abstraction based on symbols was feasible only if the symbols were universal."

Is it not striking to see this great photographer exploring at the same period these two important lines of abstraction? While theoretically the image above may have represented a setback, it was nonetheless remarkable and important formally. Although the technique was completely different, this work recalls Man Ray's and Moholy-Nagy's photograms, begun in 1921: among the most salient characteristics are the flattening of volumes, the importance given to contours, and the daring juxtapositioning of geometricized elements.

At the Bauhaus, Moholy-Nagy was in fact continuing his research on movement and light. Photography provided him with an inexhaustible field for experiment. One of the new elements brought into play by these experiments was light. For him also there was a logical continuity between painting, photography and film; this is discussed in his first book at the Bauhaus. The photographs contained in this work are now classics. Moholy-Nagy also engaged in photomontages, cutting out and pasting together parts of different photographs.

214

But above all, at the same time as Man Ray, he created his photograms. The photograph is taken by depositing the objects directly on the photographic paper: no lens, no dark room. A whole series is reproduced in his book, published at the same time as a work by Man Ray. These experiments led him to the famous "total artistic synthesis," which, in his view, involved bringing together painting, sculpture, photography, typography, stage design and architecture, to ensure that art entered into and changed the everyday life of the individual.

When Kertész died recently, Henri Cartier-Bresson, quoting René Char, wrote: "Some are inventors, some discoverers." Kertész was a discoverer. "One finds in his work," Cartier-Bresson went on, "things comparable to what Cézanne referred to as 'the small sensation.' He was one of us and one of the best of us, with an astonishing continuity, due to his sincerity, to the absence in him of photographic duplicity."

It is curious that, although they all claim kinship with Cézanne, there are two rival groups of photographers at this period, one attaching importance to "inventiveness" and to the "manufacture" of its images, the other claiming to push the button "at the right moment," as if intellectual reflection had been replaced by complete innocence. In reality it was clear that the "inventors" did not always avoid falling prey to aestheticism and that the "discoverers" were often fertile in inventive capacities.... When he said: "Kertész is one of us," Cartier-Bresson was referring to the vision they shared, which obliged them not to cheat, not to be precious, to face life as it is and to translate it into authentic images. Kertész, a

Hungarian living in New York, who photographed only to express his "feelings," could never come to terms with the vast machinery of transatlantic magazines. Kertész was without doubt among those who contributed to and invented most in the art of photography. But this man who above all gave priority to human values, a certain way of life, to observation, to sincerity, always refused labels. One can immediately identify his pictures by their tonal quality, their emotion and their severe modeling. Other than the term "reducer," however, which would be applicable to his skillful use of gray and the precision of his framing, it is impossible to define his style in a single word. At all events, he restrained himself from carrying out any "aesthetic" research, going so far as to make fun of the Bauhaus for seeking to make art "interesting." For this reason Kertész's work, although much admired among photographers, including the younger ones, did not give rise to a school: his graphic severity never admitted "gimmicks." "Art has been killed by technical exaggeration," he insisted. "Every detail which the eye cannot see has been reproduced. It is all right if you are an artist who wants to work in this way, but it is not right for everybody. In reality, your eye adjusts itself to what you are looking at and registers it.... For me, a photograph must correspond to the way you see the world."

This was far from the point of view of the Russian pioneers, whose sole thought was to develop photographic techniques to achieve, from time to time, symbolic successes. This avant-garde photography, which

278 Manaut: *Woman carrying a Tailor's Dummy.* 1930. Vienna. Photograph.

279 Eugène Atget: *Avenue des Gobelins Shop Window.* 1926. Photograph. George Eastman House, Rochester, N. Y.

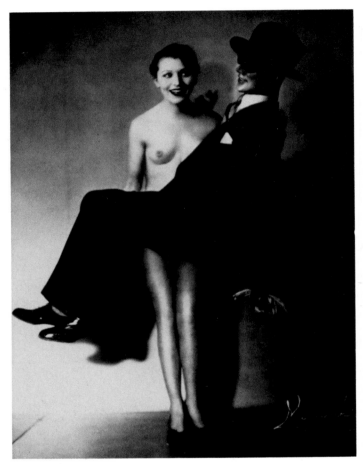

coincided in the field of technology with the advent of small, mass-produced cameras, extremely easy to handle, providing great freedom of movement, was made up, at the beginning, of those who had practised the mannered portrait photography of the time of the Czar. After the Revolution, these pioneers became the privileged propagandists of the new regime, traveling through the country from the plains of the Ukraine to the steppes of Central Asia, forging the tradition of a "concerned" photographic journalism, and establishing the ground for a militant photography which considered the act of the photographer and the power of the image to have an aesthetic ingredient.

The leading figure in this new formalist photography was Aleksandr Rodchenko, a dyed-in-the-wool Constructivist, friend of the poet Maiakovskii, by turn painter, graphic artist, designer and theatrical producer. Rodchenko staked out the ground for a new photography in no uncertain terms: the new society had created a new man; the artist and the photographer had to find a new way of illustrating him. He experimented with high and low viewpoints "to teach people to look at things from a new angle." He invented "tipping," a way of framing his subject diagonally to the picture in order to put it in relief.

280   August Sander: *Circus People*.
1926. Photograph.

**Photogaphy
with a
Message**

Aesthetic and Capitalism

281   Edward Weston: *Nude.* 1926.
Photograph.

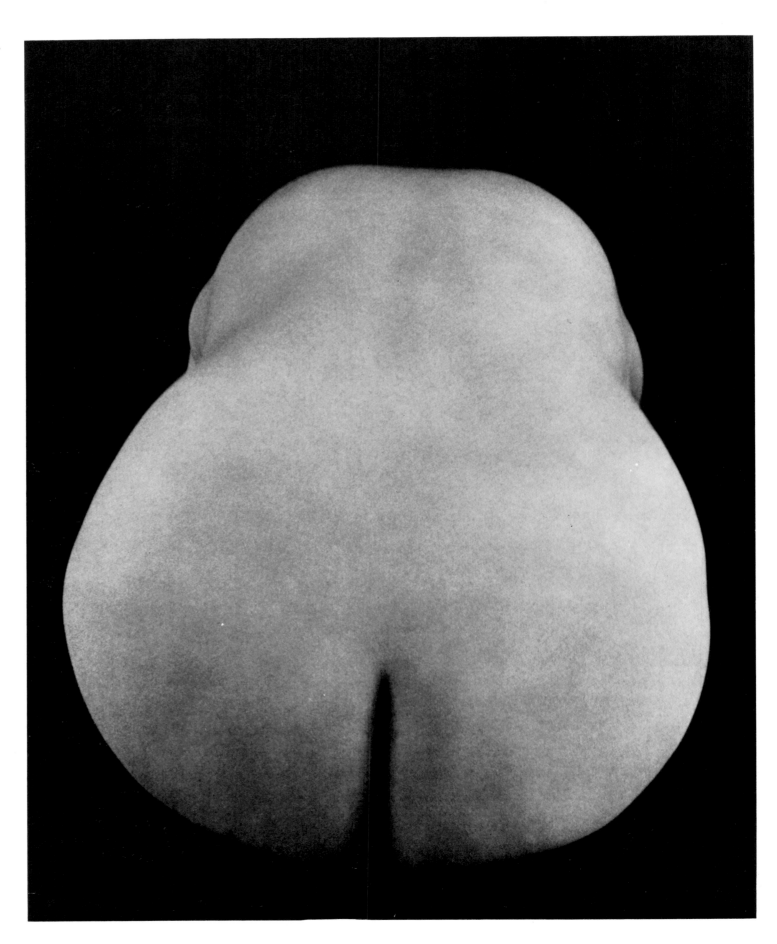

282 Edward Weston: *Nude*. 1920.
Photograph.

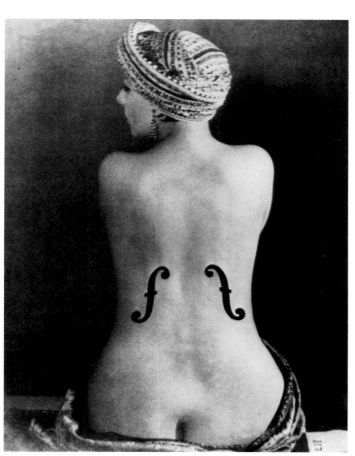

283 Man Ray: *Ingres's Violin*. 1924.
Photograph, first published in *Littéra-ture*, No. 13, June, 1924.

Rodchenko opened photography to a very wide field of experimentation. He photographed all subjects with the same boldness—solemn processions, young Pioneers, architecture, sporting events, industrial fragments removed from their environment—making his pictures veritable epic poems, brought together in albums or books.

But behind this uniform facade depicting the heroic progress of the Soviet Revolution, one inevitably finds the eternal conflict between innovators and traditionalists. The dispute turned upon Rodchenko and raised doubts about the aesthetic qualities brought to the make-up of each photo, at times to the detriment of genuine realism. Rodchenko was even expelled from the October group, of which he was founder, for "propaganda of a style foreign to the proletariat." He had been wrong to put his money on aesthetics and not on faithfulness to reality. He was expelled because he wanted to have his young Pioneers communing directly with the heavens and thus, as Dominique Carré notes, "gave them unnaturally prominent jaw-lines." Forgetting the traditions of the Russian icon, Rodchenko wished to see the figures of the Revolution in the same way as one looks at a statue in a church; from below, and with a distorted perspective. He was not forgiven. "Why is the little Pioneer looking upwards? That is an ideological mistake. Pioneers and members of the Komsomol must always gaze straight ahead."

The Dreamers

284 Man Ray: *Black and White*. Photograph, published in *Variétés*, No. 3, July 15, 1928.

285 Berenice Abbott: *Jean Cocteau*. 1920. Photograph.

As for aestheticism, that should be left to the West—to Stieglitz, Steichen, Man Ray, to Weston, Atget and the others. Let them amuse themselves by making a naked woman look like a pear or a violin, or vice versa. Let them toy with Black art or Surrealism. At least they had the merit of fiercely defending direct photography against the hangovers of pictorialism and of abandoning blurred artistic effects in favor of a clear image and the presence of the subject itself. Others, like the German August Sander, even sought to convey a social message.

Just as Rembrandt and Cézanne displayed to us in no uncertain terms the problems inherent in all painting, even clumsy painting, all these new photographers of the 1920s—whether they belonged to one side or the other—brought to light a new area of creative activity that, until then, had been hidden. It was a field not concerned with the making of things, but with the way we look at them: not with invention, but with acceptance; not with drawing, but with vision—and they were the harbingers of that new field.

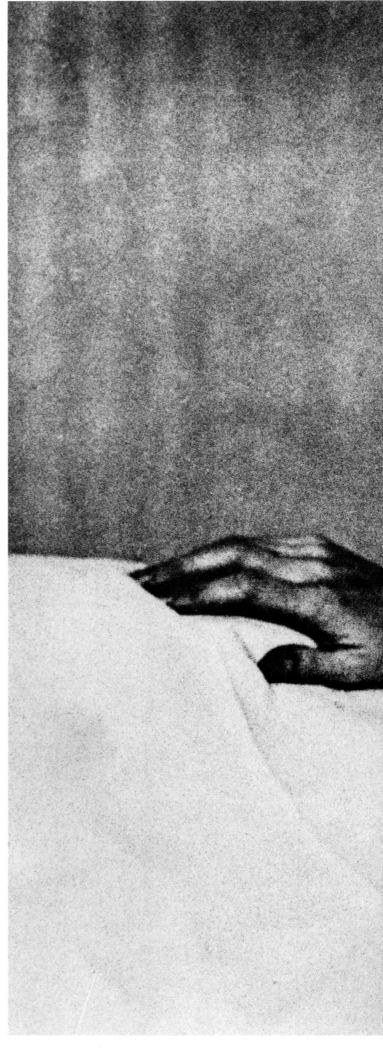

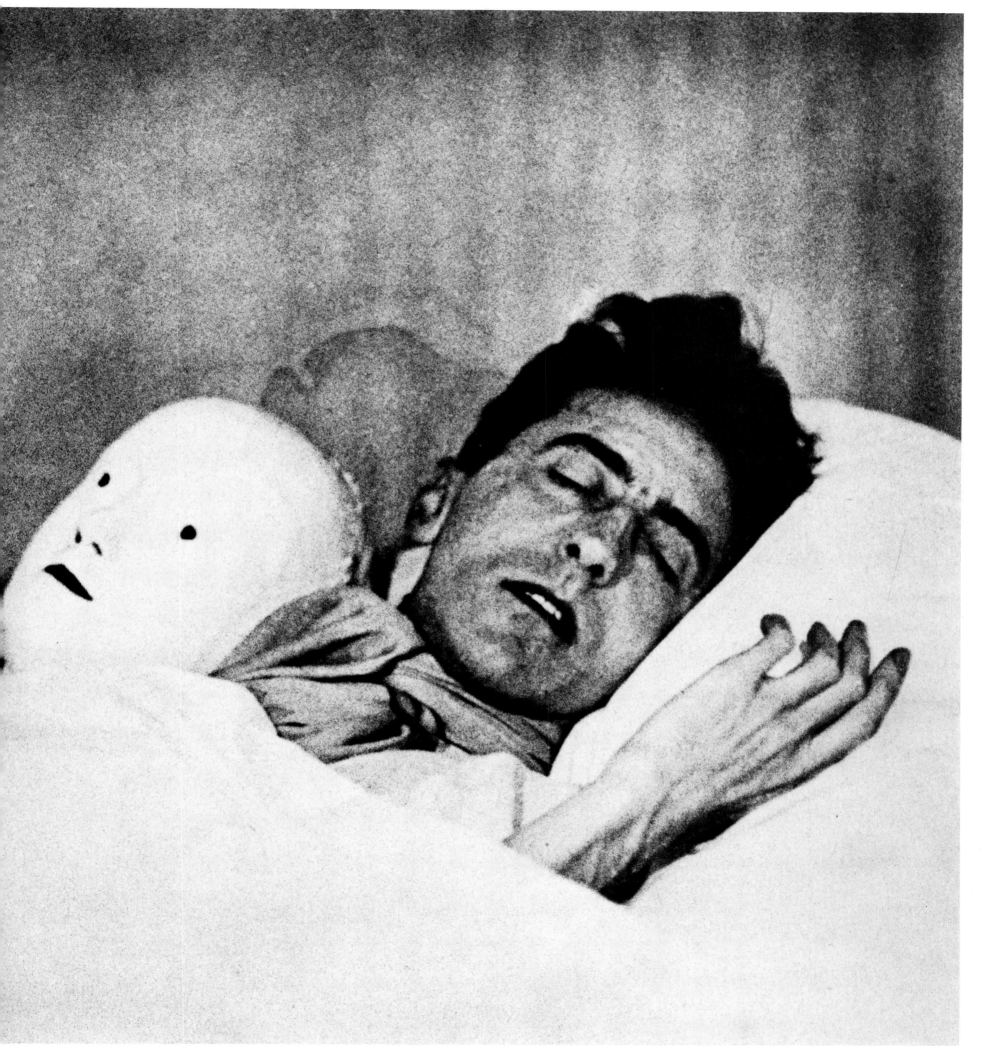

Film

286   The actor Paul Wegener in the
title role of *The Golem* by Henrik
Galeen and Wegener. 1920.

German Expressionism

287 Max Schreck in *Nosferatu, the Vampire* by Friedrich Wilhelm Murnau. 1922.

288 Otto Stahl-Arpke: Poster for Robert Wiene's film, *Das Kabinett des Dr. Caligari*. 1920. Private collection, Milan.

289 Schultz-Neudamm: Poster for Fritz Lang's film, *Metropolis*. 1926. Museum of Modern Art, New York.

Both *Caligari* and *Metropolis* anticipate the arrival of Hitler and the rise of Nazism, ten years before the event.

As we have seen throughout this book, the most characteristic feature of the art of the Twenties is the continuous dialogue between the various arts—a dialogue maintained throughout the following decades. The constant exchange also resulted, for example, in the huge-scale Hollywood productions being quickly answered by German or Russian extravaganzas. Hitherto the cinema had been a relatively unimportant form of entertainment. If *Das Kabinett des Dr. Caligari* (1920) was a major event, it was because it suddenly made known the existence of the German cinema and demonstrated the fact that a film could be something more than a more or less faithful depiction of the events of everyday life. The film in fact constitutes, through the cooperation of the various artists who assisted in its production, a genuine attempt to portray anti-realist aims. *Caligari* is essentially a film by painters, and the Expressionist artists Warm, Reimann and Röhrig were not simply the authors of the sets and costumes: they imposed their style on director Robert Wiene, whose career, with the exception of this masterpiece, was unremarkable.

We are introduced, says Georges Charensol, to a universe where the forms are as crazy as the reasoning of the heroes, since the story is presented to us as something imagined by a madwoman. We have therefore to accept that the action takes place in a fantasy world to which only the cinema can give access: it was the cinema which was able to introduce the public at large to the Expressionism which until then had been known only to art lovers.

Méliès thought up some ingenious and amusing gadgets to express the supernatural. *Caligari* was the first film to create an atmosphere of anxiety in which the decor in particular played a leading role: it was not a framework for the action, it was an essential part of that action. This pioneer film was followed by numerous others in which the lighting, the sets and the way the actors interpreted their roles were deliberately distorted in order to lead the audience into the realm of pure fantasy. There is, for example, a connecting link which leads from *Caligari* to *The Trial* by Orson Welles, forty years later. In 1938, Alexandre Arnoux was to write: "Nothing done after *Caligari* remains uninfluenced by it,

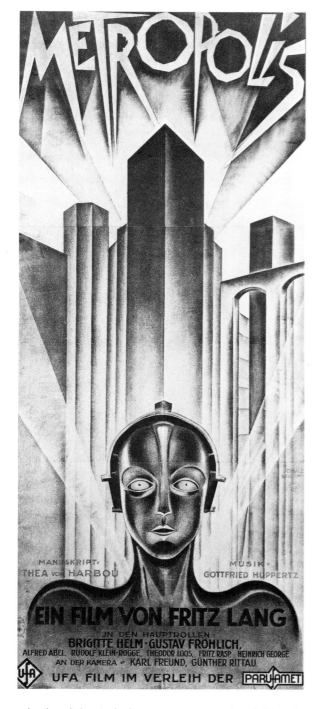

whether it be to imitate or react against it." In his book *Du muet au parlant* ("From the Silent Screen to Talkies"), Arnoux asserts that Robert Wiene gave the costume, set and lighting designers and architects the opportunity to explore the full extent of their profession. "The fact that much of today's stage design no longer shocks us at all, is due to the bold, aggressive steps taken by *Caligari*, which have taught us the corrections necessary to make to nature."

Georges Charensol concludes: "Since *Caligari*, right from the start, explored to the full the possibilities of Expressionism, a whole school has been able, often by very different means, to interpret a world on the way to disintegration. For it must be stressed that no one subsequently has gone so far as the authors of this first effort; their conception finds expression not only in the violently contrasted lighting, and in the abstract sets, but also in the caricatural make-up and the disturbing acting of the players."

From *The Golem* (1920) to *M* (1931), from *Nosferatu the Vampire* (1922) to *The Blue Angel* (1930), from *Faust* (1926) to *Metropolis* (1926–1927), this despairing art,

which sought to interpret both the tragic and absurd aspects of life, was a reflection of Germany itself. The crisis the nation was undergoing was as much moral as material in nature. After defeat in war came unemployment, inflation, and revolutionary movements, all of which were accompanied by an immense thirst for pleasure. Their world in the grip of despair is reflected in films whose dark, weird quality remains unequaled. Their authors express their own, personal suffering as well as that of a country that had broken adrift.

Fritz Lang, a towering figure, continued on the same track. In *Death of Siegfried* (1924), the narrative is of less interest to us than the decorative effects and the sets. The ancient German forest was set up in the studio, where the trees were synthesized by columns of cement. Lang created an unreal world in which Siegfried, later to fall victim to evil forces, gets lost. For in the hands of Fritz Lang, the cinema became prophetic. It also yielded to the craze for size. Throughout this period, the German cinema competed with the American superproductions, which had in turn taken over the vast stage settings from Italian films. *Metropolis*, with its immense sets, and no

290   Peter Lorre made his name in Fritz Lang's film *M* in 1931. But already in 1929 Kurt Pinthus announced "a new, horrifying face; the son of a frightful, hysterical small tradesman, whose mis-shapen, jaundiced face, with its protuberant eyes, sticks up out of his clothes." While Erich von Stroheim, although an Austrian, always symbolized the Prussian officer, Peter Lorre, for his part, incarnated one of the most disturbing aspects of the German self-satisfied middle class.

less immense crowds, foreshadowed the city of the future, and brought to life an apocalyptic world. Gradually the German cinema lost its leading figures, with the departure for the United States of Murnau, Lubitsch, Dupont, Leni and Buchovetski, precursors of the massive emigration of 1933.

In France new cinemas opened every day, and the old-style fun-fair cinema rapidly became a prehistoric relic. The cinema appeared to be the only genuinely universal language. It was enough to provide French subtitles to films from abroad to allow people to enter worlds about which they had previously known nothing. Thus, thanks to the cinema, the French discovered the vast size of America, then Germany's profound malaise. During this period of seeking, of fumbling in the dark, of countless experiments and technical novelty, France did not find it easy to come to terms with the new cinema. Some of these uncertainties are apparent, for example, in the work of Marcel L'Herbier, a director who was constantly torn between lofty ambitions and the need to reassure his producers. He wanted the cinema to express "a symbolism at first simple in character, but becoming more and more evocative," while continuing to be the "universal language of ordinary folk." *L'Homme du large* (1920), represents a major exception among works largely dominated by aesthetic considerations—which is evidence that L'Herbier did not always follow the artistic haziness at that time popular with the Americans, but was well aware of the need for simplicity then advocated by the Swedish school, and the way in which a direct contact with nature could benefit the cinema.

The personality which had the strongest impact on his time was without doubt Abel Gance. Gance, writes Georges Charensol, was an accomplished master of the plastic arts. More than any of his contemporaries, he had a profound sense of the cinema. But he also wanted to be a thinker, a sort of demiurge, and, though his destiny was not tragic, his claims were somewhat excessive. His most finished work remains *Napoleon* (1925), a character with whom he almost identified. His *La Roue* ("The Wheel") (1922) was also a landmark in the history of French cinema. For, in spite of a childish scenario, what Gance succeeded in depicting was the relationship between man and machine, though doubtless the assistance of Blaise Cendrars was critical in this achievement.

The author of *La Prose du Transsibérien* ("Trans-Siberian Prose") was in fact in close connection with avant-garde circles, where painters like Fernand Léger had discovered the beauty of steel in motion. Léger was subsequently to film *Le Ballet mécanique* ("The Mechanical Ballet"). These influences come into play in *The Wheel*, together with the influence of American films showing locomotives running at full tilt, and which accentuate the impression of speed by making full use of the possibilities offered by fast motion and editing. Gance was to go further still: the bravura section of *The Wheel* consists of a rapid piece of editing in which a succession of images is shown at an increasingly frenetic pace. Caught by the purely sculptural beauty of these forms in full action, we forget the rather crazy romanticism of the film itself and allow ourselves to be carried away by this rhythmic mechanical symphony, whose score, "Pacific 231," was by Arthur Honegger. Fast motion montage was soon, alas, to become too much of a good thing....

In its quest to break with the conventional and routine,

the French avant-garde seized every new opening and allowed itself to fall victim to the most brash effects of foreign films. Nevertheless, from time to time, a masterpiece was produced, such as *Cœur fidèle* ("Faithful Heart") (1923), in which Jean Epstein succeeded in pulling together a number of disorderly attempts by his contemporaries: the feeling for atmosphere which Louis Delluc knew how to create, Marcel L'Herbier's aesthetic analysis, together with the

French Impressionism

daring editing of Abel Gance are all to be found in the work.

The confusion among film producers in the postwar years is clearly shown by the Aubert Company's decision to give a substantial sum to an unknown director to shoot a large-scale production in the Sahara, adapted from a currently popular novel by Pierre Benoit called *L'Atlantide* ("Atlantis"). L'Herbier and Gance tried to have the best of both worlds, hoping both to attract large crowds by tackling easy subjects and to win over the elite by concentrating all their attention on technique. Feyder refused to distinguish between form and content, and the commercial success of *L'Atlantide* proved him right.

René Clair had in common with Jacques Feyder the fact that he did not want to flatter the public as innumerable craftsmen did, nor to surprise them as did the protagonists of the avant-garde. A combination of strong

291 *L'Homme du large* by Marcel L'Herbier. 1920.

In *L'Homme du large*, taken from a essay by Balzac, Marcel L'Herbier pushed French Impressionist extremes to their limit. The new generation of cinema directors saw the cinema as a means of evoking their aesthetic concerns in their own particular idiom. Rather than telling a story, or an anecdote, they wanted their cinema to be recognized as an art in itself. With this aim in view, Louis Delluc published *Photogénie*, an outline for a cinematic theory, and Ricciotto Canudo, the critic, founded a club called Des Amis du Septième Art (CASA) ("Friends of the Seventh Art"). L'Herbier's film, in spite of the brilliant acting of Jacques Catelain and Charles Boyer, was criticized for a lack of naturalness in certain scenes and the blatant discrepancies between the reality in Brittany and its portrayal in the film.

292 Scene from the shooting of the film *Napoleon*, by Abel Gance. 1925. The director with his star, Albert Dieudonné.

This epic, the result of four years of work, was highly innovative. Abel Gance effectively tripled the dimensions of the screen by means of his "Polyvision" method. The film was projected onto a screen 15 meters wide and almost 4 meters high, using three synchronized projectors, which were able to throw panoramic scenes onto the screen by lining up the three images, or three different scenes, as in a triptych. In 1927, another Frenchman, Professor Henri Chrétien, went further still, by inventing cinemascope under the name of Hypergonar. From the Lumière brothers on, the cinema has been a decidedly French invention, even if it is the Americans who make the greatest use of it.

293 Charles Dullin in a scene form the silent film *Le Joueur d'échecs* ("The Chess Player"), by Raymond Bernard. 1925–1926.

The American
Dream

taste and a broad general knowledge immediately secured him a very personal niche in the French cinema and in due time brought him academic honors. He was inventive and amusing with *Paris qui dort* ("Paris is Sleeping") (1923). With *Entr'acte* ("Intermission") (1924), a gamble, he proved without any difficulty that he could rival the avant-garde. The Ballets Suédois had asked him to make a film, which was to be called quite simply

294   Lillian Gish: "America's little sweetheart," in *Way Down East*, by D. W. Griffith. 1920.

"Intermission," to fill in the time needed to change the scenery of a ballet called *Relâche,* with a scenario by Francis Picabia and music by Erik Satie. That this film was intended as a parody cannot be doubted: all the techniques then in vogue were employed with a virtuosity, a sense of irony and imagination which remain unsurpassed. This indeed was France "the melting-pot," exploiting and criticizing simultaneously.

As one who saw the film being shot and was often at the side of Francis Picabia, Marcel Duchamp, Man Ray, Marcel Achard, Pierre Scize, Louis Touchagues and

others, Georges Charensol testifies "to the unfailing good humor which prevailed both at Luna Park, where the burial and scenic railway sequences were filmed, and at the Théâtre des Champs-Elysées, where many scenes were shot. When today much of the purely formal efforts of the period make us smile with their solemnity and pretentiousness, and when the ballet which it made famous has been forgotten, *Entr'acte* lives on as a classic. By its humor, as well as by its deliberate excesses, it demolished all rival attempts in the same field."

From this time onward the world market was dominated by films produced in America, and fear of a total takeover by Hollywood productions became one of the principal preoccupations of the European film industry. In 1924 Hollywood produced about 580 films; by 1928 the annual production had risen to approximately 850. Investment of capital in the new industry reached staggering proportions. Vast studios sprang up in what had been a Los Angeles suburb but had now become an important city. To obtain maximum profitability, the highest standards of organizational efficiency were introduced. It was at this time that many of today's largest companies were founded: Fox, Paramount, Metro-Goldwyn-Mayer, Universal, United Artists, Warner Brothers, and Columbia.

Everywhere the producer was king. Directors and actors alike had to accept his orders. Every evening the producer would view the scenes that had been shot that day and order the director to make whatever modifications he thought necessary. It frequently happened that the director was dismissed and replaced during the shooting of the film. As for the actors, they were all-powerful as long as they enjoyed popular acclaim. Suitable parts were made to order for them, and the American cinema was to a great extent based on the popularity of its stars. But once a film starring one of these sacred monsters of legendary reputation failed to please, the actor in question was ruthlessly shown the door.

1924 was a crucial year in America. Thomas H. Ince left the scene, Mack Sennett and Griffith were no longer in the front rank. Of the great pioneers, only Chaplin survived and would do so for a long time to come. The others took a back seat, giving place to newcomers. The Swedish cinema was moribund. In Germany, the Expressionist fire slowly died down and from its ashes were born the works of Dupont, Murnau and Pabst. Soviet cinema was only beginning to get organized. In France, the death of Louis Delluc marked the the twilight of the avant-garde. The age of great artistic, technical, industrial and commercial triumphs in the field of film-making was, for a time, coming to a halt.

Would the industrialized cinema know how to adapt itself to standardization? Would a stereotyped production, using techniques that were not updated because they had proved themselves, not end up by boring the public? The American cinema of this period became a collective effort, an industrial product the individual author of which could usually not be pinpointed. America had nevertheless achieved the feat of creating an international language, without cutting itself off from its national origins. It followed its own rules and these owed nothing to the conventions of classical art. It furnished a document on ways of life and modes of thinking quite unknown to the outside world. It is impossible to pass judgment on products emanating from Hollywood studios without taking into account both their social and aesthetic aspects. Would this new language fulfill the oft-proclaimed aspirations of the Bauhaus and the Constructivists? "The decline of the American cinema," prophesised Georges Charensol, "will begin when it ceases to bear witness to the times and becomes an industrial product designed purely to give pleasure to the masses."

The American film industry did not, however, despite its enormous productive capacity and its invasion of the outside world, escape the economic crisis. By December 28, 1920, some 50,000 employees had lost their jobs and production was only 84% that of the preceding year. A crisis of morals accompanied this economic decline: the cinema itself and its actors began to suffer one of those Puritan onslaughts endemic to Anglo-Saxon countries. Thus the marriage of Mary Pickford and Douglas Fairbanks following their divorces in the same year caused a scandal. And scandal meant a fall in box-office sales!

Despite these difficulties, the Hollywood cinema, mirror of American society, still succeeded in evoking "the American dream," and *The Kid* (1921), the first full-scale production by Charlie Chaplin—who was undeniably the true creator of his films, since he was simultaneously scriptwriter, director and leading actor—perfectly illustrates this point. Chaplin and his *Kid* (Jackie Coogan) symbolized that America where all things were possible and man, poor, but honest and good, could turn the most difficult situation to his advantage. The film's immense success was an indication of the wide public support for the ethical code propounded by Chaplin.

Mary Pickford in the part of *Pollyanna,* a Paul Powell film, and Lillian Gish in D.W. Griffith's *Way Down East,* both from 1920, show yet another side of the American dream, where courage and generosity triumph.

The world-wide success of *The Gold Rush* (1925) was sufficient proof of Chaplin's universal appeal. The conflicting elements of comedy and tragedy, sentiment and savagery, already present in *A Dog's Life* (1918) and in *The Kid,* found a genuine equilibrium in *The Gold Rush.* This is, moreover, a typically American film, depicting one of the most celebrated chapters in the story of America. But Chaplin never gave up the idea of being an emigrant, an outsider; a profound nostalgia for the Old World pervaded his works. While the setting of *The Gold Rush* is that of a typical adventure film, such as the United States produced by the hundred, the important thing is the figure of the little man who triumphs over cruel nature and no less cruel human beings, but who, under the worst circumstances, never loses sight of the dream.

Adolph Zukor said that the entire American cinema industry had been built on the "star system," a powerful yet fragile structure. He explained that at the origin of his "Famous Players in Famous Plays" was his conviction that the public was prepared to look at a full-length film exclusively devoted to showing stars.

The press played an important part in the development of the star system in the U.S. During the Twenties, some fifteen specialized magazines took hold of the market, from *Picture Play* to *Movie Weekly* and from *Hollywood Screenland* to *Close-up,* each specialized in the publication of photos, stars and of more or less indiscreet gossip; some did not hesitate to publish rumors of a frankly scandalous character.

The barometer was the box office, the thermometer was

the studio mail. There were the money-makers and the others. Producers were careful to maintain the popularity of their stars thanks to the tenacity of their publicity men and to the obliging and highly effective response of the world press. The year 1926 marked a high point in the cult of stardom. It was in fact the year that Rudolph Valentino died, an event that gave rise to an extraordinary outbreak of collective hysteria in all corners of the globe.

The arrival of talking films would inevitably lead to important changes in the existing star system. To be photogenic ceased to be the sole criterion for success; the capacity to use the spoken word was now a necessity. A higher intellectual level was required. From now on the qualities demanded of actors were at once more numerous and more varied. In the good old days of the silent film, the rival and competitive eccentricities of Pola Negri and Gloria Swanson had provided continuous fodder for the scandal-mongering proclivities of the major newspapers. These continued to keep their

295   Charlie Chaplin and Jackie Coogan in *The Kid.* 1920.

296　Viktor Sjöström and the Swedish cinema.

In 1920, the film which provoked the most discussion and was the most widely admired, was *The Phantom Chariot, Clay, Thy Soul Shall Bear Witness* by Viktor Sjöström. The director and actor respected the legendary tone of the narrative: the dream of the drunkard, whom Death's carter comes to fetch on New Year's Eve, remains moving because of its fantastic character. Sjöström created a new cinematographic language which was to influence the Impressionist French cinema and German film-makers like F.W. Murnau: he used superimposition for poetic ends with greater mastery than any of his contemporaries. The film was a world-wide success.

297　Erich von Stroheim between his two chief cameramen, William Daniels and Ben Reynolds.

readers informed about the no less noisy rivalries of Greta Garbo and Marlene Dietrich. But the tone would never be quite the same again. The distance that separated the stars from their colleagues in the hierarchy of the Hollywood studio was diminishing, and this development was not for the worse.

But the star system swallowed up huge sums of money. Production costs continued to increase, while audiences began to show clear signs of weariness. No one in Hollywood had any doubt that the cinema was running out of steam. It was saved by a stroke of good fortune. Warner Brothers, a relatively modest company without much to lose, found out that efforts to obtain perfect synchronization of image and sound had at last succeeded. Purchasing in April, 1926 the patent for Vitaphone, Warner Brothers immediately converted to a talkie a silent film they were in the process of producing. Given a musical accompaniment, *Don Juan*, acted by John Barrymore, was shown in New York on August 6, 1926.

Thus the cinema was able to forestall the depression which attacked the United States in 1929, bringing with it devastating economic and political consequences. Had it not been for this initiative on the part of Warner Brothers, the cinema, one of the country's most vulnerable industries, would have been hit far more seriously than it was. As it turned out, at the very moment the crisis broke, public interest in this new toy was at its height.

This synchronization of recording and image led to the

production at Hollywood of the first talkies, in particular *The Jazz Singer*, which, made in 1927, comprised a short dialogue and an important part sung by Al Jolson. The world of cinema was astounded to learn, on October 15, 1922, that Universal had well and truly dismissed the star producer of *Merry-Go-Round*. Erich von Stroheim, the director, was in fact incorrigible, just as Orson Welles would be later. The life of this one-time soldier in the Imperial Austrian army, who styled himself a lieutenant, made a most extraordinary story. Von Stroheim was marked both by the decline of the Austro-Hungarian Empire and by the rigid discipline of the Imperial army to which he had belonged. Arriving in the United States penniless in 1909, a dancer, actor and scriptwriter, he brought Universal close to bankruptcy with the film *Foolish Wives* (1921), for which he had presented so modest an estimated budget that the company had decided to let him try his luck. But he insisted on an ostentatious reconstruction of of the Casino at Monte Carlo, shot 80,000 meters of film and spent $ 1,300,000, prolonging filming for a year. According to Georges Charensol, Von Stroheim appears to have been possessed by a sort of madness and used the cinema as a means of revenging himself on a society that had derided him both in Austria and in America: he gave back a hundredfold the injuries he had received. His films are all in striking contrast to the spirit of conformism prevailing in Hollywood in the postwar years. Their extravagance excited the public, and consequently *Foolish Wives* was a success, though its brand of realism stretched to surrealism could easily have offended people. Von Stroheim's one object seems to have been to present highly unusual characters in situations equally bizarre.

An adventure rather like the affair that led to his dismissal occurred with *Greed* (1924). The film lasted seven hours and had to be shown in two parts. Von Stroheim refused to allow any cuts, though a few were made in spite of his protests; the film was notwithstanding his principal achievement. Prey to a perpetual sense of indignation, no excess, no horror could shock him. Von Stroheim, comments Georges Charensol, readapts German Expressionism to his own objectives. Everything is enlarged, distorted, inflamed. It is a painting of life in the convulsive throws of the lowest passions.

In 1928, Gloria Swanson, then one of the leading stars, asked him to produce *Queen Kelly*; he abandoned the project after shooting the first part. Pierre Leprochon rightly sees this segment as a synthesis of Von Stroheim's art, an art made up of inextricable contradictions, satire, violence, cynicism, but endowed with fragmentary glimpses of poetic freshness.

Finding that no company had any confidence in him, Von Stroheim took refuge in France, becoming an actor again. In 1937 he was given a part in *La Grande Illusion* ("Great Illusion") by Jean Renoir, a role he made striking and unforgettable. Von Stroheim's similarity with Orson Welles, also a refugee from the United States, is striking. However, the American dream died hard. It needed more than a Von Stroheim to shake it. Even the subsequent arrival of Orson Welles' Martians or *Citizen Kane* (1939) were not enough to change habits acquired over a long time. The American public, and the rest of the world with it, continued to escape into a dream world, with adventure films providing a veritable paradise for juvenile leads and for literary adaptations: among them were *The Mark of Zorro* (1920) by Fred Niblo, *Treasure Island* (1920) and *The Last of the Mohicans* (1922) by Maurice Tourneur. The success of *Zorro* was assured by the actor—the public's ultimate idol—Douglas Fairbanks, in the title role. Maurice Tourneur made use of the Impressionism so dear to France and sought to utilize outdoor locations and wide countrysides to the greatest extent possible.

Comedies of manners, light and brilliant, and musical comedies now became a speciality of a Hollywood that exploited the field of humor in depth. Among the members of the comic school, Buster Keaton founded his own company, Keaton Film Company, and produced *One Week* in 1920. The Stan Laurel-Oliver Hardy pair began their long career together in 1927. A new genre also appeared with Robert Flaherty: the "documentary." Flaherty had gone off to live with the Eskimos, to make a film of their everyday life. Hollywood production, immense and varied as it was, proved a success in spite of the crisis.

Then, beyond the star, there was the legend—a well-known phenomenon more recently personified by Marilyn Monroe and James Dean. In the 1920s the legend went by the name of Lulu. It came into being with Louise Brooks, with her boyish bangs, her "modern

Von Stroheim's Frenzy

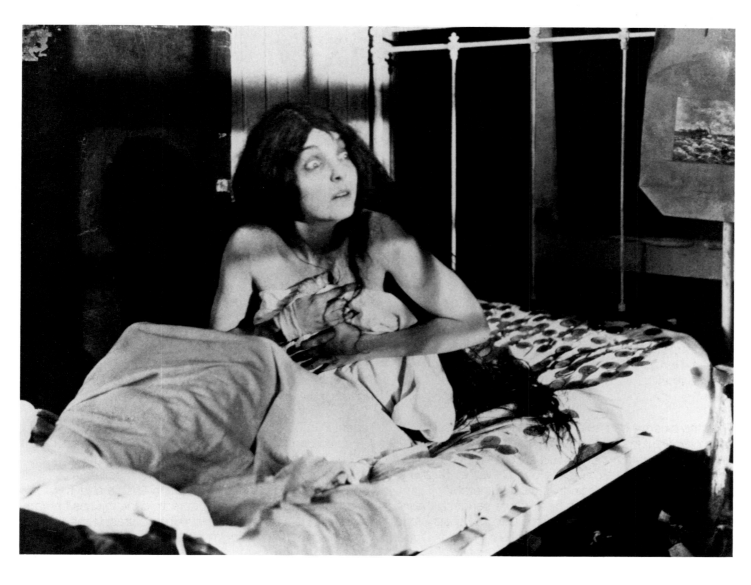

298   Zasu Pitts in the role of Trina, in *Greed*. 1924.

Rendered frigid by her wedding night, she covered her bed every night with pieces of gold to lie on. Stroheim's shooting lasted nine months and cost Metro Goldwyn Meyer $ 470,000. The director dedicated the film to his mother. "Genius," said René Clair, "how many are there in the history of the cinema, who could be so described? Whatever their number, Erich von Stroheim is at their head. He owes nothing to anyone. He died poor, and we are all indebted to him."

woman" life-style, her way of saying direct, sensible things about the cinema as she knew it. "Amoral, but totally without ego," she encapsulated an era, passing through the world of cinema without ever partaking of its pervading silliness. Ado Kyrou wrote that she was the only woman who had the ability to transform any film into a masterpiece; she was the perfect apparition, the dream woman.

Hollywood would never forgive her for was that she had had the time to pass judgment, during her meteoric career, on that processing plant of desire—Hollywood itself. After the German "betrayal," Louise Brooks made no more films, but she was ceaselessly rediscovered, decade after decade, by feverish or Surrealist cinema lovers, not the least of whom was Jean-Luc Godard, with his *Vivre sa vie* ("To Live Your Life").

Lulu in Hollywood

299   Louise Brooks at the time of *Die Büchse der Pandora* ("Pandora's Box") by G. W. Pabst. 1929.

300   The death scene of Fritz Kortner in *Pandora's Box*. 1929.

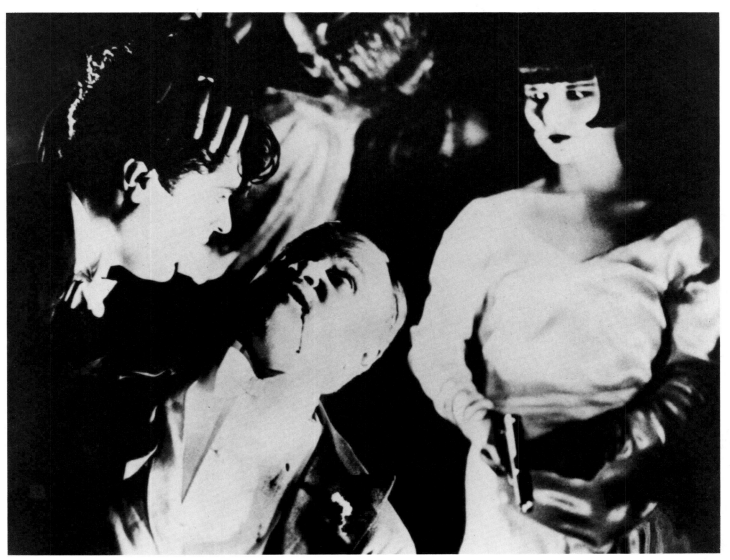

As an actress Louise Brooks literally assaulted the camera—totally, unhesitatingly. The acting that resulted was sublime, in no way resembling an interpretation. It was the antithesis of Garbo.

It was Howard Hawks, a great discoverer of acting talent, who gave her her first major role. She was the girl in *A Girl in Every Port* (1928), supposedly possessed by the sailors, though in fact the contrary was true. At this time, the transfer of stars between Europe and the United States was not difficult. Paramount raised objections, but Louise Brooks accepted an invitation from Pabst to go to Germany and make a film of which the scenario was based on two plays by Frank Wedekind. It was the right decision, for in 1929, in the character of Lulu in *Die Büchse der Pandora* ("Pandora's Box"), she passed into the history of the cinema. She was only twenty-three years old, but she gave Pabst, and many others after him, the feeling that she knew everything about love. She did, in fact, know everything, and was to write it all down in her memoirs *Lulu in Hollywood*: desire, money, men, and the explosive combination of all three. But what

Along with Nana *(Vivre sa vie)* and Lola *(The Blue Angel)*, Lulu was everybody's orphan, always escaping, just out of reach—a real "man-eater". She was the first modern woman. She was mischievous and "couldn't care less-ish," at once angel and demon, bringing together every feminine myth. She was modern, because she was a character in search of identity, and her possibilities were limitless: she displayed her contradictions in complete innocence. Champsaur speaks of her as a "pirouette": Lulu was one woman and every woman— their dream, at least; symbol and synthesis, she embodied the whole of womanhood simply by being herself. In the thirteen years of her brief career, with two or three important films, she left her mark on the era and then went on to observe, in a mocking and lively style, the innumerable repercussions of her enduring legend. With this total freedom, she did not know where she was going—but she went, full speed ahead, in the image of the new decade that was now beginning. And what better way could we find to close the decade than with this "pirouette?"

Comparative Chronology

Year	Political History	Artistic Events	Architecture
1920	Birth of the League of Nations The United States rejects the Versailles Treaty War reparations fixed by the Spa Conference War between Poland and Soviet Russia British Protectorate in Kenya The Bosphorus and the Dardanelles are declared an international zone Prohibition in the United States, Harding President Civil war ends in Russia At the Congrès de Tours, the majority of the French Socialist Party adheres to the Third International and founds the S.F.I.O. (Section française de l'Internationale ouvrière) (French Section of the Workers' International) Zionist colonies are established in Palestine Gandhi's first passive resistance campaign in India.	Moscow exhibition: *The Last Painting Has Been Painted. Constructivist Realist Manifesto* (Published in *De Stijl*, in 1921) First kinetic works by Gabo Neo-Plasticism, Purism (Beginning of the publication of the *L'Esprit Nouveau* review by Ozenfant and Le Corbusier) Arrival of Tzara in Paris. Dada at its apogee Pro Arte in Warsaw Creation of the Société Anonyme, founded in New York by Duchamp, Man Ray and Dreyer to introduce international modern art Creation of the Compagnie des arts français et de la Maîtrise Modigliani dies Grosz fined for "libelous action against the authority of the Reich"	De Klerk: "De Dageraad" group, Amsterdam Finsterlin: Project for a house of meditation Gropius and Taut publish their *Utopic Letters* Tatlin: model of the monument to the Third International Gabo: project for a radio transmitter Malevich: architectural models Vkhutemas school of architecture opened Gabo and Pevsner: *Realist Manifesto* Russia: plan to build electrical power stations voted Oud: Tusschendijken complex in Rotterdam Le Corbusier: project for the Citrohan house Prost: the new town of Rabat in Morocco Creation of the towns of Gdynia in Poland and of Canberra in Australia Soria y Mata dies in Spain
1921	Allies' ultimatum to Germany on war debts Separate German-American peace Kronstadt sailors' mutiny. Famine in Russia War between Soviet Russia and Poland ends with the Riga Treaty Japanese Prime Minister, Haza, assassinated by a Korean student Southern, Catholic and rural Ireland (Eire) becomes the Irish Free State Foundation of the Chinese Communist Party. Sun Yat-sen elected President of the Chinese Republic	Ozenfant, Jeanneret: *Purist Manifesto* November-Gruppe (November Group) Severini: *From Cubism to Classicism* Expressionism spreads to Belgium and mural art in Norway (Sorensen) Klee and Schlemmer teach at the Bauhaus Elie Faure: *L'Art moderne* ("Modern Art") Picasso: *The Three Musicians* Miró's first Paris exhibition Dada in New York: Duchamp signs the Dada manifesto *Dada soulève tout* and the publication of the only number of the *New York Dada* by Duchamps and Man Ray First Max Ernst exhibition *Salon dada* exhibition at the Galerie Montaigne: Breton, Duchamp and Picabia refuse to participate Schwitters: *Bourgeois Reactionary* 5 × 5 = 25 exhibition (Rodchenko, Popova, Exter, Vesnin, etc.) in Moscow	Perret: the church at Raincy, made of uncovered reinforced concrete Mendelsohn: Einstein Tower (Observatory), Potsdam Dudok: Hilversum Town Hall (completed in 1928) Eggerickz and Van der Swaelmen construct two garden cities in Boisfort, a southern suburb of Brussels Van Doesburg is called on, in collaboration with Van Eesteren and Rietveld, to design an artist's house and a private house. The project is not carried out, but takes the form of studies and plans that mark the architectural philosophy of De Stijl Death of Hennebique, whose role in the perfecting and use of reinforced concrete was critical Garnier publishes *Les Grands Travaux de la Ville de Lyon* ("Major Works of the City of Lyons") In *L'Esprit nouveau* No. 4 Le Corbusier's idea for tower towns appears, in total opposition to Wright's concept of the garden city
1922	First meeting of the International Court of Justice at the Hague Pius XI succeeds Benedict XV Egypt becomes independent under the reign of Fuad I Gandhi sentenced to six years in prison Rapallo Treaty between Germany and Russia The League of Nations gives Great Britain a mandate over Palestine	Siqueiros Manifesto (Mexico) for an art of the people Valori Plastici in Italy Picasso: *Figurative Forms* Constructivist manifesto by Gan *Lichtrequisit* by Moholy-Nagy and *Spatial Construction* by Naum Gabo Van Doesburg at the Bauhaus Dasburg writes *Cubism – its Rise and Influence*	Wright: Imperial Hotel, Tokyo. Earthquake-proof, it rested on a lake of mud Perret: town towers project Freyssinet: Saint-Pierre-de-Vouvray bridge Competition for the *Chicago Tribune* skyscraper: projects by Gropius, Taut and others. First prize: John Mead Howless + Hood. Second prize: Saarinen Le Corbusier builds a villa at Vaucresson and a

Design – Inventions – Discoveries	Cinema – Photography – Graphic Arts	Cultural Events	Year
Rietveld: furniture, lamps Malevich: Leningrad art pottery Inkhuk, Vkhutemas and Unovis founded in Soviet Russia Remington typewriter German telephone London Underground logo Spread of petrol pumps First kinetic work by Gabo Agitprop, Rosta Windows The Ballets Russes in Paris Rolf de Maré's Ballets Suédois First French edition of *Vogue* First broadcasting station (USA–G.B.) First acoustic recordings on records (G.B.) Superheterodyne radio receiver (USA) First passenger air services between Paris, London, Brussels, Amsterdam Use of Mercurochrome (G.B.) Eddington: *Space, Time and Gravity* Michelson measures the diameter of Betelgeuse	L'Herbier: *L'Homme du Large* (France) Wegener and Galeen: *The Golem* (Germany) Griffith: *Way Down East* (USA) Niblo: *The Mark of Zorro* (USA) Sjöström: *The Phantom Chariot, Clay, Thy Soul Shall Bear Witness* In the United States, Winnie Winkle is created by Branner; to appear in France in 1923 under the title *Bicot* *Felix the Cat*, by Pat Sullivan, created in 1917 for the cartoon cinema, becomes a strip cartoon	Hamsun (Norway) Nobel Prize for Literature Jünger: *Storms of Steel* Breton and Soupault: *Les Champs magnétiques* ("Magnetic Fields"), first texts using automatic writing Fitzgerald: *This Side of Paradise* Pound: *Umbra* Lewis: *Main Street* Gide: *Corydon* Valéry: *Le Cimetière Marin* ("Naval Cemetery"); *Album de vers anciens* ("Album of Ancient Verse") Colette: *Chéri* Mansfield: *Bliss* Christie: *The Mysterious Affair at Styles* (the first detective novel) O'Neill: *Beyond the Horizon* and *The Emperor Jones* Collet launches the Groupe des Six: Honegger, Milhaud, Taillefere, Auric and Durey, Poulenc joins later, Cocteau is their leader Stravinsky: *Symphonies of Wind Instruments; Pulcinella* Milhaud: *Le Bœuf sur le toit* ("The Ox on the Roof") Satie: *Musique d'ameublement; Socrate* Ravel: *Waltz*	**1920**
Werner Graeff motorcycle (De Stijl) Thompson machine gun Coco Chanel imposes the sporting fashion The Dolly Sisters appear at the Paris Casino Magnetron (USA) First broadcasts in Italy Anti-knock petrol Einstein wins the Nobel Prize for Physics for his theory of relativity	Feyder: *L'Atlantide* ("Atlantis") (France) L'Herbier: *El Dorado* (France) Delluc: *Fièvre* ("Fever") (France) Buchowetzky: *Danton* (Germany) Lang: *The Weary Death* (Germany) Lupu-Pick: *The Rail* (Germany) Chaplin: *The Kid* (USA) Ingram: *The Four Horsemen of the Apocalypse* (USA) Flaherty: *Nanook of the North* (USA) Gardine and Pudovkin: *Hunger... Hunger... Hunger* (Russia) Von Stroheim: *Foolish Wives* (USA) Christensen: *Witchcraft Through the Ages* (Sweden) Sjöström: *Love's Crucible* (Sweden) First Man Ray exhibition at the Six Gallery Berenice Abbott moves to Paris	A. France (France), Nobel Prize for Literature Jung: *Psychologische Typen* ("Psychological Types") Pirandello: *Six Characters in Search of an Author* Cocteau: *Les Mariés de la tour Eiffel* ("The Eiffel Tower Couple") D.H. Lawrence: *Women in Love; The Lost Girl* Huxley: *Chrome Yellow* Pound: *Cantos* Dos Passos: *Three Soldiers* Woolf: *Monday or Tuesday* (essays) O'Neill: *Anna Christie* Yeats: *The Second Coming* Maugham: *The Circle* Čapek: *The Universal Robots of Rossum*. (Čapek is the inventor of the word robot, from the root of the Slav verb meaning "work.")	**1921**
Breuer: wooden armchair Keller: cradle Bogler: teapot Stepanova: Constructivist theater costumes Meyerhold's Constructivist productions in Moscow Popova: Constructivist stage equipment for *Le Cocu magnifique* ("The Magnificent Cuckold") First broadcasts in France and Great Britain Automobile radios (USA)	Gance: *La Roue* ("The Wheel") (France) Delluc: *La Femme de nulle part* ("The Woman from Nowhere") (France) Feyder: *Crainquebille* (France) Von Gerlach: *Vanina* (Germany) Murnau: *Nosferatu the Vampire* and *The Land of Fire* (Germany) Lang: *Dr. Mabuse* (Germany) Robison: *Warning Shadows* (Germany)	Benavente (Spain), Nobel Prize for Literature Proust dies Joyce: *Ulysses*, banned for obscenity in England and the United States; the original language version first appeared in Paris, published by Shakespeare and Co. Wittgenstein: *Tractatus Logico-Philosophicus* Margueritte: *La Garçonne* Cocteau: *Thomas l'Imposteur; Antigone*	**1922**

Year	Political History	Artistic Events	Architecture
1922	The Fascists march on Rome. Mussolini named Head of Government by Victor Emmanuel III Mustapha Kemal, victorious in the War of Independence against the Greeks, abolishes the Sultanate Creation of the federal-type Union of Soviet Socialist Republics (USSR), Stalin in power	Meyerhold's Constructivist production in Moscow Man Ray: Rayograms Rodchenko and Stepanova turn to photography Heckel's frescoes in Erfurt Kandinsky leaves Russia for Weimar. He is appointed teacher at the Bauhaus, where he applies the ideas he was unable to put across at the Inkhuk El Lissitzky accompanies the Russian exhibition to Berlin. He makes contact with the Bauhaus. He publishes *The Story of Two Squares* Split between Tzara and Breton Following their return to Poland, Strzemiński and his wife Kobro, both pupils of Malevich, elaborate Unism, with the aim of going further than Constructivism The Berlin exhibition marks the beginning of the exodus of Russian artists escaping the regime, such as Gabo, Pevsner, El Lissitzky, Puni and others	house in Paris for Ozenfant. He presents his plan "for a contemporary town of three million inhabitants" Bourgeois builds the rue du Cubisme in Brussels Stam works, until 1924, on a project for overpasses for Amsterdam
1923	Franco-Belgian troops occupy the Ruhr to obtain payment of war reparations from Germany Inflation reaches its highest level in Germany Hitler fails in his Munich Putsch. Sentenced to five years imprisonment, he serves only one year, during which he writes *Mein Kampf* The Treaty of Lausanne returns the Bosphorus and the Dardanelles to Turkey USA: Vice-President Coolidge succeeds Harding on the latter's death Rivera dictatorship in Spain Mustapha Kemal becomes President of the Turkish Republic George II of Greece is deposed by the military forces, the Republic is proclaimed Tokyo destroyed by an earthquake	Monet: *Waterlilies* Kandinsky: *Circles in a Circle* Grosz: *Ecce Homo* Masson: first automatic drawings Schlemmer: mechanical ballets First exhibition of the Bauhaus's work Moholy-Nagy at the Bauhaus Van Doesburg moves to Paris, where the Effort Moderne Gallery is exhibiting De Stijl Exhibition of American art in Paris: Singer, Sargent, Dodge, Macknight, Homer, Manship and others Archipenko moves to the USA Albers begins to teach at the Bauhaus Rodchenko publishes the review *Lef* with Maiakovskii, Osip and Lily Brik, Stepanova and Tretiakov	Death of Eiffel Le Corbusier publishes *Vers une architecture nouvelle* ("Towards a New Architecture") and completes the La Roche building Rietveld: Dr. Schröder's house in Utrecht Höger: Chili house in Hamburg Häring: Garkan farm Van Doesburg and Van Eesteren: plans for houses Mallet-Stevens: Noailles villa in Hyères Perry: first studies in "neighborhood units" Wright: Lowes, Storer, Millard and Taggart houses Schindler: Pueblo Rihera courts, La Jolla
1924	Death of Lenin. The struggle for power between Stalin and Trotsky begins USSR recognized by France and Great Britain First MacDonald Labour Government in Great Britain In France, victory for the Radical coalition Churchill becomes Chancellor of the Exchequer under the Baldwin Government The "Geneva Protocol" is signed at the League of Nations In the United States, Congress tightens immigration controls The Morgan Bank lends money to France to offset inflation	Kandinsky, Klee, Feininger and Jawlensky form Die Blauen Vier ("The Blue Four") Exhibition of the Laethem-Saint-Martin group Tzara: *Seven Dada Manifestos* illustrated by Picabia, Miró and others Founding of the Prague Linguistic Circle Van Doesburg uses the first of the diagonal lines in painting which are to lead him to his theory of Elementarism Vantongerloo: *Construction within an Inscribed and Circumscribed Circle* Brancusi: *The Beginning of the World* and *Sculpture for the Blind* Rouault retrospective at Druet Breton: *Manifeste du Surréalisme* ("Surrealist Manifesto") Léger and Ozenfant open a free studio Rosenburg publishes the *Bulletin de l'Effort Moderne* ("Newsletter of the Effort Moderne") Mabille, Soupault, Péret and Breton found *La Révolution surréaliste* ("The Surrealist Revolution")	Malevich: *Architectons* Oud: Hoek van Holland workers' city and the Café De Unie in Rotterdam Gropius publishes *Internationale Architektur* Behrens: administrative building for the chemical factories in Höchst Kiesler: project for the "endless house" Steiner constructs the Dornach Goetheanum in reinforced concrete De Koninck: his own house in Uccle, using reinforced concrete Neutra: project for Rush City Reformed (worked on until 1935) Wright: Freeman house, Los Angeles Schindler: Packard house Perret: Grenoble orientation tower Sauvage: living unit with shared services in Paris Le Corbusier: House-studios in Boulogne-sur-Seine French law imposes a development plan on all towns Sullivan dies

Design – Inventions – Discoveries	Cinema – Photography – Graphic Arts	Cultural Events	Year
Insulin treatment for diabetics (G.B.) De Broglie's theories on the mechanics of waves published Nobel Prize for Physics to Bohr for his research into atomic structure and for Chemistry to Aston for his research on isotopes	Chaplin: *The Pilgrim* (USA) Stiller: *The Old Manor House* (Sweden) First technicolor film by Kalmus: *The Toll of the Sea* (USA) The Hayes Code, censoring the cinema, is introduced Man Ray publishes his first Rayograms and Moholy-Nagy his Photograms, each individually, by placing three-dimensional objects directly onto light-sensitive paper Steichen burns his canvases and becomes a *Vogue* photographer	Martin du Gard: *Les Thibault* Mauriac: *Le Baiser au lépreux* Valéry: *Charmes* Eliot: *The Waste Land* Rilke: *Sonnets for Orpheus* Huxley: *Earthly Remains* O'Neill: *The Hairy Ape* Woolf: *Jacob's Room* Lewis: *Babbitt* Fitzgerald: *The Beautiful and the Damned* Pirandello: *Henry IV* Rilke: *Sonnets for Orpheus* Gorky: *My Universities* Capek: *The Makropoulos Affair* Brecht: *Baal* Ravel: *Violin Sonata* Williams: *Pastoral Symphony* Nielsen: *Symphony No. 5* Howard Carter discovers the tomb of Tutankhamen	**1922**
Rietveld: Berlin chair Gropius: furniture Jucker and Wagenfeld: office lamps Introduction of the new Bauhaus typography Model T Ford Albers: toys Schlemmer: Mechanical Ballets The Ziegfeld Follies In Capek's play *R.U.R.*, Kiesler introduces the use of film projection; the use of the Belinograph television, to transmit photographs via wireless telegraph, invented by the Frenchman Belin, is common throughout the world Autogyro, ancestor of the helicopter (Spain) Diesel truck (German) Hearing aids for the deaf (G.B.) Le Mans 24 hours race First two-sided Victor records (USA) Calmette and Guérin perfect the B.C.G. anti-tuberculosis vaccine (France)	Cruze: *The Covered Wagon* (USA) Epstein: *Cœur fidèle* ("Faithful Heart") (France) Feyder: *Visages d'enfants* ("Children's Faces") (France) Lang: *The Nibelungen* (Germany) Grüne: *The Street* (Germany) Chaplin: *Public Opinion* De Mille: *The Ten Commandments* (USA) Von Stroheim: *Greed* (USA) Stiller: *Gösta Berling's Saga* (Sweden) Léger executes the sets for Cendrars *La Création du Monde* ("The Creation of the World") and L'Herbier's *L'Inhumaine* ("The New Enchantment") Man Ray carries out *Le retour à la raison* ("The Return to Reason"), for the *Cœur à Barbe* Dada evening Sheeler working at *Vogue* Rabier: *Gédéon le canard* ("Gideon the Duck") Schmidt: Poster for the Bauhaus Rodchenko and Maiakovskii work on posters and carry out their first photomontages Constructivist photos appear in the review *Lef*	Yeats (Ireland), Nobel Prize for Literature Freud: *Das Ich und das Es* ("The Ego and the Id") Maritain: *Elements of Philosophy* Katherine Mansfield dies Radiguet: *Le Diable au corps* ("Devil in Flesh") Romains: *Knock* Cocteau: *Le Grand Ecart; Plein chant* Svevo: *The Confessions of Zeno* Valéry: *Eupalinos ou l'architect* Hemingway: *Three Stories and Ten Poems* D.H. Lawrence: *Kangaroo* Huxley (Aldous): *Antic Hay* Stevens: *Harmonium* Block experiments with quarter tones in his *Piano Quintet* Schönberg: *5 Pieces for Piano*, Op. 25, using a twelve-tone system Milhaud: *The Creation of the World* O'Casey: *The Shadow of a Gunman* Hindemith: *Marienleben* Sibelius: *Symphony No. 6* First recordings of Duke Ellington	**1923**
Wagenfeld: Pyrex teapot, office lamp Bayer: kiosk project Cover of the *Blok* review (Poland) Breuer: "Wassily" armchair (for Kandinsky), conference chairs for the Dessau Bauhaus Kuau: tea-making machine El Lissitzky: advertisement for Pelikan carbon paper Popova and Stepanova design textiles and clothing in a Moscow factory The Ballets Suédois present *Relâche*, ballet by Picabia and Satie together with René Clair's film Diaghilev: *Le Train Bleu*, Cocteau's ballet, with sets by Picasso, costumes by Chanel, music by Auric Invention of the loudspeaker Diesel locomotive (USA) First automobile highway (*autostrada*) (Milan-Varese) First insecticide Spin dryer (USA)	Léger: *The Mechanical Ballet* (France) Clair, with Duchamp and Man Ray: *Entr'acte* ("Intermission") – short film L'Herbier: *L'Inhumaine* ("The New Enchantment") (France) Leni: *The Wax Figure Collection* (Germany) Murnau: *The Last Laugh* (Germany) Gerlach: *The Chronical of Grieshuus* (Germany) Ford: *The Iron Horse* (USA) Keaton: *Sherlock Jr.* (USA) Keaton and Crisp: *The Navigator* (USA) Walsh: *The Thief of Bagdad* (USA) Malander: *The Cursed* (Sweden) Kuleshov: *Extraordinary Adventures of Mr. West in the Land of the Bolsheviks* (USSR) Protazanov: *Aelita* (USSR) Gray: *Little Orphan Annie,* melodramatic strip cartoon recounting the adventures of a little orphan girl and her dog Sandy	Reymont (Poland), Nobel Prize for Literature Kafka dies Conrad dies and *Heart of Darkness* is published Mann: *The Magic Mountain* Bulgakov: *The White Guardsman* Gide: *Si le grain ne meurt* (1920, 1924) ("If it Die") Cendrars: *Feuilles de Route, Kodak* Saint-John Perse: *Anabasis* Radiguet: *Le Bal du comte d'Orgel* ("The Ball at Count Orgel's") Mauriac: *Génitrix* Breton: *Manifeste du surréalisme* ("Surrealist Manifesto") Forster: *Passage to India* Shaw: *Joan of Arc* O'Casey: *Juno and the Paycock* Gershwin: *Rhapsody in Blue* Strauss: *Intermezzo* Berg: *Chamber Concerto* Schönberg: *Erwartung* Respighi: *Pines of Rome* Janáček: *The Makropoulos Affair* Honegger: *Pacific 231*	**1924**

Year	Political History	Artistic Events	Architecture
1925	Hindenburg elected President of the German Republic Evacuation of the Ruhr Mussolini announces his intention to establish a dictatorship Trotsky relieved of his office in the USSR Forty-five nations meeting in Geneva sign a convention against the use of poisonous gas in times of war The Locarno Pact recognizes that Alsace-Lorraine is no longer part of Germany. Demilitarization of the Rhineland. Entry of Germany to the League of Nations Death of Sun Yat-sen Abd el-Krim attacks French posts in Morocco	Paris: International Exhibition of Modern Industrial and Decorative Arts Non-imitative Plastic Arts Exhibition *Neue Sachlichkeit* ("New Objectivity") Exhibition at the Mannheim Kunsthalle and at Dresden Ortega y Gasset publishes *Deshumanizacion del arte* ("The Dehumanization of Art") The Bauhaus reopens at Dessau Delaunay-Léger decoration for the Decorative Arts Exhibition El Lissitzky and Arp: *Kunstismen* ("The Isms of Art") Epstein: *Rima* Mondrian withdraws from De Stijl because of Van Doesburg's stand on the use of diagonals Le Corbusier and Ozenfant publish *La peinture moderne* ("Modern Painting") In New York, Neumann founds the New York Art Circle Léger exhibits in New York	International Exhibition of Modern Industrial and Decorative Arts in Paris. Perret: theater; Le Corbusier: Esprit nouveau Pavilion and Voisin plan for Paris; Horta: Belgian Pavilion; Hoffmann: Austrian Pavilion; Melnikov: USSR Pavilion; Garnier: Lyons Pavilion; Sauvage: Printemps Pavilion; Mallet-Stevens: Tourism Pavilion; Ruhlmann: Hôtel du collectionneur (private house of a collector); Mallet-Stevens, Chareau, Delaunay, Léger, etc: "A French Embassy" In the Grand Palais, Kiesler exhibits his project for a "Space City" Van Doesburg publishes *Grundbegriffe der neuen Gestaltung* ("Basic Concepts of the New Forms") in the *Bauhausbücher* (Bauhaus Books) Van de Wijdeveld publishes *The Life and Work of the American Architect F.L. Wright* Oud: Workers' village of Kiefhoek, Rotterdam Gropius: new Bauhaus buildings in Dessau Maillart employs a stiffened arch for the Val Tschiel bridge Taut and Wagner build the Britz apartment blocks near Berlin Le Corbusier builds the Frugès city in Bordeaux-Pessac and publishes *Urbanisme* Warchavchik's Futurist manifesto in Brazil Death of Rudolph Steiner, more a philosopher than an architect
1926	Ibn Saud unites two regions, thus forming Saudi Arabia, of which he becomes the first king in 1932 Steel workers go on strike in Great Britain Marshal Pilsudski's Military *coup d'etat* in Poland Morocco: End of the Riff war, Abd el-Krim deported to La Réunion Collapse of the franc and formation by Poincaré of the "National Union" Government, excluding Communists and Socialists USSR: Stalin triumphs over left-wing opposition and expels Trotsky and Zinoviev from the Politburo The Tirana Treaty turns Albania into an Italian quasi-protectorate Hirohito Emperor of Japan	Paris: Academy of Scandinavian arts Milan: *Prima Espozione del Novecento italiano* ("First Twentieth Century Italian Art Exhibition") Calder arrives in Paris. He works on his sculpture in wire, *The Circle* Pevsner: *Construction* Vantongerloo: *Construction of Related Volumes Derived from the Elipsoid* O'Keeffe: *Abstracts* Kandinsky: *Dot, line, surface* At the International Dresden Exhibition, El Lissitzky gathers non-figurative works by Léger, Mondrian, Moholy-Nagy, Picabia and Gabo. The American section includes Becker, Burroughs, Davies, Glackens, Halpert, Kent, Kuhn, Maurer, Pascin, Sheeler, Sloan and Weber The International Exhibition of Modern Art, organized at the Brooklyn Museum, includes works by Malevich and Kandinsky At Gropius's invitation, Malevich remains at the Bauhaus in Dessau until 1927	May: group of workers' houses in the Römerstadt area of Frankfurt Mies van der Rohe: K. Liebknecht and Rosa Luxemburg commemorative monument In Belgium, Van de Velde organizes the Ecole de la Cambre. De Koninck: house for the painter Lenglet in Uccle Kramer: Bijenkorf shop in The Hague Van Doesburg, Arp and Sophie Taeuber: the Aubette in Strasburg Le Corbusier: Ternisien and Cook buildings at Boulogne-sur-Seine and the "Palais du Peuple" dormitory for the Salvation Army in Paris Mallet-Stevens: group of Cubist houses (rue Mallet-Stevens) in Paris and the Saint-Jean-de-Luz Casino Moser: Saint-Antoine church in Basle Yamada: Tokyo telegraph office Founding of the Group of Seven in Italy Charkov: first Moscow radio tower Ginsburg: government building in Alma-Ata Loos: Tzara house in Paris New York International Exhibition: Kiesler exhibits his "endless house" Lavedan publishes *Qu'est-ce que l'urbanisme?* ("What is Town Planning?") Gaudí dies
1927	In the middle of civil war. Chiang Kai-shek, at the head of the moderate section of the Guomindang (nationalist party), splits from the radicals at Hangzhou and forms a provisional, anti-communist government Mao Zedong creates the Peoples' Liberation Army Trotsky excluded from the Party Franco-British agreement on war debts French troops leave the Saar	Malevich publishes *The World Without Objects*. He visits Poland and Germany, where he exhibits around a hundred canvases never to return to the USSR Faure: *L'Esprit des Formes* ("The Spirit of Forms") Ernst: *They Have Slept too Long in the Forest* Böcklin exhibition in Berlin European exhibition of abstract painting in Mannheim: Klee, Archipenko, Braque, Delaunay, Gleizes, Feininger, Kandinsky, Léger, El Lissitzky,	Tokyo *Asahi Shimbun* newspaper building The Werkbund entrusts the organization of the Weissenhof city, near Stuttgart, to Van der Rohe. Le Corbusier builds two houses with roof terraces there, Oud some row houses, Mies van der Rohe some collective apartment buildings, Stam some rows of two-story houses, Behrens an apartment block with a tower. There are also works by Gropius, Bourgeois, Hilberseimer, Taut, Scharoun, Frank

Design – Inventions – Discoveries	Cinema – Photography – Graphic Arts	Cultural Events	Year
International Exhibition of Modern Industrial and Decorative Arts in Paris: furniture by Ruhlmann, Süe and Mare, Marty, Dunand, Groult, Jeanneret and Perriand, Thonet and others. China, glass, goldsmiths' work, jewelry by Bonfils, Chevalier, Templier, Luce, Buthaud, Jean and Raoul Dufy, Puyforçat, Daum, Lalique, Bagge, Léveillé, Fouquet, Hoffman, Goulden, Marinot, Linossier, Cassandre, Sandoz, Lambert-Rucki, Fauré, etc. First tubular bent-metal chairs by Breuer, Stam and Mies van der Rohe Jourdain: smoking car Oud: facade of the Café De Unie in Rotterdam The *Black Revue* and Josephine Baker First traffic lights (G.B.) Electric phonograph (USA) First refrigerators on sale IBM horizontal sorter (USA) Milliken discovers cosmic rays	Gance: *Napoleon* (France) L'Herbier: *Feu Mathias Pascal* ("The Late Mathias Pascal, The Living Dead Man") (France) Lang: *Metropolis* (Germany) Dupont: *Varieties* (Germany) Pabst: *The Joyless Street* (Germany) Dreyer: *Thou Shalt Honor Thy Wife, The Master of the House* (Denmark) Chaplin: *The Gold Rush* (USA) Cooper and Schoedsak: *Exodus* (USA) Keaton: *Go West* (USA) Lubitsch: *Lady Windermere's Fan* (USA) Vidor: *The Big Parade* (USA) Eisenstein: *Battleship Potemkin* (USSR) Eisenstein: *Stachka* ("Strike") (USSR) Kuleshov: *The Death Ray* Tatlin accepts a post in the Kiev Theater and Cinema department Berenice Abbott meets Atget at Man Ray's studio, where she is working as assistant Hoyningen-Huene is appointed head of photography at *Vogue* Saint-Ogan: *Zig et Puce* (France) Fleischer: "Out of the Inkwell" film series (USA) Colin: poster for the *Black Revue*	Shaw (G.B.), Nobel Prize for Literature Suicide of Yesenin Hitler: *Mein Kampf* Kafka: *The Trial* Gorky: *The Artamonovs* Jünger: *The Copse; Fire and Blood* Fitzgerald: *The Great Gatsby* Stein: *The Making of Americans* Dreiser: *An American Tragedy* Loos: *Gentlemen Prefer Blondes* Lewis: *Arrowsmith* Woolf: *Mrs. Dalloway* Huxley (Aldous): *Those Barren Leaves* Montale: *Ossi disepia* ("Cuttle bone") Frondaie: *L'Homme à l'Hispano* Cocteau: *Orphée* ("Orpheus") Cendrars: *L'Or* ("Gold") Coward: *Weekend* Weill: *Violin Concerto* Busoni: *Dr. Faustus* Ravel uses a jazzo-flute and a wind machine in *L'Enfant et les sortilèges* Schönberg: *Piano Suite; Wind quintet* Gershwin: *Concerto in F for Piano and Orchestra* Sibelius: *Tapiola* Satie dies The Bible versus Darwin, or the "monkey trial": fundamentalists (conservative protestants) bring a lawsuit against Darwin's theory of evolution	**1925**
Brandt: ceiling light-fitting Schlemmer: *Triadic Ballet* American products begin to flood the world: bras, vibromassage devices, electric hairdryers, imitation silk stockings, etc. First television broadcast (G.B.) Automatic toaster (USA) Fog lights (USA) Tungsten carbide (USA) Heisenberg, Born and Jordan *Quantum Mechanics* Commander Byrd flies over the North Pole	Feyder: *Carmen* (France) Poirier: *La Croisière noire* ("The Black Cruise") (France) Renoir: *Nana* Fanck: *The Holy Mountain* (Germany) Murnau: *Faust* (Germany) Galeen: *The Student of Prague* (Germany) Keaton and Bruckman: *The General* (USA) Flaherty: *Moana* (USA) Niblo: *Ben-Hur* (USA) Kunigasa: *A Page of Madness* (Japan) Pudovkin: *Mother* (USSR) Kozintsev and Trauberg: *The Cloak* (USSR) Evans goes to Paris to take courses at the Sorbonne First number of *Amazing Stories*	Deledda (Italy), Nobel Prize for Literature Freud: *Die Frage der Laienanalyse* ("The Question of Lay Analysis") Jung: "The Unconscious in the Normal and Pathological Mind" Rilke dies Kafka: *The Castle* T.E. Lawrence: *The Seven Pillars of Wisdom* D.H. Lawrence: *The Plumed Serpent* Huxley: *Two or Three Graces* Hemingway: *The Sun Also Rises* O'Casey: *The Plough and the Stars* Lorca: *Romancero Gitano* Cendrars: *Morgavagine* Eluard: *Capitale de la douleur* ("The Capital of Pain") Weill: *The Protagonist* Lambert: *Romeo and Juliet* Prokofiev: *Romeo and Juliet* Puccini: *Turandot* Hindemith: *Cardillac* Kodály: *Háry János* Varèse: *Ionisation; Intégrales* Armstrong's *Hot Five* (jazz)	**1926**
Haring: publication on the reorientation of the applied arts Gray: "Transat" chair Mies van der Rohe: first tubular chair Diaghilev's ballet *La Chatte* ("The Cat") with stage design by Pevsner and Gabo presented in Paris and then in New York Death of Isadora Duncan Lindberg completes first non-stop Atlantic crossing	Cavalcanti: *En Rade* ("Sea Fever") (France) Clair: *Un Chapeau de Paille d'Italie* ("An Italian Straw Hat") (France) Grémillon: *Maldone* (France) Feyder: *Thérèse Raquin* (Germany) Pabst: *The Love of Jeanne Ney* (Germany) Rahn: *The Tragedy of the Street* (Gemany) Ruttmann: *Berlin, Symphony of a Great City* (Germany)	Bergson (France), Nobel Prize for Literature Fauré: *L'Esprit des formes* ("The Spirit of Forms") (Conclusion of his *History of Art*) Forster: *Aspects of the Novel* Yeats: *Seven Poems and a Fragment* Gorky: *The Life of Klim Samgin* (1927–1936) Gide: *Voyage au Congo* Benda: *La Trahison des clercs* ("The Treason of the Intellectuals") Mauriac: *Thérèse Desqueyroux*	**1927**

Year	Political History	Artistic Events	Architecture
1927	International demonstrations in protest at the execution in the United States of two militant anarchists, Sacco and Vanzetti Mustapha Kemal reelected	Moholy-Nagy, Mondrian, Picasso, Schwitters and others Juan Gris dies Davis: *Egg-Beater No. 2* The Machine-Age Exhibition, organized in New York by *The Little Review*, includes photos, paintings, sculpture and architectural projects by Van Doesburg, Pevsner, Gabo, Arp, Archipenko, Lipchitz, Zadkine, Demuth, Man Ray and others	Gropius: total theater project Berendt publishes *The Victory of the New Architectural Style* Hilberseimer publishes *New International Architecture* Plaz publishes *The Latest Architecture* Ginsburg builds collective workers' houses in Moscow, Melnikov six working men's clubs and his own house Leonidov designs the project for the Lenin Institute Malevich's *Die gegenstandslose Welt* ("The World Without Objects") appears in the Bauhaus publications Oud: working-class houses in Rotterdam Brinkman, Van der Vlugt and Stam: Van Nelle factory. Competition for the League of Nations Building in Geneva Moser: reinforced concrete factory in Basle Neutra: Lovell Health House (finished in 1929) in Los Angeles M.I.A.R. (Movimento Italiano per l'Architectura Razionale) founded in Italy Aalto: Library in Viipuri, Finland
1928	Trotsky exiled to Alma-Ata The Poincaré franc: worth a fifth of its 1914 value Nehru founds the Indian National Congress Albania becomes a monarchy, with Zogu I at its head Stalin puts forward the first Five Year Plan for the Soviet Union, with the development of heavy industry and the collectivization of agriculture as its aims Chiang Kai-shek elected President of the Chinese Republic by the Guomindang. He takes over Peking Hoover succeeds Coolidge as President of the United States The Havana Pan-American Conference raises the question of the hegemony of the United States, after the American intervention in Nicaragua	Meyer becomes director of the Bauhaus Exhibition: *Le Surréalisme existe-t-il?* ("Does Surrealism Exist?") shows works by Arp, De Chirico, Ernst, Malkine, Masson, Miró, Picabia, Roy, and Tanguy Bonnard retrospective in Paris Ernst exhibition in Berlin El Lissitzky, veritable Constructivist missionary, takes the good word across the whole of Europe, to Cologne, Vienna, Frankfurt, Stuttgart, Paris. He meets Mondrian, Le Corbusier, Léger and others Ozenfant: foundation of *L'Art moderne* ("Modern Art") Breton: *Le surrealisme et la Peinture* ("Surrealism and Painting") Basle exhibition of the Dessau Bauhaus, with works by Albers, Feininger, Kandinsky, Klee and Schlemmer De Chirico, Villon and Bonnard retrospective exhibitions in New York The U. S. Customs finally agree to grant entry to Brancusi's *Bird in Space* as a "work of art," without payment of duty	First Five Year Plan in the USSR C.I.A.M. (International Congress of Modern Architecture) founded; its first chairman is Moser and the first meeting is held at La Sarraz, Switzerland Chareau: glass house in Paris Mendelsohn: Schocken shop in Stuttgart Gropius: apartment blocks in Karlsruhe Meyer director of the Bauhaus Bartning: Pressa church in Cologne Freyssinet invents pre-stressed concrete Guimard: house in rue Greuze Garnier: living accommodation in the Etats-Unis area of Lyons Prost works on the layout of the Paris region, providing, under the Loucheur Act, for a program of 260,000 lodgings in five years Bijvoet and Duiker: reinforced concrete sanatorium in the Netherlands Wils: Amsterdam Olympic stadium Buckminster Fuller: "4-D" house Stein and H. Wright: first garden city in Radburn, New Jersey Holabird and Roche: *Daily News* Building, Chicago Schindler: Sachs Apartments, Los Angeles and Wolfe house, Avalon, Catalina Island In Italy, Fillia organizes the first exhibition of Futurist architecture under the patronage of Mussolini Ponti launches the *Domus* review Horta: Brussels Palais des Beaux-Arts Jansen builds the city of Ankara in Turkey Aalto: *Turun Sanomat* newspaper building in Finland In the USSR, Ginsburg builds the minimum one-family habitat building Howard and Mackintosh die
1929	Mussolini recognizes the Pope's supremacy over the Vatican State. The single Fascist party wins the elections Bloody 1st of May in Berlin In Great Britain, Macdonald forms the second Labour Cabinet	Foundation of the Museum of Modern Art in New York Swedish Hilmstäd group Moore: *Reclining Figure* Freundlich: *Elevation* First Dalí exhibition in Paris	Second C.I.A.M. congress at Frankfurt USSR: WOPRA (All-Russian Society of Proletarian Architects) founded Poëte: *Introduction à l'urbanisme* ("Introduction to Town Planning") Dubreuil: *Standards*

Design – Inventions – Discoveries	Cinema – Photography – Graphic Arts	Cultural Events	Year
First talking film: *The Jazz Singer* with Al Jolson Invention of the electric juke box (USA) First transatlantic telephone line First tape recording (USA) First diesel airplane engine (USA)	Brown: *The Flesh and the Devil* (USA) Chaplin: *The Circus* (USA) Arrival of talkies with Crosland's film: *The Jazz Singer* (USA) De Mille: *The King of Kings* (USA) Hawks: *A Girl in Every Port* (USA) Murnau: *Sunrise* (USA) Von Sternberg: *Underworld* (USA) Von Stroheim: *The Wedding March* (USA) Ito: *Chuji's Travel Journal* (Japan) Eisenstein: *October, 10 Days That Shook the World* (USSR) Pudovkin: *The End of Saint Petersburg* (USSR) Preobrazhenskii: *The Village of Sin* (USSR) Kertész's first exhibition in Paris *Ten Years of Soviet Photography* exhibition in Paris Cassandre: *Nord Express, L'Etoile du Nord*	Hesse: *Steppenwolf* ("The Steppe Wolf") Hemingway: *The Snows of Kilimanjaro; Men without Women* (short stories) Woolf: *To the Lighthouse* Williamson: *Tarka the Otter* Lewis (Sinclair): *Elmer Gantry* Stravinsky: *Oedipus Rex* Křenek: *Johnny Strikes Up* (jazz opera) Respighi: *La campana sommersa* (based on Hauptmann's *The Sunken Bell*) Antheil: *Mechanical Ballet* Jolson: *Sonny Boy*	**1927**
Le Corbusier: armchair in leather and chromed steel, chaise-longue De Chirico: sets for *Le Bal* The automatic telephone spreads throughout the world Bread-cutting machine (USA) Television camera (USA) First video recording (G.B.) Electronic projection tube (USA) Electric razor (USA) Liquid fuel rocket (USA) Differential calculator (USA) Nautical sounding-line (USA) Fleming discovers penicillin (G.B.)	Buñuel and Dalí: *Un Chien Andalou* ("An Andalusian Dog") (France) Dreyer: *La Passion de Jeanne d'Arc* ("The Passion of Joan of Arc") (France) Epstein: *La Chute de la Maison Usher* ("The Fall of the House of Usher") (France) Renoir: *La Petite Marchande d'allumettes* ("The Little Match Girl") (France) Tourneur: *L'Equipage* ("The Crew") (France) Pabst: *Die Büchse der Pandora* ("Pandora's Box") (Germany) May: *The Prisoner's Song* (Germany) Borzage: *Street Angel* Sjöström: *The Wind* (USA) Von Sternberg: *The Docks of New York* (USA) Von Stroheim: *Queen Kelly* (USA) Vidor: *The Crowd* (USA) Iwerks and Disney: *Mickey Mouse* animated cartoon (USA) Machaty: *Seduction* (Czech) Dovzhenko: *Zvenigora* (USSR) Pudovkin: *The Heir to Genghis-Khan* (USSR) First Paris Salon dedicated wholly to photography: Man Ray, Outerbridge Jr., Abbott, Albin-Guillot, Krull, Kertész, Hoyningen-Huene, Nadar, Atget and others First number of *Vu* directed by Vogel	Undset (Norway), Nobel Prize for Literature Jung: *The Relation of the Ego to the Unconscious* Gide: *Retour du Tchad* ("Return from Chad") Maiakovskii: *The Bedbug* Malraux: *Les Conquérants* ("The Conquerors") Giraudoux: *Siegfried* (put on by Louis Jouvet) Cocteau: *Le Livre blanc* ("The White Book") Breton: *Nadja; Le Surréalisme et la peinture* ("Surrealism and Painting") D.H. Lawrence: *Lady Chatterley's Lover* Huxley: *Point Counter Point* Yeats: *The Tower* Waugh: *Decline and Fall* O'Neill: *Strange Interlude* Brecht and Weill: *The Threepenny Opera* Ravel: *Bolero* Gershwin: *An American in Paris* Schönberg: *Variations for Orchestra*, op. 31 Webern: *Symphony*, op. 21	**1928**
Aalto: "Stool 60" Albers: chair that can be dismantled First industrial design desks Dreyfus creates the Super-constellation, the "independent pyroscaph," a fire extinguisher Loewy: Gestetner copier	Feyder: *Les Nouveaux Messieurs* ("The New Messieurs") (France) Gance: *La Fin du monde* ("The End of the World") (France) Grémillon: *Gardiens de phare* ("Lighthouse Keepers") (France)	Mann (Germany), Nobel Prize for Literature Heidegger: *What is Metaphysics* Faulkner: *The Sound and the Fury; Sartoris* Hemingway: *A Farewell to Arms* Steinbeck: *Cup of Gold* Lewis: *Dodsworth*	**1929**

Year	Political History	Artistic Events	Architecture
1929	Poincaré succeeded by Briand in France. He proposes the creation of a Federal European Union, an idea supported by Stresemann, German Minister of Foreign Affairs. Both in favor of Franco-German rapprochement, the two men had already shared the Nobel Peace Prize in 1926. Nevertheless, France goes ahead with the construction of the Maginot Line The United States joins the International Court of Justice at the Hague Beginning of the economic crisis: the New York Stock Exchange crashes (November 24, 1929)	Rivera: Cortéz Palace fresco, Mexico Seuphor and Torrès-Garcia found the Circle and Square group Ernst: *La Femme 100 têtes* El Lissitzky organizes the first polygraphic exhibition in Moscow Malevich retrospective at the Tretiakov Gallery, Moscow Emergence of the term "science fiction" in the USA. From 1926 the review *Amazing Stories* devoted itself to looking to the future Professional American artists call for the imposition of customs duties on works of art executed after 1900 coming from abroad	Moholy-Nagy publishes *From Materials to Architecture* Mies van der Rohe builds the German Pavilion at the Barcelona Exhibition Perret: Paris Ecole Normale de Musique Freyssinet builds a locomotive shed at Bagneux, with thin concrete vaults In Paris, Le Corbusier constructs the Cité-Refuge for the Salvation Army (completed in 1933), the Savoye Villa (completed in 1932) and, in Moscow, the Tsentrosoiuz (Cooperative) building (completed in 1936) Bartsch and Siniavskii: Moscow planetarium Italy: International town-planning competition for Rome Terragni: Fascio house at Como Maillart: Salginatobel bridge in Switzerland Van Doesburg: house at Meudon Val Fleury Aalto: Paimio sanatorium in Finland (completed in 1933) New York: construction of the 324 meter high Chrysler Building Jacobsen exhibits his "House of the future" in Denmark Meyer dies

Design – Inventions – Discoveries	Cinema – Photography – Graphic Arts	Cultural Events	Year
Beautiful American cars in vogue: General Motors, Pierce Arrow, Marmon, Studebaker, Chrysler, Packard, Paige, Reo, Dodge, Ford, Lincoln and others First synchromesh gearbox "Gyrator" washing machine (USA) Synthetic resins Moulinex household appliances (France) S.A.F.A.R. loudspeaker (Italy) The *Graf Zeppelin* circumnavigates the globe (Germany) Electro-encephalograph (Germany) Foam rubber (G.B.) Uncrushable material (G.B.) First 16mm Kodak color film "His Master's Voice" record player Diaghilev dies	Vigo: *A propos de Nice* ("Regarding Nice") (France) Epstein: *Finis terrae* Froelich: *The Night is Ours* (Germany) May: *Asphalt* (Germany) Fanck and Pabst: *The White Hell of Pitz-Palu* (Germany) Pabst: *Diary of a Lost Girl* (Germany) Siodmak and Ulmer: *People on Sunday* (Germany) Lubitsch: *The Love Parade* (USA) Mamoulian: *Applause* (USA) Vidor: *Hallelujah* (USA) Florey gives the Marx Brothers their start in *Coconuts* Grierson: *Drifters* (G.B.) Ivens: *Rain* (Holland) Dovzhenko: *Arsenal* (USSR) Kozintsev: *The New Babylon* (USSR) Vertov: *The Man with a Movie Camera* (USSR) Eisenstein: *The General Line* (USSR) Trauberg: *The Mongol Train* or *The Blue Express* (USSR) *Film und Foto:* First international exhibition of films, photos and photomontages organized by the Deutscher Werkbund in Stuttgart. The Russian section, under the direction of El Lissitzky, includes photos and stills from the films of Eisenstein, Rodchenko, and Klutsis. The Germans are represented by Grosz, Schwitters, Heartfield and Höch; the Americans by E. Weston, Cunningham, Steichen, Sheeler, Outerbridge, Steiner and Man Ray Hergé creates the character of Tintin Birth of Popeye, created by Segar, and Buck Rogers, first science fiction hero created by Dille and Calkins	Hammett: *The Red Harvest* D.H. Lawrence: *Pornography and Obscenity* Remarque: *All Quiet on the Western Front* Valéry: *Charmes* (with notes by Alain); *Variété II* Cocteau: *Les Enfants terribles* Claudel: *Le Soulier de satin* ("The Satin Slipper") Cendrars: *Les Confessions de Dan Yack* ("Confessions of Dan Yack") Maiakovskii: *The Bathhouse* Graves: *Goodbye to All That* Greene: *The Man Within* Woolf: *A Room of One's Own* Compton-Burnett: *Brother and Sister* Priestley: *The Good Companions* Lambert: *Rio Grande* Stravinsky: *Capriccio* for piano and orchestra Hindemith: *Lehrstück*, script by Brecht Weill, with Brecht: *Aufstieg und Fall der Stadt Mahagonny* ("Rise and Fall of The City of Mahagony") Mezzrow and his clarinet move to Paris	**1929**

Select Bibliography

Anger, Kenneth, *Hollywood Babylon,* Straight Arrow Books, San Francisco, 1975.

Besset, Maurice, *Qui était Le Corbusier?,* Albert Skira, Geneva, 1968.

Blanchard, Gérard, *Histoire de la bande dessinée,* Marabout Université, Verviers, 1974.

Brooks, Louise, *Lulu in Hollywood,* Pygmalion/Gérard Watelet, Paris, 1983.

Brunhammer, Yvonne, *Le Style 1925,* Baschet, Paris, 1975.

--, *1925,* Les Presses de la Connaissance, Paris, 1976.

Charensol, Georges, *Le Cinéma,* Larousse, Paris, 1986.

Charles-Roux, Edmonde, *Le temps Chanel,* Chêne-Grasset, Paris, 1979.

Complete Greed of Erich von Stroheim, The, Compiled and annotated with a foreword by Herman G. Weinberg, E. P. Dutton, New York, 1972.

Daval, Jean-Luc, *Journal des Avant-Gardes. Les années vingt. Les années trente,* Albert Skira, Geneva, 1980.

Delevoy, Robert L., *Dimensions du XXᵉ siècle – 1900–1945,* Albert Skira, Geneva, 1965.

Duncan, Alastair, *Art Deco Furniture,* Thames and Hudson, London, 1985.

Faveton, Pierre, *Les Années 20,* Temps actuels, Paris, 1982.

Ford, Charles, *Hollywood Story,* La Jeune Parque, Paris, 1968.

Gallo, Max, *L'Affiche, miroir de l'histoire,* Robert Laffont, Paris, 1973.

Grands Evénements du XXᵉ siècle, Les, Sélection du Reader's Digest, Paris – Brussels – Zurich – Montreal, 1980.

Gray, Camilla, *The Great Experiment: Russian Art, 1863–1922,* Thames and Hudson, London, 1962.

Guilleminault, Gilbert, *Le Roman vrai de la IIIᵉ République – Les Années Folles – 1918–1927,* Denoël, Paris, 1958.

Hall, Carolyn, *Twenties in "Vogue,"* preface by Gloria Swanson, Octopus Books, Ltd., London, 1983.

Huyghe, René and Rudel, Jean, *L'Art et le Monde moderne,* vol. 2: *De 1920 à nos jours,* Larousse, Paris, 1970.

Kertész, André, Centre National de la Photographie, Paris, 1985.

Kunst in Deutschland 1898–1973, exhibition catalogue, Hamburger Kunsthalle, Hamburg, 1973–1974.

Lanoux, Armand, *Paris 1925,* Arthème Fayard, Paris, 1954.

Le Corbusier (Charles-Edouard Jeanneret), *L'Art décoratif d'aujourd'hui,* G. Crès, Paris, 1925.

Lieberman, William S. (ed.), *Art of the Twenties,* The Museum of Modern Art, New York, 1979.

Maenz, Paul, *Art Deco 1920–1940,* DuMont Buchverlag, Cologne, 1974, 3rd. ed. 1984.

Man Ray Photographe, introduction by Jean-Hubert Martin, book-catalogue published on the occasion of the Man Ray exhibition (December 10, 1981 – April 12, 1982) at the Musée national d'Art moderne, Centre Georges Pompidou, Philippe Sers, Paris, 1985.

Mouron, Henri, *Cassandre,* Schirmer/Mosel, Munich, 1985.

Noblet, Jocelyn de, with Catherine Bressy, *Design – Introduction à l'histoire de l'évolution des formes industrielles de 1820 à aujourd'hui,* Stock-Chêne, Paris, 1974.

Oudin, Bernard, *Dictionnaire des architectes,* Seghers, Paris, 1970.

Paris–Berlin – 1900–1933, exhibition catalogue, Centre national d'art et de culture Georges Pompidou, Paris, 1978.

Paris–Moscou – 1900–1930, exhibition catalogue, Centre national d'art et de culture Georges Pompidou, Paris, 1978.

Paris–New York, exhibition catalogue, Centre national d'art et de culture Georges Pompidou, Paris, 1977.

Pauwells, Louis (ed.), *Les Chefs-d'oeuvres de la bande dessinée,* Anthologie Planète, Paris, 1967.

Photographs by Man Ray – 105 Works – 1920–1934, Dover Publications, Inc., New York, 1979.

Poiret, Paul, *En habillant l'époque,* Bernard Grasset, Paris, 1930.

Poulain, Hervé, *L'Art et l'automobile,* La Clef du temps, Zoug, 1973.

Ragon, Michel, *Histoire mondiale de l'Architecture et de l'Urbanisme modernes,* vol. 2: *Pratiques et méthodes – 1911–1971,* Casterman, Paris, 1972.

--, (ed.), *Peinture moderne,* Casterman, Paris, 1974.

Réalismes en Allemagne 1919–1933, exhibition catalogue, Musée d'art et d'industrie, Saint Etienne et Musée d'art et d'histoire, Chambéry, 1974.

Richards, J. M. (ed.) and Adolph K. Placzck (consultant), *Who's Who in Architecture: From 1400 to the Present Day,* Holt, Rinehart and Winston, New York, 1977.

Robinson, Julian, *The Golden Age of Style,* Orbis Books, London, 1976.

Roters, Eberhard (ed.), *Berlin 1910–1933,* Rizzoli, New York, 1982.

Salisbury, Harrison E., *Russia in Revolution, 1900–1930,* Holt, Rinehart and Winston, New York, 1978.

Seuphor, Michel, *La Sculpture de ce siècle,* Editions du Griffon, Neuchâtel, 1959–

Steichen, Edward, *A Life in Photography,* Doubleday and Co., in collaboration with the Museum of Modern Art, New York, 1963.

Willet, John, *Weimar Years: A Culture Cut Short,* Thames and Hudson, London, 1984.

Wilson, Charis, *Edward Weston, Nudes: his photographs accompanied by excerpts from the daybooks and letters,* Aperture Books, New York, 1977.

Photo Credits

The author and the publishers wish to thank all those who have supplied photographs for this book. The author provided the photographs which are not listed below. The numbers refer to the plates.

Bauhaus-Archiv, Berlin   153, 189, 262 (photos Hermann Kiessling)
Berlinische Galerie, Berlin   159 (photo Ernst H. Börner)
Hermann Berninger archives, Zurich   66
Mario Carrieri, Milan   187, 188
Cauvin, Paris   32
Centre de création industrielle, Paris   83, 84, 85, 93
Centre National d'Art et de Culture Georges Pompidou, Paris   5, 17, 27, 33, 35, 40, 43, 45, 50, 74, 77, 81, 82, 87, 89, 116, 117 (photos Béatrice Hatala); 65, 70 (photos James Purcell); 1, 12, 31, 34, 36, 39, 41, 42, 44, 46, 55, 58, 63, 67, 68, 69, 86, 90, 91, 92, 94, 95, 108, 124, 165, 227, 269
Chanel, Neuilly-sur-Seine   209
Sally Chapell, London   251
The Condé Nast Publications Inc., New York   218 (© 1928 Vogue)
Galerie Beyeler, Basle   57
Galerie de Varenne, Paris   243
Galerie Maeght, Paris   60, 61
Galerie Félix Marcilhac, Paris   47, 48, 49, 51, 52, 53, 54, 118, 119, 201, 203, 219, 228, 248, 249
Galerie Nierendorf, Berlin   78
Lucien Hervé, Paris   162, 164
Hans Hinz, Allschwil   64
H. E. Kiessling, Berlin   145
Lanvin, Paris   209
Sydney and Francis Lewis   174
W. Limot, Paris   28
Marion-Valentine, Paris   264
André Morain, Paris   170
Musée de l'Affiche, Paris   261
Musée de Pontoise, Association Freundlich   104
Musée des Arts Décoratifs, Paris   179, 202 (photos L. Sully-Jaulmes); 4, 7, 22, 23, 97, 161, 167, 171, 183, 184, 185, 186, 199, 208
The Museum of Modern Art, New York   3, 16, 135
Nationalgalerie, Staatliche Museen Preussischer Kulturbesitz, Berlin   72, 96 (photos Jörg P. Anders)

Paris-Match, Paris   285
Hervé Poulain   123, 177, 181, 210, 212, 214, 216
Réunion des Musées nationaux, Paris   38, 107, 109, 110, 111
H. Roger-Viollet, Paris   19, 121, 128, 129, 134, 158, 226, 293 (photos Harlingue-Viollet); 220, 221, 292 (photos Lipnitzki-Viollet); 120, 130, 133 (photos N.D. Roger-Viollet); 140, 176 (photos Boyer-Viollet); 99, 125, 131, 132, 165, 213, 224, 230, 231, 234, 265
R. Roland   26, 37
Sotheby Parke Bernet, Monaco   173
Sotheby Parke Bernet, New York   172
Staatsgalerie, Stuttgart   146
Stedelijk Van Abbemuseum, Eindhoven   30
Laurent Sully-Jaulmes, Paris   10, 175, 182, 207
Ullstein Bilderdienst, Berlin   289 (photo Lotte Jacobi)

Publishers' archives 6, 80, 126, 200, 287

Printed and bound in Switzerland

Index

This book was printed in September, 1986 by Hertig + Co. A.G., Bienne, Switzerland.
Setting: Typobauer Filmsatz GmbH, Ostfildern (Scharnhausen), West Germany.
Color lithography: Eurochrom 4, Treviso, Italy.
Black and white: E. Kreienbühl + Co. A.G., Lucerne, Switzerland.
Binding: Roger Veihl, Geneva.
Editorial coordination: Dominique Guisan, Christiane Gäumann-Gignoux and Constance Devanthéry-Lewis.
Design and production: Gilles Néret in collaboration with Emma Staffelbach.

Printed and bound in Switzerland.